CW01021674

Inherit the Earth?

I wanted to portray the earth as a beautiful and vulnerable planet spinning in space. In the centre I painted bright flowers alongside dying trees to show the damage we are doing to our beautiful planet. At the time people were very concerned about acid rain and I had seen dead trees, probably damaged by pollution from Britain, in a German forest. There are flames coming from the earth to create a feeling of danger but I was also trying to paint harmony and the beauty of the earth. Those were the sort of ideas which inspired the picture but as always the painting developed in it's own way from that starting point.

Anne Gregson

Inherit the Earth?

*Millennium Development Goals
– So Near and Yet So Far*

Barbara Butler

churches
together

IN BRITAIN AND IRELAND©

Churches Together in Britain and Ireland
39 Eccleston Square, London SW1V 1BX
www.ctbi.org.uk

ISBN 978-0-85169-381-1

Published 2013 by CTBI

A catalogue record of this book is available from the British Library

Further copies are available from:
Norwich Books and Music
13a Hellesdon Park Road
Norwich
Norfolk
NR6 5DR
www.norwichbooksandmusic.co.uk
01603 785925 Telephone direct order line
01603 785915 Fax

and from:
Christians Aware,
2 Saxby Street
Leicester LE2 0ND
0116 254 0770
Email: barbarabutler@christiansaware.co.uk
Website: www.christiansaware.co.uk

Typeset in Adobe Minion with Hevetica Neue display
Design and pre-press production by Makar Publishing Production, Edinburgh
Printed and bound in Poland by Hussar Books

Contents

Foreword

The Millennium Development Goals were always ambitious. They are inspiring because of their ambition, and in a deeply unequal world we need such a vision to encourage and cajole those who would accept such inequality. We should remember that the world's richest 1% account for 44% of global assets, while 2.2 billion adults barely speak for 1% of the of the world's fortune. In 2013 we use the word 'scandal' fairly frequently, but too often turn a blind eye to the continuing scandal of world poverty and resource inequality. We had hoped to make Poverty History!

Barbara Butler has done us a great service in writing *Inherit the Earth?* as it reminds us of the commitments made by the United Nations at the millennium. There is no doubt that some progress has been made, but there should be even less doubt that there is still a massive amount to do.

We are reminded that:

- ○ 96 million children in the world do not attend school;
- ○ One quarter of children in the developing world are undernourished;
- ○ 6 out of 10 women globally experience physical or sexual violence;
- ○ 33 million people are living with HIV;
- ○ Aid to developing countries is falling.

Reading this book will inspire you to appreciate all that has been achieved since the Millennium, but will also remind you of an even fuller list of what still needs to be done. We are in the midst of a world recession, but for millions of people across the planet this is just another day like every other day, a day to confront poverty, often against a backdrop of violence and always another day to scratch enough for survival.

Faith communities have been at the forefront of this effort to meet the MDG's, but we must redouble our efforts and work to ensure that we keep moving forward. Using the meditations and discussion material throughout this book will assist groups to refocus attention and commitment on these issues.

Let's be inspired again, let us be ambitious again, let us work together again to ensure that all our children 'Inherit the earth'.

Revd. Bob Fyffe
General Secretary
Churches Together in Britain and Ireland

Preface

My hope in writing this book is that it will be used by both individuals and groups, in churches, faith communities, colleges and schools. I have written from my own Christian perspective, but I have included contributions from people of other world faiths.

The Millennium Development Goals originated in the United Nations at the millennium, and every member country is pledged to meet them by 2015. There are also specific targets for each goal. I offer information on the progress and lack of it towards the goals. I have based the chapters of the book on the goals and their associated targets, which act as a framework or starting point for each chapter, but I have proceeded on a wide front. I include stories, poems and material for reflection.

I have realized as I worked towards this book that most of the goals will not be reached by 2015 and that some of them are a very long way from being achieved. The value of the goals is not simply that one day they will be reached, but that they have given so many countries in the developing world a vision, something to work towards, no matter how far away they may be. As a friend from Uganda said:

'The goals have given many countries and people a new energy and hope for the future.'

At the end of the book we include an account of present realities in Afghanistan, a country at a crossroads and whose future in unclear.

My hope is that when readers reflect on dire situations, which in some cases are actually getting worse every day, this book will be used for sharing the situations, with the people and with God in practical work and in prayer and meditation.

There is of course much to be encouraged and inspired by in the progress being made towards the goals. Perhaps we may all do a little more after we read, in campaigning, giving and work.

Above all, my hope is that the book may be a helpful tool towards more of us seeing the world as one place, where we and all people may work together across countries, faiths and the rich/poor divide towards a good future for every person.

Barbara Butler
Christians Aware

Introduction

There is a legend that the energy to work for a better world may be found between the horns of a buffalo. The problem, or challenge, is that in order to be energised it is necessary to climb onto the buffalo and to sit between its horns. The legend is that when a pilgrim did manage to climb up onto the buffalo and to reach its horns the animal was so furious that it jumped and bucked and at last threw the assailant to the ground. When the bruised and battered pilgrim managed to sit up many people crowded round and asked why he had done such a foolish thing as to climb up onto a menacing and treacherous animal. He replied that injured and bleeding as he was the risk had been more than worthwhile because he had glimpsed the view from the horns and had received a new and burning energy and love for the world.

Burning energy and love are needed by everyone who is concerned in working to overcome injustices and imprisonments of every sort in our world. Work to meet the Millennium Development Goal targets and to break chains of oppression of all sorts does not end with the work of the materially rich nations, important as that is for change to happen. The targets can only be reached through lives lived bravely and sacrificially. Every person and every nation must work for the future of the whole world, including those of all communities, cultures and faiths.

Martin Stern is a Holocaust survivor who was born in the Netherlands in 1938. His father was Jewish and died in Buchenwald. Martin and his sister survived Theresienstadt camp. He says that he will always feel outrage at the way he and his sister with all the Jews of Hitler's Europe were treated, and at the way Jewish people are still treated in some circles and countries. He nevertheless believes that Jewish people can never claim special rights but only the same rights and freedoms as all human beings are entitled to, and the same responsibilities. Their dignity is to be members of the human race and to work for others who are oppressed even when the outcome is not clear. Martin's inspiration comes from the Talmud.

> **'It is not given for you to complete the task, but neither are you free to desist from it.'**

In 2007 Martin joined the London march in protest against the oppression and terrible suffering of the people of Darfur, who have tried to cling to life

A dormitory at Theresienstadt camp.

in the face of hunger, illness, homelessness and despair. He saw his sharing in the march as a sharing in the suffering of people who are victims of a ruthless attempt to destroy them.[1]

Martin Stern's energy for his work for human life, freedom and dignity is urgent and compelling. He speaks of Rabbi Hillel, who said:

'If I am not for myself, who will be for me? If I am only for myself what am I? And if not now, when?'

There is an awareness here of the need to 'Love your neighbour as you love yourself.' A danger for movements and work for human development, including work towards the Millennium Development Goals, is that such work may become the obsession of those who drive it, who may risk not only destroying themselves but also everything they have worked for.

Another challenge for people who work in movements for change is for them to self-consciously do so in a way which, whilst it may be obsessive in order for the work to succeed, will also be as unselfish as possible, with the focus of attention on the other people and on the issues surrounding them, and not on the individuals or groups leading the campaigns.

One of our necessary tasks is to understand that those who may be the workers to overcome the many sufferings afflicting the world and particularly the developing world, are not just those who are in the developed world or those rich in material goods anywhere in the world. Those who are materially rich may be part of the problem facing the world, whilst others, the materially poor, may have gifts to give which none of us in the Western World have dreamed about.

There is a story, told to me when I lived in Zambia, of a farmer who had lived in Central Africa for many years. He had a huge farm of 10,000 acres, like many of his friends who had gone to live in Africa from England. He loved his life and work. Most of the people in the area worked for him. He had built a school for the children of his employees and had also put up a small clinic which was visited by a doctor from the city every week. He took a personal interest not only in his workers but also in the wider community. Everyday he walked round a section of his farm to see the workers and to make sure that all was well. One day as he walked round the farm he noticed that one of the workers was asleep under a tree. As he called out to the man to 'Wake up,' he realised that it was Moses, his oldest employee. The old man jumped to his feet and was silent for a moment before he said, 'The richest man in the valley will die tonight.' Moses walked off slowly into the field, leaving the farmer in a state of shock. Thoughts of what a silly old man Moses was were soon superseded by thoughts of what he had actually

---

1 Martin's story is told in the Lent & Easter 2008 Christians Aware magazine.

said because the farmer knew that he himself was the richest man in the valley. 'There is nothing wrong with me,' the farmer said as he continued with his walk, but by the time he reached his home he had a headache. He told his wife that he wasn't hungry and went to bed for the afternoon. By mid-afternoon he was feverish and his wife called the doctor. Unfortunately the doctor couldn't be found and, as darkness fell the farmer was much worse, experiencing heavy breathing and even higher temperatures. At last the doctor arrived and the farmer's wife rushed out to his car, shouting, 'Wherever have you been, my husband is very seriously ill, he may die.' The doctor walked into the house and went straight through to the farmer's bedroom saying, 'I'm so sorry I couldn't come earlier, I have been with your old worker, Moses. He has just died.' The farmer didn't die and later, when he was feeling better, the doctor explained everything.

Although the farmer thought that he himself was the richest man in the valley, in fact Moses knew that he was the richest man in the valley because he was the oldest person in the valley. The children and even many of the adults came to him for advice and when they wanted to know the history of the people; he was, after all, part of it. He was at the centre of his community, living with his children and grandchildren, listening to them, watching them grow. On the night when he died the whole village gathered in the little church to pray for him and they stayed there all night, keeping watch.

> **The truth of life is that everyone is a giver and everyone is a receiver. All have gifts and all have needs.**

Overcoming the degradation of poverty and all that goes with it is not simply about people struggling and moving from the dire circumstances of being materially poor, ill and marginalised; without sufficient food and drink, clothing and shelter. It includes the movement away from dependence on material things and from the notion that they constitute the only real wealth. It includes overcoming the emotional and spiritual deprivation and apathy which may exist in any person or human group at any time. It includes making the effort to make choices for good in life and going on to live them out.

The words of Nelson Mandela are important. '*You are a child of God. Your playing small doesn't save the world. We were all born to manifest the glory of God that is within us. It's not just in*

President Nelson R Mandela

SOUTH AFRICA SUID-AFRIKA **45c**

Ab1.4 1994

catwalker / Shutterstock.com

some of us; it's in everyone. And as we let our light shine we unconsciously give other people permission to do the same.'

Stocking Farm

The story of the building of the church of St. Luke, Stocking Farm, in Leicester in the mid-1950s, is a story of the building of community and confidence amongst people who had very little of either before the project began. It is a story of people who decided to take control of their lives in an extraordinary way.

Stocking Farm is an estate which was built on the edge of Leicester in the early 1950s to provide much needed housing for young ex-servicemen and their families. The Anglican Church provided a vicarage, a stipend and a church hall, and Henry Evans arrived as the first priest in 1956. He held his first services in a garage and the community centre until the church hall was built in 1957 when it became the centre of worship and of community. A mission was held and the congregations grew quickly with many baptisms and confirmations and the new hall was very soon crowded to the doors. There was space for a new church, alongside the vicarage and hall but there was no money to build it.

The members of the community decided that they would explore the possibility of building the church themselves. They did have some skilled men in the building trade and as soon as the idea was public a remarkable number of people in the community offered their services. These included a skilled building foreman who offered his services for a very small wage. Work began in 1961 with four hundred pounds in the building fund. A member of the choir was a mechanic and a lorry was bought and gifts began to arrive. A builder donated wooden scaffolding poles and the builders, all volunteers, worked every day except Sunday. As the walls began to rise more and more interest was aroused and a joiner's shop was built and second hand machines were given, so that most of the joinery was done on the site. People did not have to be members of the church to work as volunteers, in fact many of them were not, though some of them later asked to be confirmed. It was not only the men who did the building who volunteered but women also, who made tiles and provided refreshments for the builders. As the church grew so did the support and more and more donations were given, often just as the funds were running out. Soon the volunteers were building by floodlight on winter evenings and students came along in their vacations. When the time came to put on the roof local coppersmiths volunteered their services. The wooden roof beams were hauled up by hand to avoid the expense of hiring cranes. After five wonderful years the church, seating four hundred people, was completed and consecrated.

Those who built the church at Stocking Farm were always inspired by the memory of their efforts. They, like most of the people who made their homes there, were not the poorest of the poor, but ordinary people who often lacked the natural confidence of the more educated middle classes. Building the church at Stocking Farm gave people hope and made many of them realise that they had gifts and that there were choices they could make in life. One of the men said that being at Stocking Farm saved him from prison. Some people later joined the caring professions. Many people who had the experience of building the church became more socially aware and had their horizons broadened in an inspiring way.

When Henry first went to Stocking Farm he organised a mission to the parish. The mission leader was Father Gibbard from the Society of St. John the Evangelist. The outcome of the mission was that between forty and fifty people were confirmed every year for many years following the mission. Bernard was confirmed and turned his life completely around, moving from working in weights and measures to social work. He went on to pioneer the establishment of John Storer House in Loughborough, which is still the centre for social work for that area.

Derek Morton, an industrial chemist in dust control, was a complete outsider from the Church, but he joined the exciting building project and from that base he was invited to a house group run by the curate and was later ordained. His wife Janet joined the Samaritans as a listener and counsellor. She now works with Norwich Hospice Charities. Paul Billings worked as a mechanic at Imperial Typewriters and helped with the building of the church. The whole family was involved in the building in one way or another. His son Alan, who was at school during this period, went to Cambridge University and was ordained. He became deputy leader of Sheffield City Council and is now Director of the Centre for Ethics and Religion at Lancaster University.

Many still talk about the time when they built the church as a special time, of community and of hope. When Henry reached his eightieth birthday the members of the former youth club, known as 'Luke's Lot', organised a party and people travelled to it from all over the country.

Henry has a prayer diary which he uses every day. One section of the diary is called 'The Overcomers' and it includes many of the people who lived in Stocking Farm in the happy days when the church was being built. They are people who overcame huge obstacles in their lives. They include a man whose wife died when the children were very small, and who brought them up alone.

Henry, as part of the community, gave people hope and the confidence to do something themselves which was a solid contribution towards improving the lives of the other people in their communities. In his later ministry Henry was the Warden of Launde Abbey, a retreat centre in Leicestershire, and his experience at Stocking Farm stood him in good stead. He enabled a community of hope at Launde as he had at Stocking Farm and the guests who stayed there had the opportunity to learn to be in touch with themselves and to grow in confidence before going back to their work in the wider world.

The illusion of possessions...

Overcoming poverty includes the struggle of many people to overcome greed and the desire to possess, and to realise the blessedness of sharing and of giving away. Stories of people who have managed to overcome their need for luxuries have been abundant since the economic downturn in the UK, but there have also been the stories of those who have become desperate, including the man who, when he lost all his money, killed his wife and daughter so that they wouldn't have to become poor.

There is a Chinese story of a man who collected beautiful jewels and who spent a lot of his time looking at them, polishing them and drawing them. On one occasion he was persuaded to show the jewels to a friend who thought they were very lovely. The man became alarmed when the friend got up to leave and thanked him for his gift of the jewels. He quickly said that he would never give the jewels away. The friend smiled and explained that for him the gift of the jewels was the pleasure of looking at them. He did not wish to have the trouble of actually having to polish and protect them.

The Slavery Memorial outside the Cathedral of Christ the King in Zanzibar.

The Cathedral of Christ the King in Zanzibar symbolizes Christian inspiration, courage and love. It is a religious badge of hope for freedom and fulfilment for all the people of the island, Christian and Muslim alike. It was built by the people with the help of Bishop Edward Steere, who also built churches and schools. He learnt to make bricks and wheels, he learnt about farming and even started a laundry in Zanzibar. He gave the hope of new life and also gave new life itself to many people. The cathedral, opened on Christmas Day in 1880, was built on top of the former slave market, with the high altar in the place where the auctions of the slaves took place. The font stands over the tunnel where the blood of the children who were killed drained away into the sea. Children baptised in the font are offered life in abundance in stark contrast to what went before.

There is a story from the Adivasi, or tribal people, of India which tells of an attempt at the destruction of a tree, the life of the people, by one man who is jealous of the tree. He then realises his selfish mistake and goes in search of the tree in the hope of restoring it to its place at the heart of the lives of the people. He faces a long and hard journey when all of natural creation works against him, including rivers fruits and animals. At long last he goes to an island where he finds the tree weeping and asking the people:

My people, what have I done to you?
How have I offended you?
Answer me.

The people say:

You remind us of our fragility
while we want to assert our power.
You remind us of God's gifts for all,
but we want to privatise and possess.
You remind us of creation's extravagance
but we want to limit, bank and hoard.
You remind us of freedom
And we have forgotten the meaning.
You remind us of joy.
While we want only to be entertained
you remind us of sacrifice.
We don't want to die and endlessly give,
we want to live for ourselves.

There is a tree in every religion and culture of the world and the human struggle to escape into selfishness and greed is also always there. The hope is that freedom and development movements may offer glimpses of those who love the tree and who struggle to die and endlessly give, going on and ever on into an uncertain but promise filled future, always offering hope and therefore life.

But the many developments achieved, wonderful as they are, are islands of hope pointing us to whole continents of needs, suffering and near despair. The islands of hope shine as beacons not just of hope but also of encouragement to people of faith and of goodwill to love the visions of their faiths and their own visions, to embrace the trees of the world and to work for the relief of poverty, the first Millennium Development Goal, and for the achievement also of the other seven goals, and to go on, towards the eradication of prejudice against people because of their gender or race, to work for freedom with responsibility for all people.

Two things are clear. The first one is that the Millennium Development Goals will not be achieved by 2015 but must be seen as a work in progress. The work must go on beyond the chosen date, and plans are already being made for it to do so. Secondly the goals cannot easily be separated out. The success of one will lead to the success of others and the failure of one will make others impossible to achieve.

The key is to be encouraged by what has and is being done, and to go on.

This book is full of stories and challenges but it does not attempt to advise its readers how to react to the pictures it paints. When I first visited Calcutta the local bustee/slum leader said, *'I hope you haven't come here to tell us what to do because if you do this our people will feel discouraged and when you go home they will do very little. If you can simply listen and learn then when you go home our people will feel proud that you listened to them and will gain new energy to work for their futures'*. It is in that spirit that this book is written. Hopefully the reader will be challenged and inspired to respond, but how that response will come will vary greatly for we are all responsible for the common good and none of us can determine what contribution our neighbour might or should make.

The Beatitudes

Blessed are the poor in spirit: for theirs is the kingdom of heaven.

Blessed are they that mourn: for they shall be comforted.

Blessed are the meek: for they shall inherit the earth.

Blessed are they which do hunger and thirst after righteousness: for they shall be filled.

Blessed are they which are merciful: for they shall obtain mercy.

Blessed are the pure in heart: for they shall see God.

Blessed are the peacemakers: for they shall be called the children of God.

Blessed are they which are persecuted for righteousness sake: for theirs is the kingdom of heaven.

Matthew 5.3–10

Opposite: Turmoil, by Anne Gregson

'A Miracle'

Yes, it would be a miracle indeed
If everyone who needs somewhere to sleep
could find a bed;
The tired, the lost, the homeless dispossessed,
somewhere to rest...
O Bethlehem, at last we would agree
That it would be a miracle indeed.
A Miracle.
Yes, it would be a miracle for sure
If everyone who fears the men with guns
Knew no more war;
the shot, the bombed, the injured innocents
were whole once more.
Oh Bethlehem, our hearts would not ignore
that it would be a miracle for sure.
A Miracle.[1]

Voices from Ethiopia:

'We are left tied like straw.'

'Our life is empty; we are empty handed.'

'Living by stratching like a chicken.'

'Life has made us ill.'

'We are above the dead and below the living.'[2]

1 From *Manchester Carols* by Carol Ann Duffy, UK Poet Laureate.
2 From Deepa Narayan *et. al.* (eds.), *Voices of the Poor: Crying Out for Change*, New York: Oxford University Press for the World Bank, 2000: www.worldbank.org/poverty/voices.

Goal 1

Eradicate Extreme Poverty and Hunger

'Massive poverty and obscene inequality are such terrible scourges of our times – times in which the world boasts breath-taking advances in science, technology, industry and wealth accumulation – that they have to rank alongside slavery and apartheid as social evils.'

Nelson Mandela speaking in Trafalgar Square, February 2005

TARGET – halve the proportion of people whose income is less than 1 dollar a day

The poverty which must be eradicated for Goal One to be fulfilled is first and foremost absolute material poverty. To be in absolute poverty is to be without sufficient food, drink, clothing or shelter. Absolute poverty is caused by the natural environment, natural disasters and human failings, which may include war, bad government, trading systems and choices made in the use of land.

Relative poverty is comparative poverty and occurs everywhere in the world, and particularly in the Western World where the media constantly presents images and stories of wealthy and beautiful people. The poor person or people may compare themselves to others, sometimes their near neighbours, and then see themselves as poor and inadequate. This susceptibility may lead to criminality or to emotional and spiritual deprivation which may very easily draw individuals or communities into absolute poverty.

Plus ça change... an American postage stamp, c.1985. Neftali / Shutterstock.com

It is possible to sit in a wooden shack in an Indian village and not only see the wealth and wealthy of India pass across the TV screen, but also to see the wealth and wealthy of the world.

In 2010 hundreds of volunteers went out to listen to poor people across Ontario and were shocked by the extent of the poverty and suffering they found. They met people who had held good jobs and who had ended up in poverty. Comparisons between the old life and the new were there; lack of control over their own lives was the hardest thing for the newly poor to accept.[3]

---

3 Jamie Swift, Brice Balmer and Mira Dineen *Persistent Poverty: Voices from the Margins*, Between the Lines, Toronto, 2010.

Overcoming the degradation of poverty then is not simply about people struggling and moving from the dire circumstances of being without sufficient food and drink, clothing and permanent shelter. It includes the movement away from the emotional and spiritual deprivation which may exist in any person or human group.

An ancient Chinese proverb may point in the right direction towards work for the alleviation of all kinds of poverty.

Go in search of your people.
Love them.
Learn from them.
Serve them.
Begin with what they know, build on
what they have.
But of the best leaders
when their task is accomplished,
The people will remark
'We have done it ourselves.'

It is clear that what works is for local communities to develop programmes to improve their lives, though sometimes a catalyst is very helpful. This may be in the form of a visiting group, which is the hope of many of our Christians Aware visits and work camps. However, there is no lasting change when local people do not take the initiative.

Helder Camara was one of the twentieth century liberation theologians who encouraged peasants in Latin America to realise that they could do something to improve their own lives. He suggested that they form small groups to study the Gospels and then work for social change. He himself worked in the favelas or shanty towns of Rio de Janeiro and then in 1964 he became Archbishop of the impoverished north eastern region of Brazil, where he remained until 1985. He worked with the poor and also tried to persuade the Church to move away from privilege and hierarchy. At the Second Vatican Council he was known as the '*bishop of the poor*' because of his concern for the problems of the Third World. In 1968 and 1979 he took his concerns for the poor and the suffering people to the Latin American Conferences of Medellin and Puebla.

Camara was central to 'the Church of the Poor' movement, a vital group bringing together Third World bishops, priests from the Mission de France and the Little Brothers of Jesus, who were inspired by Charles de Foucauld. This group's major concern was that the Church should address itself to the gulf separating the rich and poor worlds, and then go further and symbolise its commitment by living austerely. Helder Camara's Gospel message was either embraced or hated; it has spread throughout the developing world and has never been forgotten. It is remarkable that in Helder Camara's home country, Brazil, which is now a member of the G20,[4] and where the Olympic Games will be held in 2016, he is not only remembered but is revered.[5]

All over the developing world there has been a rise in local councils and groups, and, perhaps more significantly, in informal local cooperation. An example from Ghana is the women's Village Association in Guli which used to be a rice growing cooperative. When the soil was impoverished and it was impossible to grow rice the women collected wild nuts and made nut butter to sell in the local market.[6] Most of the encouraging stories in this section have happened because people are working together. There are many locally based micro-finance schemes – see Chapter 3.

SUDAN

In the Sudan there is dire poverty largely due to warfare and violence. Recent suffering and poverty are largely due to the 2011 process of separation between the north and the south. At first there was hope of a peaceful separation but the future of oil and of the border areas has caused dire results. The greatest devastation is in the border areas. In South Kordofan more than a hundred thousand people have been displaced and many are dead. Churches and mosques have been destroyed.

Poverty in Sudan will grow now, following the separation of South Sudan and the loss of much of the oil revenue. The future for South Sudan should be more hopeful, as there is a lot of encouragement and support from around the world. However, one year after independence, half of the country's people are hungry and refugees continue to flee border fighting. The hope is that Sudan will bring itself out of isolation and away from sanctions, so that it can receive debt relief and attract investment; but first it must bring peace to Darfur.

No place has suffered more than Darfur where the peace agreement collapsed and aerial bombings and violence are increasing, with 70,000 newly displaced people to add to the 2 million who were already displaced.[7] Tabitha is from Darfur where many in her family have been killed and most of the homes have been burnt.

---

4 Group of Twenty Finance Ministers and Central Bank Governors.

5 Francis McDonagh (Ed.), *Dom Helder Camara. Essential Writings*, Orbis Books, 2009.

6 A story from Action of Churches Together in Scotland.

7 Kids for Kids is a charity working with the people in Darfur to provide goats, donkeys, blankets and much more. www.kidsforkids.org.uk.

A story of hope came to me from the Sudan three years ago. I met an Anglican bishop from Torit in Southern Sudan, where all the churches were destroyed in the war. He had lost his home and the family had scattered. He had managed to reach Khartoum where he opened an orphanage for children who were also displaced. When he was made a bishop in 2007 he returned to the South and took the children with him. He has now managed to have them all adopted into good homes. Instead of struggling to keep alive and to keep going he now struggles with planting crops to improve the health of the people.

Frances is from Liberia where there was war between 1989 and 2003. Frances fled with her children in 1993, not returning home until 1997. She lost many family members but was never injured herself. She lives with deep fear which she feels will be with her forever. A woman from the **Democratic Republic of Congo** was in tears when she told me of her traumatic experiences, including the time when an armed soldier entered her home and fired shots before running off.

RWANDA

The **Rwandan Genocide** was the 1994 murder of about a million people and the creation of about 800,000 refugees and displaced people. Over the course of approximately 100 days over 500,000 people were killed.[8] It was the culmination of longstanding ethnic rivalry and tension between the minority Tutsi people, who had controlled power for centuries, and the majority Hutu people, who had come to power in the rebellion of 1959–62 and overthrown the Tutsi monarchy.

The Rwanda Patriotic Front, which was mostly Tutsi, invaded the country in 1990 and began a civil war with the Hutu led government and its supporters. There was a cease-fire in 1993 but this ended with the genocide which followed the death of the President in April 1994. There were mass killings of Tutsis and of peaceful Hutus. The killings were supported by the Hutu who were in power and were carried out by the militias and by ordinary people who joined in. Neighbour killed neighbour in a frenzy which could not easily be believed.

The genocide had a devastating social and economic effect on the country. It led to a change in the country's demography as women today account for about 54 per cent or slightly more of the population. About 14 per cent of rural dwellers have become landless peasants in situations of extreme poverty, and a large number of demobilized young soldiers have swollen the ranks of the unemployed.

Agriculture has always been the backbone of the economy and employs more than 80 per cent of the population. It is largely subsistence farming on very small farms of less than 1 hectare each. Rough terrain, erosion and

---

8 Human Rights Watch estimate.

climatic hazards combine with geography and the lack of modern technology to create serious constraints to agricultural development which are not the result of the genocide, though the genocide has made them harder to overcome. 28% of the rural population is even now 'food insecure'.

Access to primary education has improved in rural areas (where the school enrolment rate is 77 per cent, against a rate of 87 per cent in urban areas), the enrolment rate in rural secondary schools is as low as 6 per cent, and dropout rates are higher than those in urban areas, particularly for girls.

The hope of the country is that it will move from being a poor nation and towards a middle-income country by 2017. David Dale is a Christians Aware member who is the commissary for the Bishop of Butare. He visits Rwanda regularly and leads work camps. He has written about some of the reasons for the recovery of the nation from the genocide so far:

> **I would say that the recovery in the nation is very much due to democracy and good government. The government has invested in health, education and development. This has been made possible because the developed countries of the world have been more confident that in such a relatively stable environment there is less corruption. The people themselves have benefitted from this period of comparative peace, but of course the recovery from deep trauma, sadness and anger caused by terrible and brutal loss of life is more difficult, and that will take generations to heal if at all.**

David is involved in helping to overcome poverty through the creation of work in Rwanda, including a juice and jam factory. The factory will enable Shyogwe Diocese to finance its wider work so that it can successfully fight against poverty, disease and lack of education by managing and expanding, the schools, health centres and dispensaries and the rural development advisory service for farmers. This story would just as easily fit into the section on unemployment and employment. It is a really good example of people working to raise themselves from dire poverty.

David has written:

> **The pineapple juice and jam factory, is now looking at using fruits such as papayas, strawberries and passion fruit, which grow better in the mountain areas where water is more plentiful. We plan also to use some land near the factory to provide a comfort stop for travellers on the main road, providing a pleasant environment where they can take refreshment and of course the opportunity to buy and consume our jam and juice. We hope that some of the craft items and furniture made by the 'Youth at Risk Project' can**

also be marketed there. I have always been interested in jam making and when the director of the factory asked me for help in supplying the pectin to help the jam to set I knew that we need not send to Uganda for it when we are growing lemons, a natural source of pectin. Several lemon trees are growing in the garden at Alleluia House, which I have built as a home for guests. My ancestors came from Tiptree in Essex and some are mentioned in the history of Wilkins and Sons, the producers of fine jams since 1885, and many of them worked for the company. Wilkins and Sons also provide refreshment and sell their jams to passing travellers on their factory site in Essex which inspired me to encourage this as a marketing tool in Rwanda.

Pictured above in his office in the factory is Viateur Ntarindwa who is Director of the Rural Development Interdiocesan Service (RDIS) which serves the Dioceses of Shyogwe, Butare, Kigeme and Cyangugu in Rwanda. He is responsible for the factory and also works with the 18 pineapple growing co-operatives that supply the fruit. RDIS also advises farmers in appropriate farming methods and small animal husbandry. For instance encouraging a farmer to have crossbred cattle which are part native and part Friesian or Jersey can give big increases in milk production. A native cow can give 3 litres of milk each day whereas a crossbred cow can give about 15 litres. Photographs by David Dale.

HAITI

In Haiti there is great poverty and suffering partly due to the earthquake of January 2010. But even before the earthquake more than half the people of Haiti were living below the poverty line and average life expectancy was about 57 years. There have always been natural disasters, including 4 hurricanes which hit the island 2 years ago. The 2010 earthquake was massive, killing about 217,000 people.

More than 200,000 Haitian homes were destroyed in the earthquake. When the rains arrived people were living in tents, with very little in the way of sanitation, water or even food. Vulnerability to disease was great: there was a cholera outbreak 10 months after the earthquake.

Tom Quenet of the Methodist Church visited soon after the earthquake. Many Methodists are raising support for the re-building of lives. Tom wrote, 'It felt like some giant had leapt about in a mad frenzy...' Tom went back a few months later and was at first shocked at the little progress he could see around him. But then he saw hope for the future in the children going to school, the growth in small businesses, the people moving about with stolid determination on public transport, and flowers planted in refugee camps, and he realised that the people were working together and that hope for the future was there in abundance.

Wilbert Joseph, April 2011, Haiti.

Photo by Natasha Fillion, Progressio

Progressio has been working in Haiti following the earthquake during which Wilbert Joseph's house was completely destroyed. When this photo was taken a few months later he was continuing gradually to remove the debris from his house with a shovel and wheelbarrow, building a new future little by little.

But the going hasn't been easy for Wilbert and the hundreds of thousands of others who count themselves blessed to have survived the quake. Progress to reconstruct the shattered nation has been slow. And part of the problem has been the approach taken to rebuilding. Civil society organisations, from human rights and environmental organisations to faith-based and humanitarian groups, have expressed deep frustration at the marginalisation of ordinary Haitians from the recovery process at first.

In the first few months following the disaster, UN meetings were conducted in English and Spanish, but not French or Creole. It is said that many Haitian community leaders reported feeling like passive observers of the relief operation rather than active participants. And Haitian grassroots networks were not fully used, so that valuable time was lost in the creation of new structures instead of in delivering a quick rebuilding programme.

But despite many difficulties, there are grounds for optimism. The earthquake created a great deal of solidarity between Haiti and its nearest neighbour, the Dominican Republic. Where bi-lateral engagement had proved difficult in the past, there is now hope for a collaborative future.

Lizzette Robleto, Progressio policy officer, explains: '*The extraordinary efforts made by Haitian civil society in the aftermath of this devastating earthquake are a sign of the potential that exists for the sector to take on a much larger role in the future. If, collectively, we wish to see a lasting, sustainable recovery that is owned and managed by Haitians, then the clear sense of exclusion felt by local groups must be tackled.*'

Progressio works in Haiti to bring the voice of civil society more fully into the reconstruction efforts as well as to build links of support between the Dominican Republic and Haiti. Over the long term this will ensure a better future for people like Wilbert. That's what we call 'people powered development'.[9]

Another organisation working in Haiti is **Doctors of the World**.[10] They have been there for 20 years and were therefore able to react very quickly when the earthquake struck, treating people with dreadful wounds, amputating limbs and operating on people in the open air. Thousands of wound dressings a day were used, imported from all over the world. This group also provides much needed psychological support and a malnutrition programme for mothers and children.

The struggle of the people goes on, and will go on for a long time, as they seek to reclaim their lives and their hopes for the future. A recent report from 'Tearfund' [11] points to the partial recovery so far being due to the resilience of the people, who have begun to make incredible efforts to re-build

Photo courtesy www.
doctorsoftheworld.org.uk

9   www.progressio.org.uk.

10 www.doctorsoftheworld.org.uk.

11 www.tearfund.org.

their lives. There are however more than 500,000 people still living in tents at the beginning of 2012 and it is estimated that it will take ten years for a full recovery to be made. The Tearfund approach is to work with people on a broad front, including housing, education, economic recovery and the restoration of water and sanitation. A lot of work is being done to help people to be equipped for future challenges. Carpenters and teachers are being trained and homes and schools are being built and improved.

The 2010 floods in Pakistan

Salim Yusuf Lorgat has written about his work with Islamic Relief during and after the floods. Islamic Relief raised £200,000 towards relief for the people. Salim has written the story of what happened to one baby, Fawadullah Musa, who was born during the floods in Launda village. The family lived in a mud house but as the waters rose they had to leave their home and flee to higher ground where the baby was born and they were saved by a medical team. They were fortunate; many people were not saved. Salim visited the family again a year after the floods and they were living in an earthquake and flood-resistant home build by Islamic Relief. They, like others in the new village, have clean water, sanitation and a medical centre. Reconstruction work in the flood affected areas continues as part of a two year plan to rebuild sixty villages. Local people are employed and the reconstruction includes boreholes for fresh water for each village, a good drainage system and health clinics. The farmers are being helped with tools, seeds and livestock. The children will have schools and play areas. The people have new hope for a future in which they have the tools to work for themselves and their children.[12]

Superstition and lethargy

Overcoming poverty is largely about people working with realistic hope for their futures, and with determination to bring it about. It also includes the struggle to overcome superstition and of course the lethargy that brings to any person or community in its grip.

There is a legend of the superstition of a fisherman in the Philippines. I have visited the Philippines and met many people from the fishing communities in Mindanao. A fisherman who spends all his time fishing in Lake Mainit told us that the number of fisher folk is growing whilst the number of fish is decreasing. He feels that his situation is so precarious that he has to go out at night, using a lantern, to catch all the fish he can. The fish are then sold by his wife, to support the family.

The fisherman in the legend went out fishing one night and, as the dawn was breaking, caught the biggest fish he had ever seen in one of his new nets. He could hardly hold the fish, but he clung on and the fish could not escape

12 www.islamic-relief.org.uk

from the net. Suddenly the fisherman almost dropped the net into the sea because the fish spoke to him. The fish said, 'If you let me go I will grant you a wish every week for the next three weeks.' The fisherman thought for a moment and then he gave his three wishes. First of all, he wished for a good house for himself, his wife and their three children to live in. The house would be built of bricks, with a tiled roof; it would be weatherproof and roomy. Secondly he wished for a village school, well built and with good teachers, so that his children and all the children in the village could attend. He hoped that the children would have a good education and would have choice in their work and way of life. Thirdly, and he thought a lot about his third wish, he wished to be like God. If he was like God he would be able to do so many things in the world.

The fisherman went home and told his wife what had happened. He told her about the big fish, about the three wishes and about the moment when he opened the net so that the fish could swim away. The fisherman and his wife went to bed that night, tired from all their work but also from the emotional stress of the coming of the big fish and of the promises the fish had made.

When they woke up the next morning they were shocked because they could not see the sun shining through the branches on the roof of their house. Instead the roof was a strong tiled one. When they got up they saw that the house was now built of bricks. There were several rooms including a good indoor kitchen and a separate bedroom for the children. They jumped for joy and had a wonderful week in their new home.

When the next week came round the fisherman and his wife went to bed fearfully and hopefully at the same time. When they woke up they rushed out of their new home and saw a fantastic set of buildings, the new school was there and the children were all going in carrying new books. The teachers were waiting for them.

The fisherman and his wife had a wonderful week and then came the time for the third wish to come true, a wish they hoped and dreamed would give them great powers for good in the world because they would be like God. When they woke up they were shocked to realise that their new home had gone and the rain was coming in through the roof. Worse still there was straw on the floor and animals in the house, including a lamb, an ox and a donkey. The new school had also vanished.

Brightest and Best
of the sons of the morning,
Dawn on our darkness
And lend us thine aid,
star of the east,
the horizon adorning
guide where our infant
redeemer is laid.

Cold on his cradle
the dew drops are shining;
low lies his head
with the beasts of the stall;
Angels adore him
in slumber reclining,
Maker and Monarch
and Saviour of all.'[13]

Christians Aware   Autumn 2003

The Filipino fisherman and his wife actually were like God, who had come to the world as a poor baby in a stable full of animals. They remembered that the great kings from the East, who did have worldly riches, had knelt down in front of the Christ Child. Their spirits were raised and they resolved to seek God's help in working for their family and for their community. They soon sold enough fish to buy materials for a new home. They gathered a group together to work towards building a good school for the children, and shared ideas began to emerge. There was no end to what could be done by a people full of vision, faith, hope and hard work.

It is not easy to realise the blessedness of sharing and of giving away

The art of being poor in spirit is to distinguish between use and ownership...a sense of ownership is a terrible snare, because it prevents a person's life from marching onwards towards God...[14]

In her new book[15] Anita Desai writes about the hidden inner part of every person which, no matter what the external circumstances are, is spiritual and creative. In the first of three novellas that form the book she writes about the futility of rich people collecting and hoarding. It is the story of someone who travels and collects but who does not love or care for what he has collected. He gains no benefit from the collection and it begins to rot. The live elephant he has also collected begins to eat the beautiful and rotting treasures. There is inspiration in the third story of a recluse who is happy in a secret glade where he creates beautiful patterns from natural things like

13 Reginald Heber, 1783–1826.
14 John Chrysostom.
15 Anita Desai, *The Artist of Disappearance*, Chatto & Windus, 2011.

stones and plants. His happy life is destroyed by the modern world bursting in in the shape of a TV crew who are making a film about the environment.

Refugees and displaced people are in many ways the poorest people in the world

You are the caller
You are the poor
You are the stranger at my door
You are the wanderer
The unfed
You are the homeless
with no bed
You are the man
driven insane
You are the child
crying in pain
You are the other who comes to me
If I open to another you're born in me.
David Adam

Every minute 8 people leave home to escape conflict or persecution.[16]

According to the 1951 United Nations Convention on refugees, a refugee is someone who is 'unable or unwilling to return to their country of origin owing to a well-founded fear of being persecuted for reasons of race, religion, nationality, membership of a particular social group, or political opinion.'

Those fleeing from conflict or abuse are increasing.

The United Nations statistics, included with the first target for the first goal, show clearly that there are far more internally displaced people than there are refugees who leave their own countries. Internally displaced people suffer as badly as refugees, and are included in this section. The estimate of 42 million people who are without homes is not correct, and sadly can never be correct, because this number, of oppressed people who leave home, is growing daily.

The overall numbers of refugees has risen partly because fewer people are now able to return to their own countries. 2011 marked the lowest level of refugees returning home for 20 years. The conflicts which drove people out of their countries persist; key areas are Afghanistan, Somalia, Democratic Republic of Congo, Iraq, Zimbabwe and Sudan. Forty per cent of the world's internally displaced population is in Africa but the single country with the largest number of internally displaced people is Colombia, with 3.3 million.

16 UNHCR statistic.

The majority of refugees are in countries near to their home countries, the places they had to flee from for various reasons. It is estimated by the United Nations that developing countries host 80% of refugees. Pakistan hosts the largest number, with an estimated 1.7 million.[17]

Less than 2% of the world's refugees are in the UK, where there is a long history of sanctuary, though offering sanctuary became illegal in the late 17th century. In the late twentieth century the idea of sanctuary re-emerged and churches began to offer refuge to those who were trying to escape from persecution. Sheffield was the first city of sanctuary. This movement is growing in the UK and offers welcome and hospitality to asylum seekers. Working with asylum seekers in the UK is not easy, partly because there are so many people asking for help. Volunteer helpers often have to listen to stories of torture and suffering. The Red Cross is a great partner, doing all it can to help.

Photo courtesy *Glasgow Local News* and Glasgow Campaign to Welcome Refugees

Protesting eviction of asylum seekers from their homes in the city of Glasgow, leaving them to sleep on the streets. May 2012.

There has been a crisis in the Horn of Africa for many years but this has been exacerbated in 2011 as famine was added to internal warfare and general insecurity. The camps for internally displaced people are full of disease. Large numbers of Somalis are fleeing into Kenya and Ethiopia.

---

17 UNHCR has statistics for refugee comings and goings for every country. There are also maps of 'refugee hotspots'.

homeros/Shutterstock.com

Waiting for relief aid in the Dadaab refugee camp.

Dadaab Refugee Camp is about 100 kilometres west of the Somalia border with Kenya; it is a cluster of camps, forming the largest refugee camp in the world. The UNHCR base for the region is here and CARE International manages the camp.[18] Most of the refugees are from the Somali wars, even though Kenya closed its border with Somalia in 2006. The camp has suffered floods, terrorism and most recently drought. The 2011 drought, in a naturally dry region, brought an estimated 1,000 people a day into the camp from the surrounding area, making an unbearable total of around 500,000 people.[19] Cholera, an intestinal infection which is spread through contaminated water, broke out in November 2011 and is an incredible challenge for the camp workers. Most of the children in the camp were malnourished before they arrived there, another challenge.

18 CARE International is 'Cooperative for Assistance and Relief Everywhere'. It is a leading aid agency, working in 87 countries.
19 Figures from Medecins Sans Frontieres.

Dadaab camp offers its occupants few opportunities. Kenya does not encourage refugees to work, seeing them as temporary 'guests' who are causing deforestation and, more realistically, trouble, including the October 2011 kidnapping of aid workers. The refugees are seen as privileged by local people, because they have some running water and some education for the children.

Even when a minority of refugees do manage to reach Europe they have to struggle to be heard and, following hard times as asylum seekers are often returned to their home countries.

A novel by Rose Tremain tells of a man who is not actually a refugee in the UK because he is from Eastern Europe and, as he tells the policeman who accosts him, he is therefore legal. However, he suffers the same initial agony as those who are refugees and asylum seekers. On his arrival he is homeless and hungry, he sits on cardboard boxes throughout the night and is exhausted and depressed. When he does find work it involves very long hours of cleaning in a restaurant kitchen and he is still exhausted. Later he moves to the countryside to a life of labouring in the fields all day and sleeping in a caravan.

There is hope in this book, but it is a long time in coming.[20]

Conversations with many lead me to realise that their hopes and dreams are about the need to rise above hunger but also about the need for recognition and love. One man told me that he had been in the UK for ten years before he began to feel like a real person, a human being with hope for a future.

A story of hope

Jeremy Fowler's life is a story of hope for the people of Burma and for refugees everywhere, and an appeal that more of us may choose to live in freedom, love, bravery and responsibility.

The estimate of displaced Burmese people is now 66,000, mostly from Karen State. There is huge environmental damage in the North, due to gold mining and logging. One hundred rhousand young people have died of HIV related illnesses. Only 10% of the children in Burma complete their primary education.

Jeremy Fowler has lived a changing and many sided life, beginning in Burma and moving to the UK, where he grew up, married and had a family; and then, never forgetting and always in touch and moved by the suffering people of Burma, journeying back to the borderlands between Burma and Thailand to work with the people who have escaped from the Burmese military regime.

He goes to the border camps every year, to take medical supplies, clothes and food for the refugees.

---

20 Rose Tremain, *The Road Home*, Vintage Books, 2008.

A painting entitled 'They must eat as soon as the meal is cooked.' The children must not complain about the food, even when they are hungry, even when it is time to eat and there is nothing available. They cannot choose what to eat. They must have a meal whenever it is ready, for during hiding the situation can become dangerous at any time. The artist is Maung Maung Tinn, himself a refugee from Burma. He was born of a Karen mother and a Shan-Burman father in 1969. He has lived at Mao Tao clinic in Mae Sot, Thailand, as a health worker and artist, since he left Burma in 1995. He helps poor people displaced in Karen State and working as labourers around Mae Sot.

In January 2008 Jeremy Fowler had a very strange experience when he received a telephone call from Bolton in Lancashire. He had never been to Bolton and he knew no-one there, but as he listened he realised that the last time he had seen the speaker, in 2007, she and her family of twin daughters and a son were in a refugee camp on the Thai/Burma border. They had been taken to Bolton by the United Nations High Commission for Refugees following the determination of the Thai Government to reduce the numbers of people in the camps. They had faced a traumatic time on the journey and when Jeremy found them they were completely disorientated and unhappy. Jeremy was able to enlist friendly neighbours to help.

Jeremy was born into a Eurasian family in Maymyo, a small hill station outside Mandalay. Their home was a bungalow with a large garden and fruit trees.

The family was middle class and prosperous; many of them musicians and teachers. Jeremy's father was the Telegraph Master for the whole of Burma. His mother was a seamstress who also taught English and her children were brought up to speak the language beautifully. His great uncle was in the Burma police and remembered working with Eric Blair, or George Orwell as he became famously known.

The family members on Jeremy's mother's side were all prisoners of war in Burma during the Japanese occupation in World War Two. His mother was 23 years old when the occupation began. She and her sisters were very attractive and narrowly escaped being taken by the Japanese as 'comfort women', because their mother threatened to kill them rather than let them go into such a future.

The registration of foreigners was introduced in the 1950s and the teaching of English was banned. Anglo-Burmese people all faced a special levy. Jeremy's family was also vulnerable because they were Christian. Burmese Buddhist nationalism was very strong.

Jeremy left Burma with his mother, father and younger brother in 1958 to travel by boat to the UK. He was 8 years old. Other members of the family went to live in Perth, Australia. Many members of the family moved from Burma gradually, between 1958 and 1996. The last member to leave Burma was an auntie who was helped to leave in 1996. Auntie Marina has settled well in Perth and now, in her seventies, organises community groups and social welfare for many of the Burmese people who live there. There are in fact around sixty thousand Burmese people in Western Australia now. They are the largest Burmese community outside Burma itself.

Jeremy's family arrived in Liverpool to a thick fog, a new and bleak experience for them. They travelled by train to London where they rented accommodation in Hornsea in the north of the city. They were shocked by the rows of terraced houses. The parents both worked in factories at first and then Jeremy's father became a letter sorter with the Post Office and his mother became a dress-maker. At first they rented a small house and had two Jewish landlords followed by a Greek and then a Maltese. Jeremy thinks that his commitment to multicultural and inter-faith living and working was born at that time. He also developed a dedication to work for human rights which began when he made friendships with Jewish people who had been in concentration camps in Germany during World War Two. The family soon took out a mortgage on a terraced house and had managed, by great thrift, to pay for it in only seven years. Jeremy remembers that his mother sewed the money she earned into bags and hid it towards the mortgage. Jeremy sold newspapers, tea and coffee as a child. He delivered groceries round the neighbourhood on a cast iron bike. He faced racism in his secondary modern school, but he never lost his hope and confidence or his belief in himself as a person. He developed a career in interior design and decoration. He tithes the profits from his business to support the Burmese people, especially those in refugee camps. Many of his clients and associates also tithe their incomes and give the money to support the people in the border camps. Jeremy has only once returned to Burma when he celebrated his second marriage there in 1997.

The family remaining behind in Burma suffered a great deal, many dying of malnutrition. There was a caretaker government from 1958 until 1962 when the military coup occurred. The family in England remembered watching TV films of the war in Vietnam and at the same time thinking of their cousins in Burma who were also suffering a similar fate to many of the people of Vietnam. Jeremy has childhood memories of requests coming from the family in Burma for very little things like make up and chewing gum. Today only one auntie and uncle remain in Burma. They are Buddhists and are now in their 80s, living in the belief that 'Next time life may be better.'

Jeremy goes on working with the suffering people of Burma, on the border with Thailand, in Australia and in the UK. He offers friendship, material support through the money raised in his work, but above all he offers hope for a future of work, dignity and freedom to people who had almost lost hope.

Shadows in our own cmmunities

Michael Morpurgo has written a book for older children called *Shadow*.[21] Shadow is a dog who befriends an Afghan boy. This is the story of the boy and his mother, who manage to escape persecution and set off to walk to the Iranian border and from there on to Turkey, France and England. The journey is perilous. One day, in Afghanistan, the boy writes, '*There were no orchards and fields here, just desert and rocks…so hot and dusty by day that you could hardly breathe; and cold at night.*'

They reach England and manage to live in Manchester for six years, where the boy goes to school. Then disaster strikes when permission to remain is refused and the police take them to detention in Yarl's Wood in Bedfordshire, where, '*…inside its all locks and guards. They put us in a prison. We were locked up.*'

The boy in the story represents the many hundreds of Afghan children who travel to Britain, no matter what the hazards are, to seek a safe haven. 547 lone children applied for refuge in Britain in 2010. Caroline Brothers has written a new book about Afghan boys in Europe. There are amazing stories of boys who walked all the way from Afghanistan to European countries, overcoming terrible cruelties both at home and on the journey.[22]

The UK law has now changed and refugee children are no longer sent to detention centres; instead they are separated from their parents, who continue to be sent into detention. The parents are often in detention for a very

---

21 Michael Morpurgo, *Shadow*, Harper Collins, 2010.
22 Caroline Brothers, *Hinterland*, Bloomsbury, 2012.

long time. It is possible to argue that the situation of the children is worse than when they did go into detention. They suffer from terrible insecurity and sadness. Sometimes they are put into foster homes but the evidence seems to be that they are moved around a lot.

It is alarming that some European countries, including Britain, are contemplating sending teenage children, aged 16 and 17 years, home to Afghanistan if their families can be found there. The Refugee Council has pointed out that it is unlikely that the families will be found and that if the children go back they will end up in orphanages in a war zone, where they will be extremely vulnerable.

The other group of refugees in detention in the UK who suffer greatly are the women, who are separated from babies as young as a year, and who are held in detention when they are pregnant. [23]

> And they shall build houses, and inhabit them; and
> they shall plant vineyards, and eat the fruit of them.
> They shall not build, and another inhabit;
> They shall not plant, and another eat: for as the days
> of a tree are the days of my people,
> and mine elect shall long enjoy the work of their hands.
> Isaiah 65.21–22

---

23 See work of Refugee Council for UK.

TARGET - achieve full and productive employment and decent work for all, including women and young people

The **Global Compact**, introduced at the World Economic Forum in Davos on 31st January, 1999, is a learning network with participation from UN bodies, companies, business associations, NGOs and trade unions. It has 9 principles focused on the bringing about of responsible business practices in the areas of human rights, labour standards and environmental performance. The Global Compact asks companies to keep to the 9 principles. They are that businesses should: support the protection of human rights, make sure they are not complicit in human rights abuses, uphold freedom of association & recognition to the right to collective bargaining, work to eliminate forced labour and child labour and discrimination in employment, undertake initiatives for greater environmental responsibility and encourage environmentally friendly technology.

> **Paulo Coelho tells the story of a pilgrim, a shepherd boy called Santiago, who, when he was penniless in Tangier, stayed with a very depressed crystal merchant. He offered to clean the dusty and neglected crystal glasses in exchange for food and then agreed to work for the merchant, who had no heart to do anything himself. As the months went by people not only bought the glasses but were offered tea in them and the merchant's well being and business improved. When Santiago left him the merchant was a new person, full of commitment to his work. Santiago was also enriched for his onward journey to cross the desert and reach Egypt, partly at first by the money the merchant had given him but more by new life, confidence and hope.**[24]

Without movement away from the dominance of feelings of deprivation and helplessness and towards awareness of acceptance and of an ability to do things and thus an awareness of self-respect, people are not able to take a hold on their own lives. With movement and change self-confidence and new life are possible in every country and culture though it is sometimes hard to believe this. In the Western World the issue of lack of employment is growing, and especially for young people.

75 years after the Jarrow Crusade, when 200 unemployed and really poor men walked 330 miles from Tyneside to London, a group of young people walked along the same route, arriving in London on November 5th 2011.The first walk had hoped to highlight the dire poverty of the north east following the closure of the main shipyard, and the second hoped to highlight one

---

24 Paulo Coelho, *The Alchemist,* Harper, 2006, pp. 42–58.

aspect of 21st century poverty, youth unemployment. For instance almost half the 2.5 million unemployed people in the UK are young. The end of the education maintenance allowance means that fewer young people can seek qualifications to improve their chances of finding work. The marchers hope to raise interest in the plight of the young and to give young people themselves confidence to go on.

At the beginning of December 2011 The Joseph Rowntree Foundation published a report.[25] The main thesis is that in 2011 the UK government helps the old and children but continues to neglect young adults, the working poor and the underemployed. The underemployed are estimated to be 6 million people. The report points out that incentives to encourage people to enter work will mean that more people will scramble for the inadequate number of vacancies. The real need is for more work to be available.

Photo courtesy Youth Fight for Jobs and Education campaign

The Post-Industrial North

I recently moved to live in West Yorkshire, a region of both material wealth and extreme material poverty: and because in West Yorkshire the wealthy areas and the poor areas are often only a few miles apart from each other

25 'Monitoring Poverty and Social Exclusion', Joseph Rowntree Foundation, December 1st, 2011.

the experience of poverty is heightened. In this there is a similarity between West Yorkshire and many areas of the developing world, particularly some of the large cities where wealth and dire poverty may be side by side.

Many materially poor villages and small towns in West Yorkshire are poor because they are former mining areas, where most of the men worked in the coal mines and most of the women were home-keepers. The UK miners' strike from 1984 to 5 was a major industrial action greatly impacting upon the British coal industry. The strike was a defining moment in British industrial relations, and its defeat significantly weakened the British trades union movement. The strike in fact became a symbolic struggle, since the National Union of Mineworkers was, if not the strongest, then one of the strongest in the country, viewed by many, including Conservatives in power, as having brought down the Heath government in its 1974 strike. The strike ended with the miners' defeat and the Thatcher government's consolidation of its free market programme.

Soon after arriving in Yorkshire in 2011 I visited **two typical former mining villages.** After the miners' strike many of the more energetic people managed to move away to other regions, perhaps near to family members living in other parts of the country. Those who remained, and still remain, are disillusioned and also proud, but with little confidence either in themselves or in their country, or in the government of any political party.

The villages I visited have been described as the most deprived in Yorkshire. The material poverty of the villages can be measured in the fact that the average age of death here is at least five years below the national average. There are many more teenage deaths than there are nationally, due to suicides, drugs and road accidents. Crime is high, even amongst primary school children of 8 years. There are many teenage pregnancies and there is drug taking and alcoholism. The most difficult housing area has now been demolished largely because it was a terrible eyesore, a situation caused when houses became vacant and the local community robbed and vandalised them. The population of the two villages is about 4,000 and there are only 5 graduates amongst them. Professional people who work in the village, including the teachers in the two village primary schools and doctors and nurses in the clinic, travel in to work from elsewhere.

Most of the village men are now unemployed and some of the women work part time. The work of some of the people in the village, usually part – time, includes a variety of work with the local authority, factory work, caretaking, warehouse work, domestic cleaning, sales assistance, assistance in offices and care homes, school dinner supervision, chicken farming and one fire-fighter. The poverty of the villages has not been overcome even by the money given by the Coalfield Regeneration Trust when the mines were closed. The money was taken for very few projects, including a resource centre which is now mainly used by people who come in from outside the village. The two nursing homes and the local dog track only benefit very few people.

The Anglican Church is the only one left in the area. The Roman Catholic and Salvation Army churches have now gone. There is a problem dating back to 1910 for the Anglican Church, because in that year the local pit owners evicted people from their cottages by raising the rents until they were higher than the salaries, and the Church took the side of the pit/landowners. Some suspicion of the Church remains into the twentyfirst century. There are also different but much stronger divisions dating from the time of the miners' strike in the 1980s. The communities are divided into those who supported and ran the strike and those who opposed it.

The Church, following the normal Anglican approach, focuses on the geographical area of the parish, and relates to everyone living in the parish and not just to those who go to church. The priest decided early in his ministry to specialise in working with families and he has managed to do this for more than ten years, his only problem being that he has not always found it easy to identify the members of each family. It is normal for a mother to have several children, but each child may have a different father. The families are matriarchal, often with a grandmother who has a lot of responsibility.

Now that the priest has been there for ten years the church has won the trust of the people in the villages, so that the vicarage garden provides a lovely colourful and green space which everyone can enjoy. Ten years ago, when the priest and his family were new to the area, there was no trust and the vicarage was robbed. Today there are many baptisms in the bright and modern church. There are also weddings and many funerals.

One simple story amongst many from these two West Yorkshire villages will offer a pointer to the great need all poor areas have for time to

be spent on the people; for care, concern and loving partnerships towards hope and change. The vicarage in the villages I visited has over the years offered a haven to local children who had no food to eat in their homes. On one occasion a woman asked the vicar and his wife to look after her daughter for a few days, because she knew that the police were coming to search her house. The girl in fact stayed at the vicarage for nine months, and when she returned home she kept in close touch. Shortly afterwards, because she was so unhappy in her own home a way was found for her to go to live with her grandmother. She has worked well and is now applying for university entrance.

The work of the church has made it possible for many of the people to grow in self-respect and in confidence so that new life is possible, especially for the children.

Sikh gurdwaras

The Sikh religion offers love, hope and good food to people who are poor, unemployed, homeless and suffering, and also to anyone, rich or poor, who visits the worship centre or gurdwara. The work of the Sikh kitchen or 'langar' is as much part of the worship in the gurdwara as is the worship in the prayer hall; the reading of the scriptures in the 'Guru Granth,' the prayers and the hymns. The 'langar' is open to anyone, Sikh or non-Sikh, and all are treated equally. I have enjoyed meals in many gurdwaras in the UK and in India. The food is always delicious and there is genuine interest in visitors by members of the gurdwara who welcome them and look after them.

Peter is someone who lives in Leicester. He suffered a breakdown in 2007 and became destitute, but due to the help he received from the Sikh community he now goes to college, has a part-time job and lives in a flat.

Here is a letter written by Peter to the members of a Leicester gurdwara. 'I was on the streets for two months until I got a hostel place. I had no money, no friends or family, and nowhere to go. I was starving hungry. After a week or so I was told that I could get a meal at the Guru Nanak Gurdwara in Holy Bones. I was warmly welcomed, told to cover my head and then given the loveliest meal I had ever eaten. The meal was rice, cooked in a marvellous way, a thick soup of peas and cheese, bread and rice pudding. I was also given a drink and a banana. I was also asked if I wanted more, which I did.

I was so deeply touched by the generosity, sincere kindness and the warmth shown to me by the Sikh people when I was in great need and thoroughly depressed.

I have recently been reading the history of the Sikh people. You have suffered so much, including fighting in World Wars One and Two. You are truly amazing and courageous people. I am so glad you live alongside us in our community because you add so much richness of culture. We are so lucky

Lunch at a Sikh gurdwara in Leccester.

Meeting Sikhs

Christians Aware

here in Leicester to have you. The gratefulness, respect and appreciation from me and the homeless in Leicester is huge. I feel indebted for everything you gave me, not just the meals but the warmth. May God bless you.[26]

The Care-Co Story

Paul Draper has worked for most of his life to enable employment for people who are not only poor but also disabled. He pioneered 'Craft Aid' in Mauritius and now lives and works on the small volcanic island of Rodrigues, which is one of the outer islands of the republic of Mauritius where the people, mostly fishermen and farmers, are of mixed African and French descent. The population is about 40,000. The stories Paul tells are of hope arising out of situations where there was no hope.

Paul has written about his work on Rodrigues where he is the Director of Care-Co:

Here on the remote and isolated Indian Ocean Island of Rodrigues, Care-Co is seeking to provide training and employment for people with disabilities.

This our goal. We run a rehabilitation and production workshop and have up to 35 people with disabilities all working together in a 'sheltered' workshop situation.

We once had a visitor who told us, *'This isn't the way to do it. You should set up each of these people on their own, in their own homes with their own mini enterprises . They should be independent, not serving a boss'.*

Others have observed. *'You are trying to set up a small collective business on this remote island which has no culture of production and no raw materials and no resources. Furthermore there is almost no local market for the goods*

---

26 Letter included with the permission of the Guru Nanak Gurdwara in Leicester.

produced, so you have to either export or sell to visitors. On top of that you are seeking to employ on regular wages the people everyone else rejects.

You're mad.!'

That was their SWOT analysis.

Well, that's one way of looking at it.

Yes, the ideal would be to look for income generating activities that people could do on their own and not in a group. But in the 'real world' is this attainable? For the disabled there are issues to bear in mind.

We have a blind man here who is one of those people with a disability but he will try to find his way round any difficulty. You tell him it can't be done, and he will find a way to try and do it. But even he can't do the impossible.

That is why the very laudable term – 'differently abled' when applied to people with disabilities is questionable. It implies that there is no negative aspect and that people are not disabled, but different. This may be true and applicable in some cases but not in all. For the blind man, however hard he tries, is going to find that, on his own, direct competition with an able bodied person is a tall order . However in a group with all working together there is a chance for him. That has been our experience. Of course it all depends on the way it is done, and even the group can't succeed without help and assistance.

In the CARE-CO workshop there are those who are blind and partially sighted, those who have a hearing impairment, severe or profound, and those with physical disabilities and some with 'intellectual challenges'.

The administration is mainly done by the non-disabled who have imported skills and experience. The people with disabilities are as high up the involvement ladder as possible at present. Two of the Board of Directors, the receptionist/telephonist, the shop sales assistant are all people with disabilities as well as 80% of the production workshop workforce.

Care-Co has now been going for 24 years and has received help for the purchase of equipment and for infrastructure, but is self sustaining for running costs. We are attached to a Special Learning Centre for children with disabilities and learning difficulties. The young people from the Centre are given training in the production activities practiced at the Care-Co Centre and full employment is offered as and when it becomes available.

There is also a turnover of people in the workshop on a natural basis as some retire, move to Mauritius or set themselves up as and when possible on a de-localised basis. Care-Co has found a natural operating environment in the Rodrigues context.

The Care-Co Beekeeping and Honey Story

Paul has also written about this. In the 1980's, the European Union funded a Beekeeping and Honey Production Project in Rodrigues. As I understand it, the Beekeeping aspect started well. Local people who were interested in

Care-co
beekeepers.

beekeeping, were recruited and assisted to get basic beekeeping skills and
were offered beekeeping equipment and supplies on a subsidized micro-
credit scheme. The Project was initiated through the Mauritian Ministry
of Agriculture through the Rodrigues Department of agriculture. A Honey
Centre to bottle and market the Honey was constructed and staff employed.
It was from this aspect that,(as I understand it), some problems arose, eventually leading to an abandonment of the scheme as it was originally planned.

In 1989 I arrived on Rodrigues and set up what is now the Care-Co
Rehabilitation and Production Centre. It was suggested by the Island Commissioner at that time, who was aware of the problems with the Government
scheme, that maybe honey bottling and marketing could be an activity that
the disabled could be trained in, and this activity could be included in the
Care-Co programme.

As I did not have any experience in beekeeping or honey bottling and
marketing I requested some advice and help through my contacts and in
1993 the British Executive Overseas organization sent us an elderly beekeeper from the UK to help our organization with techniques for the disabled and to advise on the project. A plan for setting up a well-designed
honey processing centre at the Care-Co site at Port Mathurin was drawn
up and a model teaching Apiary was set up with 5 beehives initially. Our
consultant was always aware that the main objective of the project was to
provide a remunerative and creative activity for the disabled.

Training courses in beekeeping and honey production were started for those disabled people who were in touch with Care-Co and those who were attending the Gonzague Pierre Louis Special Learning Centre. Soon there were over 20 new beekeepers trained and set up, and all of them had disabilities. Some were trained alongside members of their families, so that the beekeeping could be done as a joint effort by all the members of the family, and could be done at home and not involve travelling to a centre.

However as certain norms of handling honey out of the hive needed to be observed to respect the local & international regulations regarding the handling of foodstuffs, the Honey Processing Centre at Camp du Roi obtained help and advice on these matters and is now run under strict procedures and an audit is done every two years.

The trained disabled beekeepers and their family members therefore do their beekeeping at home but the honey processing and bottling is always done at Camp du Roi. The main aim of the activity is therefore social rather than commercial, but the highest standards of beekeeping and honey processing and bottling have been observed and practiced from the outset.

In 1994 our consultant (who visited the project regularly for the following 10 years or so, at his own expense) exhibited the honey at the national honey show in the UK. The honey from Rodrigues was awarded First Prize (Silver Medal) in the Classification 'Honey from all countries of the world except the British Isles and Ireland.' In 2009 our honey won First Prize in the category again and was awarded the Medal of the Brotherhood of Ukraine Beekeepers.

In 2006 the Care-Co Beekeeping and honey producing project was selected as finalist in the BBC Shell, Newsweek World Challenge Contest, and a TV coverage of the project was made and was screened several times on the BBC World TV Network and other networks.

In 2009, with a grant from the EU, we opened up a second model teaching apiary at Petit Gabriel in Rodrigues and obtained the services of Gladstone Solomon, a beekeeper from Tobago to advise on further developments. Today we have the two model teaching apiaries and regular training courses for the disabled graduates from the special learning centre. We bottle on average a total of up to 5 tonnes of honey in presentations of 30 grammes, 240 grammes and 450 grammes in specially designed honey pots imported from the UK, and we sell most of this in our two sales outlets in Rodrigues. We have in the past supplied small pots for the breakfast trays on Air Mauritius and to some selected hotels in Mauritius. Our activities are mentioned in the Rodrigues pages of most tourist guidebooks on Mauritius and the Indian Ocean Islands. and this brings a string of visitors to our premises to see the beekeeping and to purchase the honey – prizewinning 'Miel La Caz.'

The Zaytoun Story

Zaytoun is a fair trade cooperative company founded in 2004 to develop work for Palestinian people and also a market in the UK for the resulting Palestinian produce. The profits made are invested in the development and improvement of products and projects and in the buying of stock. The aim is always to give the maximum income possible back to the local Palestinian communities.[27]

Zaytoun sells a range of products in the UK including olives, dates, almonds, couscous, soap and herbs. By far the main product Zaytoun sells is the olive oil. Olive trees and olives are the mainstay of Palestinian society. The trees are not valued simply for the income they produce; they are also part of the lifeblood of the people; many are hundreds of years old. Farmer Abu Suleiman, one of the producers for Zaytoun, has said,

> **The olive trees root and anchor us in our land, provide a sense of belonging, home and hope.**

Najwa Farah, a Christian Palestinian, has written about the olive tree many times. One of her poems is about olive trees in Jerusalem:

It was a Sunday afternoon,
A wind blew
And those special trees of Jerusalem
Swayed and bent.
Their deep foliage engulfed me with joy mysterious.
The trees were there for many, many years,
by a hospital, church, school, embassy.
They were more ancient than any hospital or church,
There was something about them – profound – an essence.
Many winds had visited these trees,
These Jerusalem trees.
And told of their birth-place, of their journeys
But this is where they want to linger, to stay
to rest and belong… [28]

The olive industry makes up 18% of total agricultural production and 15 to 19% of agricultural output. It is estimated by Zaytoun that 100,000 families depend upon the olive harvest for their income and food security. As the olive industry is developed it does have the potential to lift thousands of Palestinians out of the poverty most of them live in.[29]

Problems which prevent the improvement of the olive industry, and thus of people's lives, include the major one that many of the groves have been destroyed by the Israeli government to build their settlements.

---

27 The Ecumenical Accompaniment Programme in Palestine and Israel (EAPPI) brings internationals to the West Bank to experience life under occupation. See www.eappi.org.

28 Najwa Farah, 'The Colour of Courage', Christians Aware, 1991.

29 Christian Aid report on Palestinian poverty.

An Olive tree in the grounds of St Georges's Cathedral, Jerusalem. Painting by Najwa Kawar Farah.

There are also shortages of water for the remaining olive groves because a lot of the water is used up by the Israeli settlements.[30] Further to this, because the Israeli settlements have mostly been built on the tops of the hills it is not unknown for their sewage to run down the hills and to pollute the Palestinian villages and olive groves. Raja Shehadeh has been walking in the hills of Palestine for many years and has written a book about his adventures.[31]

---

30 The issue of water is tackled by Andrew Ashdown in Chapter 7.
31 Raja Shehadeh, *Palestinian Walks Notes on a Vanishing Landscape*. Profile Books, 2008.

It is lovely to read about the beauty of the area which Raja experienced in his early walks, but is is very sad to realise that much of this landscape has now gone, crushed and covered in concrete during the building of the settlements. One horrible piece of writing is in relation to the sewage which pollutes Palestinian villages and farms.

> This settlement might have had a rubbish collection system but it
> did not have one for treating sewage, which was just disposed of
> down the valley into land owned by Palestinian farmers. We tried
> to step lightly so as not to drown our shoes...[32]

The Palestinian farmers also have great difficulty in accessing their olive groves. This is largely because the separation wall built by Israel between Israel and the Palestinian territories, often cuts the villages off from the olive groves. Often only a very few people are allowed to harvest the olives and they find it challenging, and sometimes impossible, to carry out their routine duties. This restriction not only makes it hard for the farmers to earn a living but it also destroys the spirit of the communities.

Moments of community during the olive harvest are captured by Paula Cox:

A moment of heaven In the hell of the holy land
With the friendship and laughter of the women
Harvesting these ancient ancestral trees
Combing the black and green olives
From the silver branches
Onto sheets laid over red and yellow ochre earth
Under sapphire blue sky
The sweet bitter smell of olives baking in the hot sun
Shovelled by beautiful strong hands
into hessian sacks, sewn up with a huge needle and string.[33]

Percussion of
Falling Olives

32 Raja Shehadeh, page 166.
33 Picture and Poem by Paula Cox from an exhibition 'Celebrating the Life of Palestinian
     Women', 2005.

TARGET – to halve the proportion of people who suffer from hunger

A child dies every 6 seconds from chronic hunger. 40,000 children are blinded each year through a Vitamin A deficiency

Food security exists when people have access to sufficient, safe and nutritious food to meet their needs for an active and healthy life. Food sovereignty exists when people have control of their food from production to distribution, to consumption.

People who suffer from hunger obviously have no food sovereignty and no food security. According to the 2010 UN Food and Agriculture Organisation Report there are 925 million people in the world who are chronically undernourished. The good news is that this is 98 million fewer than in 2009. The bad news is that this huge number of people is still hungry. This target for Goal One is still very far from being realised.

Ghana is the only country in Sub-Saharan Africa which is on course to meet this target by 2015. The overall number of hungry people has increased during the last decade in Sub-Saharan Africa. Women and children are the largest hungry group. People in the rural areas are more vulnerable than those in the cities.

The challenge of feeding the world is huge and many 'experts' are searching for ways forward. Some would say that we need to develop higher yielding seeds, most probably genetically modified. Others propose dams to irrigate the land and fertiliser to improve the soils. But these ways have been tried and have so far failed to feed enough people. There is also the problem of the dependence on non-renewable fossil fuels and of long term use of fertiliser leading to damaged soils.

The cost of food is rising rapidly and governments all over the world are reluctant to invest in farming. Europe and North America particularly are turning to the use of bio-fuels which leads to a reduction in available food crops. The USA consumes one fifth of the world's energy. There is also a growing demand for meat, especially in Argentina and in Asia. It is estimated that only 15 countries account for over 75% of beef and veal imports in the world.[34] The issue of climate change adds uncertainty to the future of farming.

---

34 *Farmers' Weekly*, 6 January 2012.

The world population reached 7 billion in 2011 and it is often said that this is the main reason for food insecurity. However, it may be that many farming systems are not as focused on feeding people as they should be. Many groups are working to improve farming and thus to provide more food.

CAFOD's policy statement on population and development makes it clear that the CAFOD approach is that high population is linked to poverty. The approach is *'Fewer people through less poverty, not less poverty through fewer people.'* It is necessary for poor people to have control of their lives and thus to rise above the poverty line and to choose to have fewer children. The empowerment of women and primary health education are crucial. CAFOD, in line with the teaching of the Roman Catholic Church, does not support artificial contraception or any population control programmes. Many other churches do support artificial contraception and have developed family planning clinics to enable this.[35]

Jonathon Porritt, writing in the 'New Internationalist in January/ Ferbruary 2010, focused on the link between population and poverty, especially the poverty of women and stated, *'...there is a clear link between high population growth in many countries and the continuing failure to address life-crushing poverty...'*

The huge challenge of feeding the hungry and indeed of feeding all the people of the planet does depend on the education and empowerment of the people and must also include consistent work to improve the eco-systems of the world, and additions to the variety available in the food chain. The evidence seems to be that the traditional variety of food crops is being reduced everywhere, though the developing world has more species than the developed world.

When I visited Kenya in 2011 I met an elderly woman whose husband had died. Far from being someone to feel sorry for she was full of energy and every day was spent working in her 'shamba' or small farm. I was taken round the farm and was astonished at the variety of crops she grew including tomatoes, cabbages, kale and turnips. She also had a large fish tank, ducks, chickens and goats. She grew coffee and had joined a coffee cooperative. She had organised a simple system for drip feed irrigation, so that the crops were always moist. She was able to employ about 4 people and also to sell produce in the local market. This woman was remarkable because of her age, but she is not unusual amongst the Kikuyu people I know so well. They are natural farmers who work hard and find a balance between the soil, water, energy, plants and animals. Their way of working could be copied elsewhere in Africa and in the rest of the world.

If more people are to be lifted out of hunger it is vital that every country and people, like the Kikuyu, work hard to nourish the soil and to improve

---

35 The Catholic Agency For Overseas Development. See www.cafod.org.uk.

Kikuyu woman in greenhouse and her shamba (small farm).

the supply of water for the crops. Water is an essential part of sustainable development; a fundamental resource that underpins both life and livelihood. But the poorest are often at particular disadvantage when there is competition over water resources.

Irrigation is important, but also the sensible use of rainwater, much of which is wasted at the moment. More crop diversity is needed, including crops other than grains. The development of trees, and thus the reduction of carbon dioxide in the air, included in Goal 7, is also vital. Agro-forestry is quite normal now in rural Africa. Trees planted on small farms are planted with food crops underneath them, and the trees chosen are fodder and food producing. Old crops can be used for fertilizer, legumes can also be placed between the crops.

It is estimated that less than half the rainwater which falls onto small African farms is used for crops. Some small farms have recently found ways to capture rainwater. When travelling around in African villages it is now easy to spot water tanks which collect the rainwater as it washes off roofs. Sometimes walls are put round hilltops and the water collected there before being piped down into fields and farms. I have taken part in many projects for rainwater harvesting. A memorable one involved the digging of a channel

Rainwater harvesting in Kenya.

down from a mountain in Tanzania and into a large pond in the middle of a village, where fish and ducks were then introduced. The moment when the water gushed into the pond for the first time was magical.

The scarcity of water can plunge whole communities into hunger, especially in rural Africa. Mid-season droughts make farming increasingly hard to depend on. Families may survive on as little as $1 a day, so there's not much to fall back on. But a little know-how goes a long way. Progressio's local worker in Zimbabwe, Melody Kwanayi, works with Environment Africa, a small NGO doing big things to help local communities across southern Africa. Melody has a wealth of knowledge about farming practices that are more sustainable in times of drought, including how to conserve water and how to grow crops that need less of it. Melody's knowledge in partnership with the determination of the people in rural Zimbabwe is a powerful combination.

Patricia Mhike and Blessing Shayanewako who farm in Wedza, rural Zimbabwe.

Hope in Bangladesh

A story of hope for the poorest and hungriest people of the world comes from Bangladesh. Floating nurseries provide a way to grow food despite increasingly severe annual water logging/flooding of hundreds of hectares of fields in the marshy central lowlands of Bangladesh. This technology was learned from a small region further south where farmers have been using floating gardens to grow food on a large scale for hundreds of years. Such adaptation technology is vital for increasing numbers of Bangladesh's population who are forced to live a 'floating life' for the wettest months of the year, due to changes in the climate and environment. These conditions mean that crops do not produce their usual yields causing hunger and malnutrition.

A floating nursery in Banglaesh.

Photo © Steve Buckely, URC

The Soil Association was founded in 1946. It has always worked for safer and healthier food and sustainable agriculture, based on establishing and working with the link between healthy soil, healthy food and healthy people. Organic farming standards have been developed. The Soil Association has often pointed out that more people in the world could be fed if the type of food produced could be changed. They suggest a move away from meat production, reliance on locally produced food and much less reliance on expensive chemicals.[36]

The Campaign for Real Farming is working for *'Farming that is expressly designed to feed people without wrecking the rest of the world.'*[37]

John Pritchard, a former General Secretary of the Overseas Division of the Methodist Church, has written a book on the history of the international work of the church. John has included a section on Merfyn Temple, someone who was converted to organic farming whilst he was in Africa and who went on to spend his life working for it in Africa and in the UK until his death in January 2012.

---

36 www.soilassociation.org.

37 www.campaignforrealfarming.org. See also *Good Food for Everyone Forever*, Colin Tudge, published by Pari, 2011.

Merfyn Temple, long after his retirement, was an ardent advocate of organic farming. In 1965, seconded at the request of President Kaunda for government service in newly-independent Zambia, he was Acting Commissioner for Land Settlement in the Gwembe Valley, where 50,000 Batonga had been resettled when Lake Kariba flooded their territory. The area was seriously overpopulated, and the land was rapidly degraded. At the time Temple was dazzled by the prospects of the Green Revolution, and made small loans to some of his neighbours in Chipapa, the village where he was living, so that they could buy 'miracle seed' and fertilizers. In the first year, the results were spectacular, harvests as much as ten times the norm. But in the second year the rains failed, the crops withered, and the farmers were left deep in debt. The chemical fertilizers were of no help In these circumstances. '*Perhaps,*' he mused twenty-five years later, '*if the benefit of chemical fertilizers had been introduced gradually and selectively, in conjunction with careful measures for soil conservation, rotation of crops, and liberal manuring, little damage need have been done to fragile African soils.*' He became a convert to the organic method:

> '**The organic farmer ensures that the soil's fertility is constantly renewed through the natural processes of life, death, decomposition and rebirth. The chemical nutrients which a plant needs for its growth are created in the manure heap, the compost heap and in the soil by millions of micro-organisms. The organic method of agriculture gradually improves soil fertility and is therefore indefinitely sustainable. As it requires no external inputs, it is available to anyone with access to soil, water, sunlight and a crop to grow. The incorporation of livestock into an organic farmer's system provides valuable manure for increased soil fertility. When this livestock includes draught animals such as horses, mules, donkeys, camels or oxen, the farmer has an additional renewable energy source for cultivating crops.**'

When he retired, Temple put his convictions to the test and devoted eight years to a two-acre organic market garden near Reading. Then in 1989 he marked his 70th birthday with a tour of East and Central Africa, some of it by bicycle, both to look at organic farming and to encourage the friends who had taken it up. He enthused his old friend Kenneth Kaunda, and Kaunda was impressed by the organic farm at the David Livingstone Teacher Training College – but by that time Kaunda's days at Government House were numbered. Organics were still a minority interest: Temple described in poetic vein the more general picture:

> '**With their axes they have cut down the trees to plant their crops and make charcoal for their cooking fires. With plough and hoe they have scorched the earth, turning soil into dust, to be driven on the wind, or washed in muddy rivers down to the sea**'.

In fact, he could see, the damage had two causes. There were the foreign agribusinesses, to whom he wanted to say *'Keep your dangerous herbicides to poison your own land … and let the women and children of Zambia destroy their weeds with their own hoes.'* And there was the pressure of runaway population growth, with so many mouths to feed making excessive demands on the soil. In this Zambia was not alone. One of the most outstanding, and provocative, missionaries in the final half of the Twentieth Century, Merfyn Temple was a passionate evangelist with a 'life-inclusive' gospel.

Nutrition insecurity

If all the world's people had easy access to local fruits and vegetables there would be a huge reduction in hunger and also, in the Western World, in obesity. Nutrition insecurity means that people are often eating the wrong mixture of foods. Most obese people are in this group together with the malnourished.

On one of my regular visits to Calcutta I was taken aback in a bustee community hall when, as we were being introduced I noticed a poster on one of the walls. It had the large heading 'How To Increase Your Weight'. How sad that we so often see posters in the developed world which read 'How to Reduce Your Weight'.

In the developing world there is a need to improve the preservation of food, and the transport of food to market.

Further, farmers in the developing world could do more to take their basic commodities to the next stage of production, thus making them more saleable. For example, chocolate could be made in cocoa producing countries, peanuts could be made into peanut butter, pineapples and other fruits could be canned. I included the good example from Rwanda earlier, where pineapples are being made into jam and juice. However,much

Photo: John Daniels

processing of African crops is currently done in the Western World or by the large companies who normally take most of the profits and do not even pay appropriate taxes.

In the last 50 years the amount of value added to agriculture per person has doubled, except in Africa where it has declined, and where people have become more dependent on imported food. This situation has meant that food speculation has hit the poorest people in the world very badly.

Food speculation by investment banks and hedge funds is a recent problem which has meant that food prices have gone up so much that many poor people can no longer buy anything to eat. Food prices have been rising steadily over 2011/12 and are now higher than the prices during the food crisis of 2008, when the number of hungry people reached over a billion. Now the number of those who are hungry is scandalously higher.

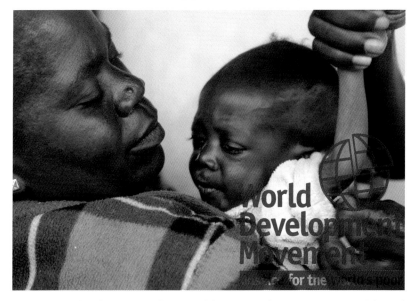

Commodity futures markets need better regulation to ensure stable and affordable food prices for the benefit of consumers, producers and businesses in the UK and globally. This is especially important for the world's poorest countries and people. The World Development Movement is asking that everyone campaigns in Westminster and Brussels to bring change to:[38]

○ Ensure transparency on commodity futures markets, by requiring all deals on food derivatives take place on regulated public exchanges.

○ Prevent excessive speculation from distorting food prices by introducing position limits to restrict the number of food futures contracts that can be held by financial institutions at any given time.

---

38 For more information see: www.wdm.org.uk/food-speculation.

Solomon Raj is an Indian theologian, a Dalit and artist who has always accentuated the social aspects of the Gospel message and the inculturation of the Gospel within the culture of the poor and despised ones in India. For that reason, the Gospel of St. Luke seems to be his favourite Gospel, Luke is also the patron saint of artists.

Solomon created a book of wood block prints and meditations inspired by St. Luke. One of his meditations was inspired by Luke 12.22–23:

> **Hunger, cold,**
> **sickness and death**
> **are razing around.**
> **Children are dying**
> **Masses of people are starving.**
> **May we think of the hungry**
> **and the naked**
> **Before we ask –**
> **'What shall we eat,**
> **or what shall we drink.'**
>
> (P. Solomon Raj, 'Liberation in Luke's Gospel,' St. Luke's Lalitkala
> Ashram, Vijayawada, Andra Pradesh)

Two wood block prints by Solomon Raj – We and They *(left) and* The Lord Remembers the Hungry *(right).*

A recent book written by Solomon is *Biblia Pauperum ~ The Poor Man's Bible*. Solomon explains that originally the bible of the poor was printed with simple wooden blocks. The words and pictures were cut onto the blocks and then printed manually directly onto the page. Often the wooden block books were produced in the period between the illuminated manuscripts and the books produced by the printing presses.

> '**For I was an hungered, and ye gave me meat: I was thirsty and ye gave me drink: I was a stranger and ye took me in: Naked and ye clothed me: I was sick and ye visited me: I was in prison and ye came unto me.**' Matthew 25–35 & 36

Purim

All the great world religions have an obligation to relate to and help the poor people of the world. One of the Jewish festivals when the poor are remembered is Purim. People observe the festival, which takes place in March, by helping the poor, by giving to charity and by giving gifts, including food, to friends. The story of Purim is found in the Hebrew Bible in the Book of Esther, and it takes place in Persia in the reign of King Xerxes I, around 481 BCE.

The story is that the minister of the King falsely accused the Jews of disobeying the laws because they would only bow to God, and not to him. The Jews were condemned to death but the Jewish Queen Esther and Mordecai, her guardian, persuaded the king to let the people defend themselves. The success of the Jews and the defeat of Haman are celebrated by the holding of a feast when pastries filled with prunes, poppy seeds, apple, apricot and dried fruit are made in the shape of Haman's ears.

Leave This

Leave this chanting and singing and telling of beads!
Whom dost thou worship in this lonely dark corner of a
temple with doors all shut?
Open thine eyes and see thy God is not before thee!
He is there where the tiller is tilling the hard ground
and where the pathmaker is breaking stones.
He is with them in sun and in shower,
and his garment is covered with dust.
Put off thy holy mantle and even like him come down on the
dusty soil!

Rabindranath Tagore, *Gitanjali: Selected Poems*, MacMillan India.

Opposite: Good news to the poor, by Jyoti Sahi.

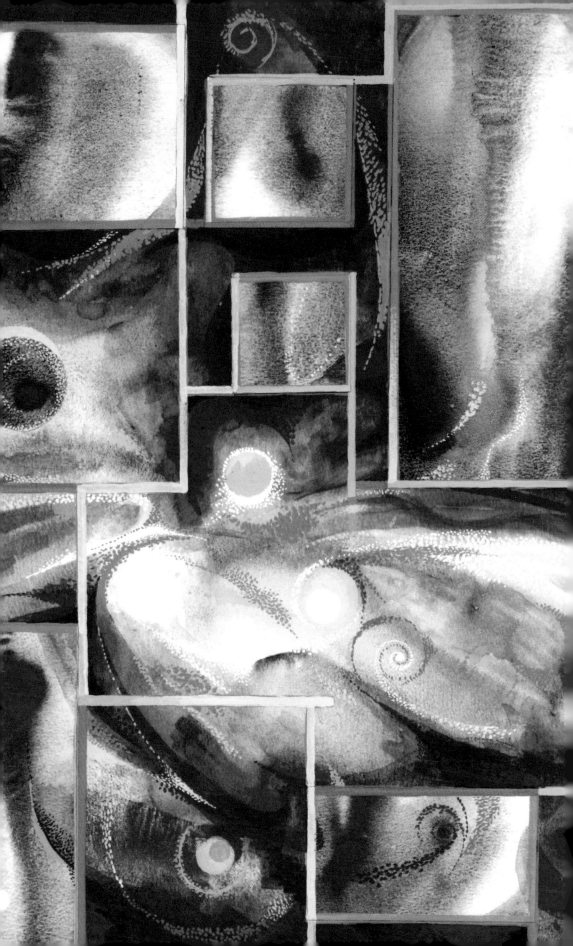

Goal 2

Achieve Universal Primary Education

Many of the things we need can wait,
The child cannot.
Right now is the time his bones are being formed,
his blood is being made
and his senses are being developed.
To him we cannot answer, 'Tomorrow'.
His name is 'Today'.

Gabriella Mistral

If you're thinking a year ahead,
SOW a seed;
ten years, PLANT a tree;
a hundred years,
EDUCATE THE PEOPLE.

A Kikuyu saying ... good character must be cultivated from an early age.

Children are obviously the most valuable resource the world has and their education is vital. I would want to go further and to say that if primary education is good it will naturally lead on to lifelong learning. I have focused on primary education in this chapter but I have also included some examples of secondary and adult education.

The number of children in primary education is growing as we move towards 2015 but what do we expect and hope for from growing schools all over the world? Does the increased number of children in primary schools point to real improvements in the lives of the children or not?

TARGET – by 2015, children everywhere, boys and girls alike, will be able to complete a full course of primary schooling

Good progress is being made all over the world and in 2010 only 10% of children of primary school age were out of school. However, this 10% represents 72 million children and half of them live in sub-Saharan Africa.

Opposite: Windows on the Universe, by Anne Gregson.

Huge efforts have to be made to overcome tremendous problems in much of the developing world before the children can learn in any real sense. Children are often malnourished, ill and hungry, sometimes they are living in homes which are dark and impossible to read in. I have stayed in such homes. I spent a summer holiday in Africa, helping to build a girls' dormitory for a new technical college, where there was simple **solar panelling** so that the girls could do homework for an hour or two each evening. Mityana Diocese in Uganda is remote and undeveloped but serious attempts are being made there to improve the lives of the children. In 2010 an appeal was made and solar panels and lighting equipment were sent out, so that now the primary school children can study after dark in their homes. The educational opportunities for the children have been vastly improved and their families have a better quality of life. Mosquito nets and antibiotics to fight typhoid have also been bought. In most places many simple improvements still need to be made for the children and for all the members of the communities.

The potential for harvesting solar energy in Africa is immense.

African school using solar power.

Learning in Community

To do justice to the children of the world primary schools must above all be places of purpose and of hope. Teachers should be able to believe that their contribution will make a difference and to go on to work in a way which will enhance the potential of all their pupils. Teachers must also be able to respond to the communities around them, offering the children relevant and useful skills so that they can adapt and change as their environment changes. If education does not make a difference to the lives of children, no matter what their background is, then it is not education. The development of each child is vital. Sometimes the families children come from are so deprived that teachers also have to seek to work with parents and to offer them resources and suitable skills training.

A YMWS Pavement School.

One community we send the Christians Aware groups to, which I visit regularly in Calcutta, is the interfaith Young Men's Welfare Society. The society offers learning opportunities to children of all ages, from three to eighteen years old. There are pavement schools and night schools, where the children from the bustees or slums are offered the same conditions and teachers as the fee paying day pupils. The parents are closely involved in the education of their children and opportunities are offered to them also, to learn basic skills including reading and writing. Many Muslim parents had reservations about the education of their daughters, so the Society now has a Muslim girls primary school and also a girls secondary school from which the girls may go on to university education. I have visited the Muslim secondary school for girls and it is a place of work and of hope. The YMWS began in the 1960s and now there are teachers who began life as bustee children and who have moved through the Society schools to achieve their university education and teaching qualifications. The name of one of the YMWS schools sums up their hopes in focusing on education, which is the 'jewel in the crown' of their wider developmental work. The school is called 'Young Horizons'.

Learning in Groups

Learning, begun in primary school, should go on naturally throughout life, never ending. Schools should be places where new thinking is encouraged, where shared hopes are released and where pupils and teachers are always learning how to learn together. Learning in teams is vital, as in a sports team, where there is a common purpose even though every person might be doing something different from the others. Success and happiness depend on trust and risk.

A community which developed trust and risk together was the community of peasants in Solentiname, a remote archipelago in Lake Nicaragua. They were encouraged by Ernesto Cardinale, a poet and Roman Catholic priest, and they included writers, poets and artists. The group met every week to discuss the current Gospel reading. Books were published in the 1970s and finally one volume emerged.[1] The power of the book even today is that it is a record of the good news of the Gospels from the perspective of truly poor and oppressed people. It was in fact banned by Somoza, the dictator who ruled Nicaragua until 1980. The art work of the peasants is creative, bright and inspiring.

Beate Dehnen is an artist who works with Christians Aware and who has run a series of interfaith workshops for primary school children.[2] Beate normally works with groups of children, beginning with discussion of subjects to be drawn or painted and looking at some works of art. The children may then go on to create a shared work of art. In 2012 a shared calendar was created by the children of one primary school in Leicester. The children began by singing together and then singing in rounds:

> **may there be peace in the East,**
> **may there be peace in the South,**
> **may there be peace in the West,**
> **may there be peace in the North,**
> **may there be peace throughout the world,**
> **peace throughout the world.**

The children then shared their thoughts and feelings about peace for themselves and for others. They then talked about how to produce the calendar for peace. They prepared the sketches, transferred them onto foam sheets which they used as print blocks, inked them up in different colours and printed the calendar.

---

1 The Gospel in Solentiname, Orbis Books, 1982.
2 Beate Dehnen, *Stepping Stones…*, Christians Aware, 2011.

may there be peace throughout the world

inter-cultural and inter-faith calendar   2012

PEACE

STEPPI   STONES towards each other

If children are enabled to share their hopes and dreams together, in academic work, in discussions and in practical work, then they are likely to become well-adjusted teenagers and adults who are useful to their societies and countries.

The Learning Process

In every discipline the learning process itself may be neglected. What is learnt is valuable but how it is learnt is more valuable. Awareness of the learning process may actually be a spiritual experience which may carry the pupils forward. This is not something that can be captured or measured. There is the need for expressing feelings, tackling conflict, waiting for consensus, valuing colleagues as people, group development, recognising inadequacy, building trust, risking and responsibility. Above all pupils and teachers must work on real issues.

Learning Practical Skills

Many schools and teachers all over the world make the huge mistake of valuing academic gifts and success as more important than practical skills. Countless children are gifted in a practical way and their work and contributions need to be recognised as just as valuable as academic disciplines.

In his book *The Wrong Boy*,[3] Willy Russell writes through his anti-hero, Raymond Marks, who comes from a dysfunctional family and faces a life of persecution, near tragedy and suffering, because he has been classed as troublesome. The book is about Raymond's journey back to normality, after he has met someone who believes in him. He writes – about playing his guitar –

After I'd rescued it from under the stairs and polished it up and got new strings, I practiced and practiced every day, my fingers aching and stinging in agony from making the shapes and pressing the strings, until gradually my fingers became supple enough, the tips grew smooth and hardened up and I could press the strings and play the chords without feeling any pain.

Raymond had learnt to be happy, to become himself and to be a learner.

The School of Barbiana

Children have to work on real tasks and awareness of this need is not new. The School of Barbiana was founded as long ago as the 1950s by Don Lorenzo Milani in the remote mountainous community of Barbiana in Italy for boys who had dropped out of school. The community is about thirty miles from Florence and near to where Giotto was born. Attendance at the school was voluntary and often the older pupils taught the younger ones. The pupils also decided what they would learn, which would be useful to them in their adult lives. Don Lorenzo ran the school until he died in 1967 and then it was run by the pupils. There is a book, *Letter to a Teacher*,[4] written by eight pupils in 1969 to a state school teacher and comparing their experiences at their state school and at the School of Barbiana. Briefly what the students are saying is that the state school existed as a closed system, where the teaching and exams were based on the culture of the middle class children and were therefore mostly irrelevant to poor children. It is pointed out that the pencil is the tool of the middle class child whilst the shovel is the tool of the poor child. What was most hurtful was that the state school

---

3 Willy Russell, *The Wrong Boy*, Doubleday, 2000.
4 *Letter to a Teacher by the School of Barbiana*, Penguin Books, 1972.

excluded the life experiences of the poor pupils from the school, which badly affected the poor children whose families lived very practical lives, often as hill farmers. The School of Barbiana in contrast made real links with the real world of the poor. In 1969 the school was moved to Calenzano, where it continued in the same way for boys and also for adult pupils. This school was developed a long time ago, but its message is still needed all over the world in the twentyfirst century.

Barbiana and beyond

I recently met a young British man who had been thrown out of his school about ten years ago because he refused to listen to lessons and was disruptive. A local farmer was asked to take the boy on and to give him the opportunity to do practical work. The farmer agreed and ten years later the young man is one of his most responsible workers. He often stays late at night when there is lambing or when other work needs to be done. He is even left to look after hundreds of animals when the farmer and his family are on holiday. What a pity it is that the school could not offer some real life experiences which could have led the boy on to listen and to learn from the wider curriculum.

Understanding what is taught

A friend who worked in an African university was uneasy about the progress his students were making. They always did well in his tests however, so he decided to try an experiment. He prepared extracts from his textbooks with questions to be answered at the end of each paper. But, he changed a key word in almost every paragraph of all the papers and inserted a new word, something like 'gibberish.' And his suspicions of the understanding his students had of his teaching were confirmed. The answers were perfect in terms of what was written on the paper, but, because they included the new words they made no sense. He started again.

If university students in the developing world, whose first language is most probably not English, do not easily understand what they are being taught, how much more is this the case for many primary school children. When we say that enrolment in primary education is going up, what exactly do we mean? I have visited many schools in the developing world and some of them are excellent. Many, however, have very large classes and very little equipment. Often the teachers are struggling to keep order in classes of more than fifty children. One teacher told me that he did little more than run up and down the aisles between the desks, shouting and calling for order, and if it was raining even this was impossible. I am left wondering what many children are learning.

I have of course visited good schools in the developing world, in Africa and in India. Good schools are often those which are privately owned, so that classes are smaller and teachers have a better chance of engaging with and helping the children as individuals. There are many privileged schools, where the children come from middle class families whose parents pay the fees, but I am not referring to those schools. Some schools in the developing world are run by churches and other charities and they offer the places to poorest children. I went into Highbridges school near to Nairobi in Kenya in 2011, where the children mostly live in rural slums and are receiving excellent education from a dedicated head teacher and creative and committed staff. There are about twenty children in each class and they do understand the lessons. They mostly get places in good government secondary schools. In the local government primary school I visited the children just did not have the same opportunities. The teachers were excellent but the classes were too large.

Happy Children

I went to a primary school in Othaya in the north east of Kenya, where the small boarding school is linked to a very new teachers' training college, so that the students at the college go into the primary school with their lecturers. The primary school and teachers' college have both been established by a private benefactor, who is himself a teacher and who is dedicated to improving the standards of education in Kenya. He is also interested in the children being happy, something not always considered in education everywhere in the world. He has made sure there is a field for the children to play in and that the dormitories are comfortable and the food good.

The happiness of children, at home and in school, is a new idea in much of the developing world, where survival is often the priority. Timothy Ranji is someone who has worked to provide home and school environments where children are happy. When I visited his diocese towards the end of 2009 I became aware of a person who is totally dedicated to the children of Kenya. I saw a wonderful display of photographs from his climb to the top of Mount Kilimanjaro, which at 19,000 feet is the highest mountain in Africa. This was not an easy climb for Timothy but he simply put one foot in front

Crispus Ngungire is a teacher at Othaya Teacher Training College. He is son of the founder, Godfrey Ngungire.

of the other and did reach the summit, largely because he was urged on by thinking of his hope of raising money to build a children's home for those in great need in his diocese, including those who are HIV positive.

Timothy climbed the mountain and therefore 'got things started'. Then he involved as many people as possible in the project. The first thing he did was to ask parishes throughout the diocese to identify children in great need who might be included in the new Mothers' Mercy Home. This was not hard to do and there are now eighty five children who have a home and a future.

Timothy challenged every archdeaconry to share the responsibility for fund raising for the home. When I was at the home I met about twenty young people who had come to work with the children from one of the

archdeaconries. They were a good mixture, including school & university students and those running their own businesses. They were happy and obviously enjoying their work together, including playing with the children, hairdressing, preparing food and farming.

Whilst I was working at the children's home with the Christians Aware group I was very conscious of one corner of the 'campus' where a clinic had been developed. This was obviously no ordinary clinic because the buildings were new and strong. We were shown round and discovered that this clinic was fitted with the very best equipment for many of the conditions affecting the children and the surrounding community. What was even more amazing was the rota at the front of the

Timothy Ranji, Anglican bishop for the Diocese of Mount Kenya South.

clinic, which listed specialists who would attend for a short time over the next month or so. I realised that the specialists were not Kenyan but came from Germany.

Timothy told the story of how this came about. The Mothers' Mercy Home lies between an airport and a hotel. Sometimes, after long flights, air crew members walk across country to reach the hotel. Fokko Doyen, the captain of a Lufthansa flight from Germany walked that way many times and became interested in the people living in the area and also in the Anglican children's home. He met Timothy and together they created a remarkable scheme for the building of the clinic and for the free return travel of medical personnel who could work in the clinic for whatever time fitted in with their normal programmes in Germany. A plan has been worked out so that responsibilities are shared between the Church in Kenya and a German charity.

Timothy's vision for the children of Kenya has produced wonderful results but he is not resting. He is now building a school for boys in Tharundi. Timothy feels that many boys are neglected at the moment, because most publicity and work are for women and girls. There will be more mountain climbs, more travels round the country and more talks, this time to help the boys. The men's association has been enlisted to run the school. There is also an annual initiation programme for boys between 10 and 14, run by the church and taking them through the traditional circumcision rite, with counselling before and after the ceremony.

I saw the new buildings of the boys' school going up when I was in the country in 2011 and since returning home I have received photographs and news of the form one boys who have now started their studies.

Timothy's main aim is that as much as possible should be done for the children of Kenya, in their own homes and in

Mother's Mercy clinic and dormitory.

Tharundi school under construction.

community homes and schools when there are no parents or carers. When children become destitute, as many do, special homes should be, and must be, provided for them.

Above all children should be children, able to play and be happy. When I was at the Mothers' Mercy home the children were undoubtedly happy. This is their home, from which they go to school in a bus provided by the Mothers' Union of Kenya, and to which they return to do homework and household tasks as any other child might. The children have a farm and animals providing milk. They are healthy and bright, some with the prospect of university ahead of them. One girl won the national prize for English.

Timothy Ranji is a man of love, prayer and action for all the people and especially for the children.

He prayeth well, who loveth well
Both man and bird and beast.

He prayeth best, who loveth best
All things both great and small;
For the dear God who loveth us,
He made and loveth all.
Samuel Taylor Coleridge

Telling Stories

When I was in the Mothers' Mercy Home in 2011 I noticed a large poster in one of the classrooms. The poster read, 'Books are our Friends'. Reading and telling stories are the best ways to give children and also adults the skill of listening and learning. In visualising a story children and adults may yearn to learn to read. The use of story also helps to build bridges between people of different ages, backgrounds, cultures and religions

Beullah Candappa is from Burma. I saw her hold a Christians Aware conference entranced when she told them the story of her own childhood when she was a refugee in Calcutta during World War Two. She spoke of how she would always remember her Jesuit teacher and that she wanted to return to Calcutta with one of the Christians Aware groups in memory of him. She joined a group in 1997 and asked to visit her old school. She met many pupils and teachers in the school but then was completely bowled over when she spoke of her old teacher and was quickly told that he was in his mid- nineties, alive

and well and still living in the school. The re-union was extraordinary and up-lifting. The re-telling of the story was even more up-lifting for those who listened.

A story may give hope and new energy to children and adults alike. A legend which brings this home is the one about the old rabbi who lived in a village somewhere in Poland. He was a good rabbi and the people loved him, but somewhere in his heart he was dissatisfied with himself and he began to

lose his confidence. One night he had a dream, that if he walked to Krachow, a beautiful old town more than two hundred miles from his village, he would find treasure hidden under a bridge which would transform his life. He decided to set off to find the bridge, taking a very small bag of clothes and food for the journey. He walked for several weeks, at last coming to Krachow, where he found the bridge of his dreams. He rushed to the spot under the bridge where he had dreamt that the treasure would be and he began to dig. He dug a deep hole, but found nothing. A little girl watched him as he dug and finally asked what he was doing, so he told her his story. 'I know a story like that,' she said. 'I have dreamt that many miles from here there is a village where an old rabbi

Old Paloc story-teller entertains the crowd at the Easter Festival at April 12, 2009 in Holloko, Hungary.

lives, and in the corner of his small home there is buried treasure.' The rabbi stopped digging and turned and walked all the way back to his home, where he began to dig up the floor. At last he heard the clank of a tin, and sure enough he had found treasure, more than enough to build a school for the village children. The treasure had been at home all the time, waiting to be discovered.

The story of the rabbi always gives listeners energy and may set them off on new paths, realising that the resources they already have are enough to make a real difference.

I visited a small village primary school in India which bases much of its work on telling stories and where the children are well cared for, well taught and happy. Jane Sahi's school is in Silvepuram near Bangalore. She started the school about forty years ago for children from poor families who would otherwise have had no education. She has created an atmosphere where the children, from Hindu, Christian and Muslim families, are able to learn. She realized early on that the children might learn best by listening to each other telling stories. Stories give hope and creativity. She also offers art, drama and dancing to the children. On more than one occasion I have listened to stories, watched plays acted out by the children, enjoyed dancing, including the local stick dancing, and viewed wonderful exhibitions of the children's painting. I have also been given beautiful calendars which the children have produced, sharing together in groups.

Created by the children of Sita School, Siluvepura, Bangalore North, South India, 560090
ಸೀತ ಬಾಲ ಮಕ್ಕಳಿಂದ ರಚಿತವಾಗಿದ ಸಿಲುವೆಪುರ, ಬೆಂಗಳೂರು ಉತ್ತರ ಭಾರತ 560090

This calendar is about night and day and was painted by the children of Jane's school. Many images were generated working on the themes of village, forest, light, dark, memory and imagination, with a story as the starting point. Some of these were put together into a single composition. The images were then translated into clay seals, which were used to print the final calendar. The children wrote:

'A calendar year is made up of days and months. Every day divides into light and dark – day and night; but not every night is dark. When the moon shines it lights up the night and when it doesn't the darkness can be overwhelming. This rhythm of the phases of the moon is what the months of the year were once based on, which still remains significant during times of celebration. For this calendar we worked on a picture of the dark. In one part of the picture the moon lies buried in the forest and creatures of the dark haunt the village. The other part shows the memory of light-filled nights when the moon shone down from the sky'.

A new school for very young children is the Little Elephant Pre-School in Thayyur in Tamil Nadu, which is being created so that young children in South India can be healthy and happy. The school will offer good food as a first priority for the children of poor parents. There will also be plenty of time and equipment for play and relaxation, followed by listening to stories and basic education. The hope is that the children will have such a good start in life that they will be able to learn throughout their lives in a country where it is estimated that more than 60% of children do not even complete their primary schooling.

Mentally Disabled Children

It is especially important that there is love and education for mentally disabled children. Vital work is going on in India. The Census of 2001 states that 2.13% of the Indian population has such disabilities. However, this data is keenly disputed, with alternative estimates invariably much higher than the official ones. The population of people living with disability in India's neighbouring countries is substantially higher, 5% in China, 5% in Nepal and 4.9 % in Pakistan. One WHO report states that 10% of the entire world's population lives with disability, and there are more such people in India than in any other country.

In India, the National Policy for the Mentally Handicapped was formulated in 1988, which gave an impetus to the development of Persons with Disabilities (Equal Opportunities, Protection of Rights and Full Participation) Act. Coming into force in 1995, this act envisages mandatory support for the prevention, early detection, education, employment and other facilities and social security benefits for the welfare of people with disabilities in general and with mental retardation in particular. In addition, this Act provides for affirmative action and non-discrimination against such people.

There are over 30 million mentally retarded children in India, of whom only a few attend special schools or get vocational training. For the vast majority there is no help because of the lack of resources. Realising the difficulties, the **Martin Luther King Centre for Democracy and Human Rights in Orissa** started Utkarsh, a residential school for mentally disabled children, in the 2008–9 academic session, with seed money from the Diocese of Derby, routed through Christians Aware, with whom there has been a friendship since 1983. The idea was to meet some of the long felt needs of the people of Mayurbhanj.

'He who passively accepts evil is as much involved in it as he who helps to perpetrate it. He who accepts evil without protesting against it is really cooperating with it.'
Martin Luther King (1929–68). His statue at Westminster Abbey.

Shanti Ranjan Behera writes about Utkarsh

We have gradually admitted 41 children, sent to us by the government institution. The Children are given disability certificates by a medical board consisting of experts from different departments. The 'Rights of Children to Free and Compulsory Education Act', which was passed by the Indian Parliament on 4th August 2009, describes the modalities of the provision of free and compulsory education for children between 6 and 14 in India under Article 21 A of the Indian Constitution. India was one of the 135 Countries to make education a fundamental right of every child when the Act came in to force on 1 April 2010.

Education is a fundamental human right and essential for the exercise of all other human rights. It promotes individual freedom and empowerment and yields important development benefits. Yet millions of children and adults remain deprived of educational opportunities, mostly as the result of poverty.

We have opened a home for the children during 2010-2011. We have admitted 11 children who have lost one parent and some who have lost both. Some children were working as child labourers. In addition to this we have also rescued 3 children, including a new baby and a 3 month old baby. All the children have been admitted in Indapahi Primary School.

Basically, we are making a humble effort to meet the Millennium Development Goals with special reference to Goal No 2. We do focus on the education of the girl children. Incidentally, full and equal enjoyment of human rights and the elimination of all forms of discrimination against women have not yet been attained anywhere.

Here are the stories of some of the children in Utkarsh. They all come from very poor families so that the school is paying for food, accommodation, uniform, bedding and clothing and learning materials. During their short stay in the school they have learnt life skills like going to the toilet, knowing cleanliness, brushing teeth and taking a bath.

Gita Majhi was 12 years old when she was admitted to the school. She was illiterate and had 65% of disability. Now she has learnt the alphabet and numbers. She can recognize the coins and has developed social skills and communicates in the Oriya language.

Runumani Mohanta, was 9 years old when she was admitted to the school. She was illiterate. Now she is learning the alphabet, can recognize the coins and has developed the social skills and communicates in Oriya language. She is a slow learner.

Deblal Hansda was approximately 7 years old

when he was admitted in Utkarsh. He was illiterate when he was admitted. He is having 70% of disability. He has come from an extremely poor family below the poverty line. The family gets rice under the government anti-poverty programme. He is a slow learner and requires more time than others.

Gouranga Naik was approximately 10 years old when he was admitted in Utkarsh. He was illiterate when he was admitted. Now he is learning the alphabet and has developed social skills. He is a slow learner and requires more time than others.

Bishop Sargeant School is for the 'Mentally Disabled' in Palayamkottai

One of the teachers in this school worked in the Christians Aware office and has shared many stories of the work with the children. One of the stories is about the bakery training programme.

The Tirunelveli District Women Welfare Project arranged a bakery training programme for 25 members of the self-help group. This training was giving by Mr. Ganesamoorthy, the differently abled mentally retarded person of our school and other bakery staff for a period from 13.09.10 to 18.10.10. At the end of the training programme certificates were issued to all the participants. We bought a new bakery oven and a mixture machine.

New bakery oven.

Literacy is the key to healthy and happy families

I have included a detailed account of the work of Janice Clark, a Methodist Mission Partner, in Sierra Leone. It gives a valuable insight into how the adult literacy classes work, into the huge difficulties the communities face and into some of their hopes for a new future. Janice's writing highlights the struggles and also the hopes of literacy training in a developing situation where people are hopeful of teaching and learning but are hampered in so many areas, not least ill health. In Sierra Leone the work is going well, but sadly the same cannot be said everywhere in the developing world.

It had been decided that the newly trained literacy facilitators should have a few weeks of teaching, on their own, before I made a visit to see how they were getting on. On 1 November 2010 they were invited to attend a meeting, where they would receive their allowances for October, share stories of how things were going, and for me to give them additional activities and ideas to encourage active participation of their learners. "There were 10 in the bed and the little one said 'Roll over'" went down really well!

During the first week of November I visited 3 classes, 2 in Wellington, an hour's drive from Freetown on a good day, and one in Waterloo, 3 hour's drive from Freetown on a bad day, 90 minutes on a good day! All of the adult literacy classes take place from 4 to 6pm. The first class I visited was that of Deen. He and Sahr should have been teaching together, but Sahr has been quite sick for the last three weeks, and has been diagnosed as having TB. His wife goes to a clinic each morning to get his medication for him, and once the treatment has started to work, it is hoped that he will be back in the classroom.

Deen was teaching at one end of a small church, built from local materials, in Wellington, not far from the 'Methodist Church Sierra Leone People Living with HIV project'. During the day, the building serves as a nursery and primary school, and is the church Sahr attends. Emphasis on confidentiality is very important in relation to the facilitators, and people in the community are not aware of their HIV status nor of that of many of the learners. Although 14 have registered for the class, not all of them manage to get there for every lesson, and punctuality is not a strong feature. Most of those registered are women, and are clients of the 'Methodist Church Sierra Leone support group for people living with HIV'. Deen was working on the alphabet and in particular looking at the vowels and the consonants, referring to how they can be found in the learners' names. Having had only 2 weeks of training,

the facilitators are operating with limited background knowledge of teaching and resources. For people in Britain this would appear formal and passive, but for both learners and facilitators there is always enthusiasm for what is going on.

I then went to Lifeline School, a large independent school, about 10 minutes drive from the first group, and up a rather steep and rough track. Mohammed, Emma, Osman, and Watta were using classrooms belonging to the school, and had started out with 2 classes, but for the last week, had joined the classes together, due to the unpredictability of attendance. 14 learners in total have registered, each of them paying 1000 leones registration fee (17p). There are some within their groups who have had some primary schooling, and so they have decided to split the group into two, with those having had some schooling, working together.

Work was being done on number recognition, and the four facilitators gave a very good demonstration of team teaching, with each of them doing a few minutes and then handing over to another person for a different activity. Flashcards had been made and replicate activities from their training were practised. Again, enthusiasm for all that was taking place was obvious.

Three days later, on Friday afternoon, I headed out for Waterloo, a 90 minute drive on a good day, but on Friday afternoon, with broken down vehicles, and just general congestion the journey out took two hours. Chris and Agnes M have 23 learners registered and they come from either MCSL or are from a similar support group in Waterloo, Progressive Union, whose building they are using for their classes. I met the project officer Mr Lebo, who expressed much appreciation for what the project is doing, and

Particpants in the lieteray programme in Sierra Leone.

emphasised to me that both he and the learners are HIV+. Agnes was not there, as she was not feeling well.

On the day of my visit, there were 18 learners there, in good, clean and comfortable facilities, with chairs for them all to sit on. None of the learners present had been to school, and the majority of them were women. All the learners had name tags, and Chris was working on revision of the alphabet. Agnes was not there, not all the learners had exercise books, and so I was able to help out, with a few sheets of paper and pens. There are also some learners, who were not present, who have been to school, and so the group is split appropriately. The centre provides two rooms that can be used and as a result the groups can operate independently.

The return journey to Freetown took 3 hours, but fortunately I was not driving, and so did not need to concentrate on the traffic with its lights on full beam, or without any lights.

The enthusiasm shown by both learners and facilitators is to be admired. One of the learners in Chris's class, Alie, has the ambition to go to Fourah Bay College, part of the University of Sierra Leone. Hopefully not just Alie, but many of the others will develop skills which will not just improve their own lives, but that of their families as well.

Janice made her second visit to the literacy project in February 2011

The enthusiasm of the literacy facilitators continues to be buoyant, working well with their groups, and attending the monthly meetings that have been established, for sharing what is happening, practical support and ideas and to receive their monthly allowance. The latter is probably the main reason for coming to the meeting, but although the amount is about £15 a month, it does give a regular income. One of the facilitators used his first allowance to pay the fees for his partner to finish her training as a secretary.

There have been joys and sorrows amongst the group. Chris had been enjoying much better health, having got TB, and he and Agnes, another of facilitators were planning for a "marriage" to take place in Chris' village at Christmas. They had spent time together, sent each other texts, Agnes had made Chris a cake, and both were looking very happy. Right at the end of November I received a text to tell me that Chris had died, following a severe coughing bout, just about the same time that the news arrived on our compound. Chris worked in a media office just across the road from where we live, so visited us frequently. Agnes was able to attend his funeral and burial in his home village. When asked how she is, she says, like many other Saloneans "I'm managing".

Sahr's partner was expecting a baby. He was owing her family money as part of the traditional bride price. Once that was paid he would be accepted by her family. A couple of months later I received the news that the baby was born alive, but within a short time had died. The cause was not known.

It suddenly became noticeable to me that Tina was pregnant. She kept saying that if the baby was a girl then she would be called Janice, if a boy then Peter. Peter arrived safely at the end of December, and I am happy to announce that mother and child are doing well.

Mariama had come into Freetown from the provinces to live with her sister. She passed the door where a class was taking place, had a look in, was invited to come inside and has been attending class ever since. Aged about 17, she has not been to school, speaks little Krio, no English, but is fortunate that one of the facilitators for her class speaks her language that of Temne. At present she is still at the stage of practising writing letters on a slate but is keen to learn, ably assisted by Deen. Mariama is a Muslim, and may have attended Arabic classes. She started her writing at the right, and wrote all the letters backwards. Yet another skill to be tackled, to work from left to right, from top to bottom.

Mr Ellie was not able to teach for a while as he was coughing blood. He went to the hospital and had an X ray, and TB was diagnosed. For two weeks he was too weak to go for his medication, which is taken daily, so his wife went for him. She does not know that he is HIV+. Once the medication started to take effect, then the smile on Mr Ellie's face returned and he was back in the classroom. When I spoke to him recently, he told me he was having problems with his chest again.

Such is the precariousness of life in Sierra Leone, and even more so for those who are HIV+. This precariousness also affects the attendance at the literacy classes. Malaria is constantly reoccurring, and the government at present has a programme for the distribution of bednets to all households, and, if properly used, they greatly reduce the incidence of fever.

Supervisory visits continue to be made to all the classes. Considering that the facilitators have only had two weeks of training, they are doing their best. In a couple of classes seeing women carefully hold a pencil, and with great concentration write their name, or copy words off the blackboard, brings home just how difficult it is to learn such skills, taken for granted once we are literate. The speed of learning is slow, and one facilitator commented that it was as though they forgot everything over the Christmas break, which was just a couple of weeks.

Those who may have had just a little schooling are able to work more quickly, and so with two facilitators for each group, one facilitator is able to help the learners who find things more difficult, while the other one works with the rest of the group. The age range of the groups varies, one group having the grandmother of the facilitator as one of the students. Vowels and consonants have been a favourite topic, and appear to be an essential piece of drilling. Fortunately many groups have now moved on to two letter sounds and are encouraged to identify the sounds they have on a chart in their books in their own names, and the names of their colleagues. "Aminita"

"Mabinty", "Adama" being just a few examples. All the learners are now able to write their first names without assistance though they muddle up capital and small case letters.

As well as literacy skills, numeracy skills are also being developed. There has been a move on from basic counting to add numbers together, and some have now moved on to adding two digit numbers.

When the facilitators meet together, one of the recurring issues is how to encourage the learners to come on time, and to attend regularly. The facilitators acknowledge that the learners encounter all sorts of difficulties, whether through reasons of health, family responsibilities, domestic chores or employment. There is a concern that the classes are not being taken seriously by all, but certainly are by some. The classes have been open to the local community where they are held, and so all groups are now made up of clients from the Methodist Church Sierra Leone Clinic and community members. One group is in partnership with another support group for people liveing with HIV.

The clients of the MCSL clinic on occasions receive food from the World Food Programme. The suggestion was made that an incentive for those who as yet have not attended classes, might be that if they are not able to sign their name by a certain date, they will not get their food ration. "Food for learning." The expectancy that everything will be free is common, and work is taking place to reduce this dependency syndrome. No decision has yet be taken on this suggestion.

At present there are about 80 learners registered. Things are progressing quite well. The facilitators should be observed in the near future. In July there will be a short refresher course, when it is hoped that they will all receive official certification to be Adult Education Facilitators.

The learners and facilitators continue to be grateful to all those who have contributed to making this project possible.

A third visit was made to the literacy project in April 2011

It is just over six months since the Positive Lives Literacy Project started. Many of the learners who came to the first class continue to be regular attenders and are making good progress. A few have found it difficult to keep the commitment of meeting twice a week, but there have been a number of new learners. The project was originally to support women who are clients of the Methodist Church Sierra Leone Community Care Clinic for people living with HIV. They continue to be the largest number of learners that attend. When the classes were initially being set up the facilitators discussed whether they could include people from within the community where their classes are located. It was decided that this would be good, and by being open to the community, it would avoid an exclusive group, and the question "Why them and not me?" and encourage integration of HIV+ people with others in a learning situation. A few learners have sneaked into the classes who have already had some schooling, but for one man it was over 35 years ago. He attends regularly, and is enjoying retrieving information stored in his long term memory.

The class that is in partnership with another HIV support group is working very well. Although it is quite a distance away from Freetown, 25 miles, the supervisory visit is always worthwhile. All the learners are HIV positive and the classes give another reason for hope in their lives. It is the getting out and into Freetown that is the problem, not the distance, so dense is the traffic.

The content of the lessons has moved on considerably and the repetition and rote learning has been somewhat reduced. Now the learners are practising greetings and having conversations about hygiene and cleanliness around their homes. One of the positive outcomes is a lot more fun and humour. Another outcome of the project is the sense of belonging to a new group, and being concerned about each other. New friendships have been formed and the atmosphere in the various groups has changed considerably since the first classes.

The facilitators decided recently to introduce merit cards, to give incentives to come on time, to bring a friend and to bring their books, and this too has had a positive effect. Like all forms of learning, initial progress seems slow, but once improvement can be seen then personal motivation sets in.

Another facilitator has given birth. Watta informed me for the last 4 months that she was carrying baby Janice. I visited the school where she was working on a Monday, to be told that she had rung to say she was not feeling well. I saw her, the following Friday, and there she was with baby Peter! Both mother and child are doing well.

I am happy to report that Mr Ellie is much better, and has a big smile on his face. The health of the other facilitators is good, although Agnes had serious chest problems which seem to have cleared up.

The staff of the MCSL Community Centre are giving serious encouragement to those who initially indicated they wanted to attend classes, and the proof of the commitment of the learners is the ability to write their names when they attend the monthly meetings, and when they receive allowances of food. No signature, no food!

The programme has now reached the stage where it is necessary for PADECO, who led the original facilitators' training, to monitor them in the classroom, and to run a refresher course in July. This was not in the original budget, and therefore both facilitators and learners are most grateful to all those people who in different ways have contributed to the project. There have been a number of unexpected contributions recently and these are just so important for all the unexpected expenses that occur.

Ah tell yu bohku bohku tenki (I thank you very much).

Olga Popova/shutterstock.com

Child Refugees are a link between the developing and the western worlds

The children who move to the west alone are vulnerable and lonely. In the UK they no longer go into detention, but may be placed with foster parents and in children's homes. Their lives have no security and are frequently disrupted as they are moved from place to place. Such treatment does not help them to move on from their traumatic pasts.

A sign of hope is the Leicester Unaccompanied Child Initiative (LUCI). Established in 2006 as part of the city's Baptist Central Poject, LUCI runs a freedom club where the children are offered education, information and support.

One of the offerings to the children is art projects. Beate Dehnen leads the classes and says, 'Art functions as a shelter. It is an opportunity to find new skills and to find self-esteem and confidence. The exhibitions give the young people appreciation and a voice.'

A poem written by one of the children –

'My name is B – I am from Darfur,
I'm 16. I've never met you before.
Sudan, Libya, Italy, France
I came to England to have a chance.
I travelled across many different nations,
But now I'm here I can get an education.
We are the boys of the Freedom Club,
All we really want is peace and love.'

Refugee Children's Art Project.

A Celtic Prayer of thanks for Saint Hilda of Whitby

Blessed are you God of each land,
For giving Hilda as a radiant jewel
to light up the darkness of her people.
Faithful in both achievement and adversity,
constant in disappointment
wise mentor, generous host,
counsellor of rulers, friend of cowherds,
encourager of talents,
able teacher, noble in bearing,
unceasing in praise –
light up our lives and our lands today.

From *Liturgies from Lindisfarne: Prayers and services for the
pilgrimage of life,* Ray Simpson. Kevin Mayhew Publishers, 2010.

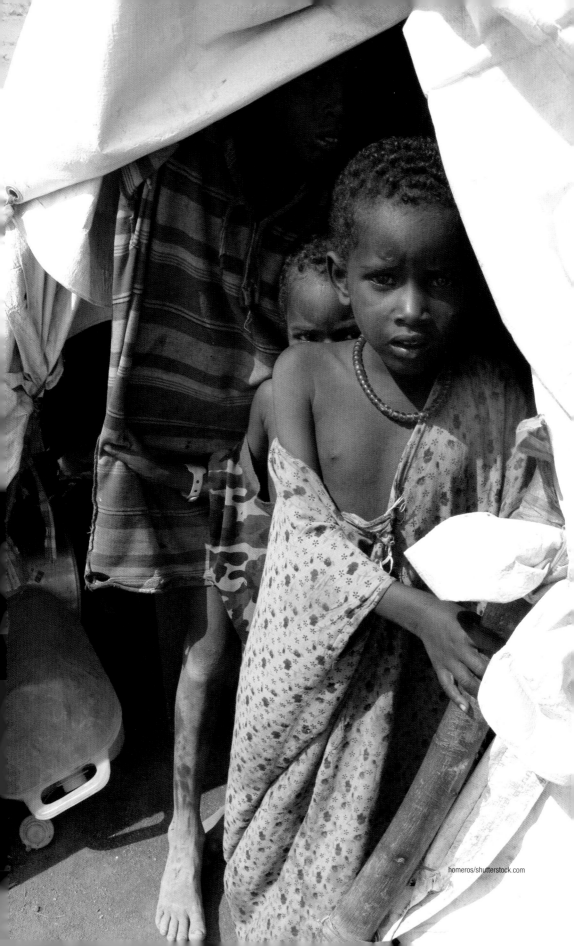

Declaration of the Rights of the Child

This is the plain language version of the Rights of the Child.

1 All children have the right to what follows, no matter what their race, colour sex, language, religion, political or other opinion, or where they were born or who they were born to.

2 You have the special right to grow up and to develop physically and spiritually in a healthy and normal way, free and with dignity.

3 You have a right to a name and to be a member of a country.

4 You have a right to special care and protection and to good food, housing and medical services.

5 You have the right to special care if handicapped in any way.

6 You have the right to love and understanding, preferably from parents and family, but from the government where these cannot help.

7 You have the right to go to school for free, to play, and to have an equal chance to develop yourself and to learn to be responsible and useful. Your parents have special responsibilities for your education and guidance.

8 You have the right always to be among the first to get help.

9 You have the right to be protected against cruel acts or exploitation, e.g. you shall not be obliged to do work which hinders your development both physically and mentally.
   You should not work before a minimum age and never when that would hinder your health, and your moral and physical development.

10 You should be taught peace, understanding, tolerance and friendship among all people.

Goal 3

Promote Gender Equality and Empower Women

'The principle which regulates the existing relations between the two sexes....is wrong in itself, [it is] now the chief hindrance to human improvement and it ought to be replaced,.... admitting no power or privilege on one side, nor disability on the other.' John Stuart Mill, *The Subjection of Women*, 1869

This English nineteenth-century vision has not even been fully realised in the western world. In the rest of the world there is a very long way to go. It is shocking that a millennium goal of achieving gender equality remains necessary. The United Nations Commission on the Status of Women was established in 1946 as a global policy making body to promote women's rights in practically every sphere of life. The commission made a contribution to the Universal Declaration on Human Rights and since then has met every year to promote women's empowerment. Much of the work is fact finding followed by efforts to remove discrimination. There has always been a strong focus on community and rural development, and on family planning. It is very sad however to realise that female genital mutilation was not seen as a type of violence until the mid-1980s and it is still practised. Attitudes at the time included that of one African bishop at the 1988 Lambeth Conference, who spoke of female circumcision as being morally neutral, a practice which could be lived with, whilst cattle rustling was morally wrong and had to be eradicated.

Female Genital Mutilation (FGM) includes 'all procedures involving partial or total removal of the external female genitalia or other injury to the female genital organs for non-medical reasons'.[1] An estimated 100 –140 million girls and women currently live with the consequences of FGM, most of them in 28 African countries.[2] Opposition to FGM goes back to the nineteenth-century voices of some European missionaries, but the beginnings of real change came with the 1995 Beijing Conference of Women when opposition to FGM was presented as a health and human rights issue.

---

1 World Health Organisation definition.
2 Research carried out by Feed the Minds in 2011.

An anti FGM poster produced by Population Media Center for Ethiopia.
"NO, WE DO NOT WANT OUR DAUGTHER BE (or get) CIRCUMCIZED.

Delegates also understood that if change is to be made it has to be from within the communities. Local pioneers have to be identified. There is a long way to go in spite of international statements.

In 1997, a joint international statement against the practice of FGM was issued by the World Health Organization (WHO), the United Nations Children's Fund (UNICEF) and the United Nations Population Fund (UNFPA). In 2008, a new statement was released, with wider UN support and a stronger focus on the human rights, legal and policy dimensions.

There are many reasons for the continuation of FGM into the twenty-first century, not least the long-standing habits of the women who carry it out. Women, often those who oppose cultural change, feel that they have gone through the procedure of FGM and they expect their daughters to do the same. When Cheryl Bentsen spent time with the Kenyan Maasai in the 1980s this became obvious to her. Cheryl was there during an 'operation' and she wrote that the women laughed when the cutting was carried out, even though the girl being cut was screaming. When asked why they laughed the women said that the procedure was normal and part of the Maasai culture. They were happy that they had kept the culture of their people.[3]

FGM is a rite of passage from girlhood to womanhood and many girls see it as the doorway to social acceptance and a good marriage. It is also sadly seen by parents as a way of reducing the sexual desire of girls and women and thus making sure they are faithful wives. As with many traditional customs in many parts of the world, it is the women who are restricted, or who restrict themselves, whilst few people ask what the men are doing. Some people may say that women's restrictions have developed because women are central to the life of the families and communities, whilst men are more peripheral and therefore freer.

The evidence from the research carried out by Feed the Minds points to the Kenya Demographic and Health Surveys (KDHS) which show that the overall prevalence of FGM has been decreasing over the last decade. In 2008/9, 27% of women had undergone FGM, a decline from 32% in 2003 and 38% in 1998. Older women are more likely to have undergone FGM than younger women, further indicating the prevalence is decreasing. However, the prevalence has remained highest among the Somali (97%), Kisii (96%), Kuria (96%) and the Maasai (93%), relatively low among the Kikuyu, Kamba and Turkana, and rarely practiced among the Luo and Luhya (less than 1%).

Young Kenyans against FGM.

---

3 *Maasai Days*, Cheryl Bentsen. Collins, 1990.

In Kenya, approaches used, with varying degrees of success, to encourage communities to abandon FGM include: health risk/harmful practice approaches; educating and providing alternative sources of income to circumcisers; alternative rites of passage, including talks and ceremonies; addressing FGM through religion; legal and human rights; and the promotion of girls' education and empowerment programmes. FGM was made illegal for girls under eighteen in Kenya in 2001 and the evidence is that the practice is reducing.

Health professionals now always encourage all women to abandon FGM. They point out that it is a form of torture which is very dangerous. It can lead to death.

1976 to 1985 was the United Nations Decade for women, which raised women's issues and spread them through other UN commissions. In 1979 the Convention on the Elimination of all forms of discrimination against women was adopted by the UN General Assembly. It committed Governments to take:

> **...all appropriate measures, including legislation, to ensure the full development and advancement of women, for the purpose of guaranteeing them the exercise and enjoyment of human rights and fundamental freedoms on the basis of equality with men.**

The convention, whilst obviously failing to achieve its aim, has remained a useful instrument in tackling injustice, and has also been widened to include HIV/AIDS, disability and general violence against women, which is now approached as a public instead of a private matter. The Commission undertook the drafting of the 'Declaration for the Elimination of Violence against Women' in the early 1990s. In March 1994, a Special Rapporteur on violence against women was appointed, with a mandate to investigate and report on all aspects of violence.

The United Nations definition of violence against women includes any act or threat which leads to mental, physical or sexual suffering. A world-wide WHO study found that between 15 and 71% of women reported experiencing violence by a partner, leading to many health problems, including vulnerability to HIV. These figures may be the tip of an iceberg, because they do not include those who are too afraid to speak. Violence against women can be almost invisible.

Women likely to be most vulnerable to domestic violence and other forms of oppression are those with low education and those who have had bad treatment as children. Sometimes they may also witness violence as children. There is also alcohol abuse and attitudes of acceptance of violence and gender inequality. Sometimes poverty can lead to oppression. The same criteria may be applied to those who perpetrate violence.

This poem was sent to me from Uganda. It speaks volumes.

Families are reluctantly violent, promoting HIV&AIDS rampancy.
A penniless husband leaves home, asks his wife to improve things.
He comes back late in the evening, and asks for food with vigour,
and yes, the wise woman has improvised:
Isn't prostitution improvising?

In situations of war or other conflict, and of displacement, women are especially vulnerable to violence. Women refugees are at great risk and not infrequently women and girls are moved across borders for sexual exploitation. It is estimated by the United Nations that about a million women and children a year are trafficked for sex. A small minority are trafficked as forced labour. The use of the internet and mobile phones now means that trafficking is increasing. In the UK women are brought from many countries all over the world and are sometimes rescued and sometimes not. A recent book tells the story of an English girl who went to Italy for a holiday with her boyfriend, who then forced her into prostitution to repay his debts. [4]

Courtesy unitescotland.org

It is normal for women, girls and boys to be deceived by the traffickers, or even by their own families who sell them into this modern slavery. They are often raped and beaten after they arrive in the new country, so that they are mostly afraid to do anything to save themselves. Their documents are taken away and they are normally used as prostitutes. [5] It is illegal in the UK for a man to have sex with a trafficked woman, but this does not seem

---

4 *Trafficked: My Story*, Sophie Hayes. Harper Collins, 2012
5 Churches Alert to Sex Trafficking across Europe is 'CHASTE' – www.chaste.org.uk

to be a deterrent. Efforts are now being made to make it illegal to arrange trafficking anywhere in the world.

The issue has been by addressed by many artists and writers. Uwem Akpan is a Jesuit priest in Nigeria who has written a book of stories about Africa's children and one of the stories is about a brother and sister whose uncle tries to sell them into slavery in Gabon.[6] And as far back as the mid-ninties the British crime writer Ruth Rendell read about sex slavery in Sheffield and wrote *Simisola*. The eponymous Simisola was a young Nigerian girl who was already dead early in the story. When her body was found a web of selfishness, greed, deceit, and oppression was gradually unravelled, and it became clear that the abuse of human rights is not limited to poor and uneducated people who try to get rich quickly.[7]

Amnesty International[8] has called for human rights reform in the new Egypt, including the ending of the thirty year state of emergency, arbitrary detentions and torture. The call includes an appeal to the new government to give women equal rights with men in public life and before the law, in marriage, divorce, the custody of children and inheritance, and further to protect women from domestic violence, including rape. It is very sad that the Amnesty call has to include the appeal for 'FGM' to be made illegal and for abortion to be allowed when women and girls have been raped or where their health is at risk.

Many women in the west also suffer from violence. According to the NSPCC[9] – a quarter of all girls and 18% of boys have experienced some form of physical abuse. Three quarters of girls and half of all boys have experienced some form of emotional abuse. A third of girls and 16% of boys have reported sexual abuse.

In the UK in November 2009 a cross government strategy was set up to tackle violence, and in December 2011 the government announced plans to make domestic abuse include emotional abuse. The plans have now been implemented. The Home Office defines domestic violence as any incident of threatening behaviour, violence or abuse, whether it is psychological, physical, sexual, financial or emotional. In recent years abuse has come to include cyber bullying. Young people may be oppressed and abused through internet web sites and through e-mail messages. This can be a terrifying experience.

Erin Pizzy started Chiswick Women's Aid in 1971 – and gradually a network of safe houses developed all over the country. This work continues today and there are now 500 women's refuges in the UK. The police also take violence more seriously. Erin Pizzy is against the new government plans and maintains that domestic violence is the correct description only when people, mostly women, are in fear of their lives. She has written,

---

6 *Say You're One of Them*, Uwem Akpan, Abacus, 2008.
7 *Simisola*, Ruth Rendell, Arrow, 1995.
8 Amnesty International – www.amnesty.org.uk.
9 nspcc.org.uk.

Affected by domestic abuse?

Join the Survivors Forum!

Want to talk to other women who have experienced domestic abuse?

Post messages, share your thoughts and get support at
www.womensaid.org.uk/survivors-forum

women's aid
until women & children are safe
www.womensaid.org.uk

Supported and hosted
by Women's Aid.
Funded by The Body Shop.

' ...there is always clear evidence in domestic violence cases, bruises, cuts, internal organ damage or scars. Unless you have seen real shocking abuse as I have, it is difficult to imagine some of the awful violence that people can inflict on each other in the home.' (Daily Mail. Dec 15th, 2011)

Education is obviously crucial in achieving gender equality but it is hard to know whether this will automatically lead on to women seeking employment. Will education also give women more confidence and therefore the strength to resist abuse? It is possible that the first opportunity women need is to be employed and to have some independence, including choices to make for themselves and their families, including the education of their

children, especially the girls. It seems to be the case that when women raise the living standards of their families they earn respect and thus freedom.

Until perhaps the beginning of the twentieth century women all over the world were severely restricted in their life choices, with the exception of those who were from privileged groups or of outstanding health and personality. Marriage was the lot of most women, childbearing took up most of their time and energy and often caused their deaths. Chapter Five focuses on maternal health or lack of it in the twentyfirst century. We have seen that over the last hundred years or so great changes have come in what is known as the 'developed world', including Europe and North America, but most of the women of the world, with a few exceptions, are still struggling.

Programmes to combat violence are very badly needed. Some work is done in schools but what is most successful in the developing world is training for women in micro-finance which gives them the ability to become financially independent and able to help their families. Improving communication within the family and the reduction of alcohol intake are also important.

Muhammed Yunus

Muhammed Yunus is someone who has brought new life to women, first in Bangladesh and now in many developing countries, by introducing micro-finance through the Grameen Bank. Yunus targeted women borrowers who used the small amounts of money they borrowed to set up businesses. The borrowed money was then paid back to the bank for others to borrow. This pioneering work led to Yunus being awarded the Nobel Peace Prize.

Muhammed Yunus

Yunus grew up in Bangladesh and, following university in the West he became a professor of economics and a government adviser. As part of his work he began to ask why so many people in his country were poor. He later told the story of one woman who made baskets, but when he asked her why she was so poor when the baskets were so beautiful he discovered that most of the money she earned went to a middle man who supplied the materials. He gave her a loan to buy her own materials and within a very short time she had doubled her income and also repaid the debt. He went on to try the experiment with more people and eventually decided, when the commercial banks refused to be involved, to set up his own bank. The Grameen Bank now has more than 5 million borrowers, who are amongst the poorest people in the country. The loans continue to be small, somewhere in the region of £60, but they lift most borrowers out of poverty. It is interesting that 95% of the borrowers are women, who are able to develop their work and also help their families. When the loans are returned to the bank they include interest. Borrowers have become savers who are able to buy land and enlarge their businesses. In Bangladesh the borrowers have normally chosen to work within their communities and to improve sanitation and the health of all.

A micro-finance group.

Microcredit has spread from Bangladesh to many parts of the world. Yunus has set up the Grameen Trust to train people who want to introduce microcredit projects and to adapt them to local situations and needs. Large donations have been given to the Grameen Trust and Yunus has been able to set up the 'Consultative Group to assist the Poorest.' He also works with 'Results', an international lobby organisation which campaigns for governments to work to end poverty.

BRAC is an anti-poverty organisation working with the poorest women in Bangladesh to save lives and raise incomes. This system has spread from women to men in many places. I saw a wonderful example in Kiambu on the edge of Nairobi when I sat in the small bank, set up by the diocese of Mount Kenya South, and saw the queues of people file through, to borrow money for their small businesses and also to pay in money so that new people could borrow.

Kashf, which means miracle, is a microfinance organisation in Pakistan which lends mostly to women. The women work in groups of twenty five and they guarantee each other's debts. They begin by borrowing small amounts of money each and when the businesses grow they are allowed to take a second and larger loan and thus to expand their work. They meet regularly to discuss their businesses, and they also share issues facing them and their communities and families. Family planning is an important topic for discussion and also action as is girls education and how to help victims of rape. Kashf was started by Roshaneh Zafar, a well educated Pakistani woman who learnt about microfinance from Mohammed Yunus and then translated his vision from Bangladesh to Pakistan. Yunus is currently talking about bringing his system of small loans to the UK, because he has heard about the high rate of unemployment.

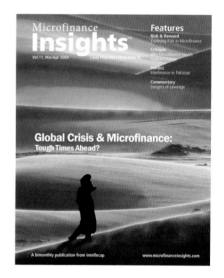

Roshaneh Zafar at India Economic Summit, 2005.

The World Conference on Women was held in Beijing in 1995. The Beijing recommendations were reaffirmed in New York in 2000 at the time of the Millennium Declaration. The conference's main document states:

> **The Platform for Action is an agenda for women's empowerment. This means that the principle of shared power and responsibility should be established between women and men at home, in the workplace and in the wider national and international communities. Equality between women and men is a matter of human rights and a condition for social justice and is also a necessary and fundamental prerequisite for equality, development and peace.**

In July 2010, the United Nations General Assembly created UN Women, the United Nations Entity for Gender Equality and the Empowerment of Women. This creation came about as part of the UN reform agenda, bringing together resources and mandates. It merges and builds on the important work of four previously distinct parts of the UN system, which focused exclusively on gender equality and women's empowerment:

○ Division for the Advancement of Women (DAW);

○ International Research and Training Institute for the Advancement of Women (INSTRAW);

○ Office of the Special Adviser on Gender Issues and Advancement of Women (OSAGI);

○ United Nations Development Fund for Women (UNIFEM).

Goal 3 is perhaps the hardest one to reach. It is obviously for this reason that the targets are limited to the easier to record areas of the education, employment and the political involvement of women. Even in these areas this goal and Goal 5 are the ones where the least progress has been made: when the assessment of the goals was held in September 2010 warnings of failure were given and promises to try harder were made.

TARGET – to eliminate gender disparity in primary and secondary education

It is not possible to isolate education, employment and political activity from other areas of what makes for gender equality and the empowerment of women, or more realistically the lack of it. I have approached this chapter in a broad way and have included many of the impediments to women's empowerment and gender equality all over the world. There is little point in women being educated and employed if they continue to be subject to violence in their communities and homes and to rape, often as a weapon of war, to genital mutilation and to many other forms of violence and abuse.

It is crucial that gender equality in its widest sense is reached, even if this seems to be a long way away, because it links to so many of the other goals, and especially the first one, of reducing poverty, and the fourth one, of reducing infant mortality. There have been a number of reports, from the United Nations, World Bank and others, arguing that the achievement of gender equality is the key to eliminating world poverty. The United Nations Charter strongly affirms the equality of women and men.[10] In the introduction to the Christian Aid report on poverty it is pointed out that the achievement of gender equality is a very long way away.[11] A key commitment to 'Gender Minimum Standards' has been made by Christian Aid in this document.

---

10 The 192 member states must comply with 'fundamental freedoms for all.'
11 *Poverty: We're All in this Together.* A Christian Aid Report.

THE RICH, THE POOR AND THE FUTURE OF THE EARTH: EQUITY IN A CONSTRAINED WORLD

POVERTY

Courtesy Christian Aid

christian aid

'All Christian Aid supported programme work...must recognise and take account of these gender dynamics, ensure women's participation...'

It seems obvious that when women are empowered they help their families. Educated women with equal status to the men in the family are more able to keep their children clean and healthy, to feed them on nutritious foods and to struggle for their education. Educated women also make a huge contribution to society. There are some wonderful examples of what women do in our world today. It is also encouraging to reflect on women's development in the UK over the last hundred years, when so much has been achieved.

Rook76/shutterstock.com

It is hard to believe that as late as November 1910 there was fighting between suffragettes and the police in Westminster and more than 100 people were arrested. In 1913 Emily Wilding Davison sought to bring the women's cause to the public in a drastic way when she threw herself in front of the king's horse at the Epsom Derby and died four days later. It was as late as 1918 that women over the age of 30 were given the vote, at the same time as women in Germany, Austria, Latvia and Poland. Women were given the vote on the same terms as men in the UK in 1928, when they were eligible to vote at the age of twentyone. World War Two was the watershed for women, and since then there has been a steady improvement in women's lives, with growing education, freedom and responsibilities.

Kenya

It is possible to misunderstand a situation in another culture and country and to assume that women are in need of liberation when they may or may not be. I visit Kenya regularly and have sometimes organised exchanges, so that Kenyan groups come to the UK to meet people, stay in homes and learn about work and life. Some years ago when I was in Kenya I went to stay with old friends in their home on the edge of the Abedare Mountains. They have four children, who were then very young, and both mother and father were teachers in local schools. The father of the family had been to the UK in one of the groups I had invited and hosted and it occurred to me that it would be good for the mother, to come in one of the future groups. I shared the idea with her but she was not very keen. She explained that her husband goes away quite often, and she and the children just carry on with their lives and work. Then she said, 'If I went away he could not manage.'

I have often thought about this family because until she told me how she felt I had seen her almost as an oppressed woman whose husband travelled whilst she remained behind doing all the work. She saw herself quite differently, as the person who was essential in keeping the family together. She had no desire to do anything else. She was an educated woman and also a free woman. I visited the family again in 2011 and found the grown up children and some small grandchildren sharing the family home. The father, and now grandfather of the family explained to me that his wife was not actually in Kenya because she had gone to visit one of their children who lives in America with his own family.

I remember another Kenyan woman I used to visit, who lives with her family in the rich farming area to the West of Mount Kenya. She is the headmistress of the large local primary school where she starts work at 8.00 am and finishes at 6.00 pm every day. She is considered an important person in the community by most of the adults whose children attended her school, but this does not stop her from being a good mother. She keeps a beautiful kitchen garden, cooks wonderful meals for the children and also serves the community around her. When school is over she walks for long distances to visit sick people and to nurse them and give advice. There is no room in her day for feelings of importance, she has chosen to serve and is one of the most fulfilled people I have ever met. I went back to her home in September 2011 and she retained the same indomitable spirit.

The struggle continues

The women's movement has always been about the right of women to be educated and to be recognised as capable of running their own lives, of making decisions about their vocations and about living them out. The struggle for freedom and dignity for women has always included the struggle for education. It has never been about women working in the world, but about them deciding for themselves whether to do so or not. The struggle has been for women to fight against low self-esteem and low status and to know themselves as human beings in their own right and not as appendages to others, whether parents, husbands or children. Education gives women choice.

Maya Angelou was born in Stamps, Arkansas in 1928 and, unlike many of her contemporaries, has managed to overcome a difficult early life which included her being assaulted when she was seven. She has in fact lived a rich and very colourful life as a writer, dancer, singer, teacher, actress, black activist and film-maker. She wrote, '*I decided many years ago to invent myself. I had obviously been invented by someone else – by a whole society – and I didn't like the invention.*'

Maya Angelou's move away from her childhood of oppression and stereotyping as a Southern American black child sounds fairly smooth but she is in no doubt that the gap between her vision and the achievement of her dream was filled by many hard times and determined consistent work. She has spoken of struggling to be free every day of her life, of making a little progress but then feeling that she almost had to start again. Sometimes her struggle to be free felt like a struggle to survive. Part of the struggle was her growing realisation that home, in America, was her home, that she was not living in someone else's country. She never saw the need to divide people

*Maya Angelou
delivers a poem
on Bill Clinton's
Inauguration Day
January 20, 1993 in
Washington, DC.*

into groups, but always felt that it was necessary and good for all Americans to recognise each other and to work together to tackle the disease of racism.

It is noteworthy that such a strong and famous woman as Maya Angelou can speak eloquently about the grace and goodness of service. She has always felt that service is a wonderful gift to others, when it is freely given and not forced on people.

It has very sadly to be acknowledged that the achievement of many aspects of gender equality has been slowed down and even stopped in many countries and cultures by the influence of some of the world religions. In the area of life where women are often more committed than men and where they might expect to be recognised as of equal status with men, they often find themselves restricted rather than free to choose their path in life.

The creation stories of Judaism, also taken into Christianity, have led to the development of a theology which has understood God's dealings with the world through men, although one of the creation stories gives no indication that man was created before woman, the other story is that Adam was created first, whilst Eve was created from Adam. Christianity today is not exempt from the oppression of women, especially in countries and cultures where the bible is still taken literally. The Anglican report on the possibility of women bishops in England [12] wasted many pages in reiterating the traditional Christian theology of women as second to men in the life of Christianity and the Church. Most Western Christians today do not take the bible literally and would not accept that women are in any way second

---

12 *The Rochester Report*, Church House Publishing, 2004.

to men. The life and culture of most churches now promote equal status and equal responsibility for women.

In the developing world Kenya is an exception in having women priests in the Anglican Church and in some dioceses they are now forty per cent of all clergy. This became possible when the Church moved from a strong focus on the written word of the bible to a focusing on the gifts of the spirit and on the reality of women's contribution to life and society.

Women of other Faiths

Muslim women are often seen as the most oppressed in the world. It was Ataturk who was a pioneer in the Muslim World when he recognised women's equal rights in Turkey in 1926. He abolished polygamy and brought in mixed sex schools and colleges. Women in some Muslim countries and societies however suffer great inequality in the Twenty First Century. The rate of literacy amongst the Muslim women of the world is the lowest.

Some would say that the women of Afghanistan are the most oppressed. A global survey by the Thompson Reuters Foundation, published in 2011,[13] points to Afghanistan as the world's most dangerous country for a woman to live in. The report includes public violence against women, bad healthcare and dire poverty. Siba Shakib grew up in Iran, is a writer and film-maker and has travelled to Afghanistan many times. She has written the story of Shirin – Gol, a woman whose life under the Taliban can only be described as horrendous. We read of rape, enforced prostitution, and attempted suicide.[14]

Fawzia Koofi was the first female member of the Afghan parliament in 2005 and she is hoping to stand for election as President of the country in 2014. For this reason she is under constant threat of being murdered. She was born in the north eastern area of Afghanistan, the nineteenth child in the family. Her mother, the second of her father's seven wives, was illiterate, but made sure that her daughter was the first girl in the family to go to school. She has written her story in the hope that the progress women have made since the Taliban were defeated in 2001 will not be lost.[15] Oxfam has reported that there are now 2.7 million girls in school, compared with only a few thousand under the Taliban. Nearly 30 percent of the MPs in the new Afghan parliament are women. However, many ordinary women still find it hard to live with dignity in their own country. Many are living under the daily threat of violence, suffering and death.

My Muslim friends are as horrified as I am by the lives some Muslim women live. Many educated Muslim women realise that their religion is being used for oppression rather than, as was intended by the Prophet, for liberation. The spirit of the faith has, over the years, been clouded by

---

13 Reported in *The Guardian*, June 15th, 2011.

14 Siba Shakib, *Afghanistan, Where God Only Comes to Weep*. Century, 2002.

15 Fawzia Koofi, with Naden Ghouri, *One Woman's fight to lead Afghanistan into the Future*. Palgrave, 2012.

Supporters of Women Workers Helpline (WWH) rally on occasion of the World Women's Day on 8th March 2011 in Lahore.

male dominated cultures and politics even though there have been Muslim women who have been significant in their communities and for the faith. There are women's groups in Muslim countries working for the recognition of equal rights, but they are a minority.

My Muslim friends firmly point to egalitarian accounts of human creation given in the Qu'ran and believe that God has created men and women as equals. They point to references to Adam in the Qu'ran and explain that Adam is interpreted as humankind.

> **The Qu'ran even-handedly uses both feminine and masculine terms and imagery to describe the creation of humanity from a single source.**[16]

The Sikh and Baha'i religions both affirm women's equality.

The Baha'i faith teaches that the equality of men and women is a spiritual and moral necessity. Equality does not mean that men and women are the same, there are differences and special roles, but this does not alter the fact that men and women are of equal value and status. The faith teaches that the equality of the sexes is essential for the wholeness of humankind and for religious peacemaking. The Baha'i teachings are that equality must be practiced in every aspect of life; in the family, community and nation.

Wendi Momen with
Moojan Momen

*Understanding the
Baha'i Faith*

16 Dr. Riffat Hassan – University of Louisville.

'And among the teachings of Bahá'u'lláh is the equality of women and men. The world of humanity has two wings -- one is women and the other men. Not until both wings are equally developed can the bird fly. Should one wing remain weak, flight is impossible. Not until the world of women becomes equal to the world of men in the acquisition of virtues and perfections, can success and prosperity be attained as they ought to be.'

1 'Abdu'l-Bahá

What remains to be done?

Gender inequality still sadly exists in every country of the world in one way or another. In the West it often focuses on unequal pay, though there are many hidden inequalities which are almost impossible to measure. One simple example serves to make the point. There are twice as many women living on less than one US dollar a day than there are men.

The 2003 World Bank Report on gender and the MDGs included a graph with the heading, 'In no region of the world are women and men equal in legal, social and economic rights.' The report brings out the benefits to all the MDGs of working for gender equality. One of the many impoverishments of women, especially in the developing world, is 'time poverty.' This is caused by long hours spent in collecting water and in other tasks, leaving little or no space for education.

In writing about International Women's Day 2012, Polly Toynbee pointed out that even in the UK women do twice as much unpaid caring work as men, they earn less, own less and have less secure jobs. [17]

In the developing world 'time poverty' as part of gender inequality is still very obvious in day-to-day life. A UNICEF, WHO and UNESCO paper describes women as follows:

They grow most of the developing world's food, market most of its crops, fetch most of its water, collect most of its fuel, feed most of its animals, weed most of its fields.

And when their work outside the home is done, they light the third world's fires, cook its meals, clean its compounds, wash its clothes, shop for its meals and look after its old and its ill.

And they bear and care for its children.

It is sadly still true that women do two-thirds of the world's work, earn a tenth of the income and own a hundredth of the property.[18] It is also true, as in the case of my Kenyan friends, that many women, who are not struggling for the survival of their families, are happy to be the key workers at home and also to be earners in the communities.

---

17 Polly Toynbee, *The Guardian*, 8th March, 2012.
18 *Mind the Gap: Rich World – Poor World, the Unfinished Agenda,* John Bennett, Barbara Butler, John Moore & Florence Nyahwa (eds.), Leicester, Christians Aware, 2006.

Asianet-Pakistan/shutterstock.com

Most serious of course is the abuse of the human rights of women and the resultant loss of life around the world. *'It has even been claimed that simply because of their sex, more girls have been killed in the last 50 years than all of the people slaughtered in all of the world genocides.'*[19]

At the beginning of December 2011 a UK report from the Iranian and Kurdish Women's Rights Organisation reached news and press headlines. The report indicated that the number of women suffering violence and intimidation at the hands of family members is growing rapidly and that as many as 3,000 cases were reported in the UK in 2011. The information comes from the records of some police authorities. The violence includes threats, acid attacks, beatings, forced marriage, mutilation and murder. On 3rd December 2011 there was a picture in *The Guardian* of Banaz Mahmod who had been strangled in 2006 on the orders of her father and uncle because they thought her boyfriend was unsuitable. This scandalous situation is most probably the tip of the iceberg because some police forces do not collect data and many crimes are unreported.

The issue of honour violence was tackled by Mona Siddique in her 'Thought For the Day' on Radio 4 on 6 December 2011 and she was very clear in her condemnation, asking: *'How can we talk of a God given human dignity for all and at the same time care so little for individual human life.'*

Girls normally grow up more easily than boys, having less vulnerability to disease. In countries where there is equality, especially in health care, between women and men, it is the women who live longer. The cultures of some areas of the world mean that the reverse is true and boys grow up as the favoured children and there are therefore more men than women in the communities.

---

19 *Half the Sky. Turning Oppression into Opportunity for Women Worldwide,* Nicholas D. Kristof and Sheryl Dun, Alfred A. Knopf, New York, 2009.

The dissappeared

The research of the economist Amartya Sen has pointed us to the astounding fact that more than a hundred million women are missing from today's world. It is estimated that two million girls disappear every year. In China it is estimated that almost forty thousand baby girls die every year due to rejection and neglect. Parents focus their attention on their sons, giving them love and all the care they need often to the exclusion of their daughters. Some people in China have seen medical developments like ultrasound, which reveal the sex of foetuses, as wonderful because they can now abort female foetuses. This is forbidden but the attitudes remain and are not limited to China. Even in the UK there has been recent concern about women asking for abortions because the sex of unborn babies was not to their liking.

The Third Century poet, Fu-Hsien, wrote,

Most bitter thing it is to be born a woman...

Much has changed for women in China, but there is still truth in the poet's reflection.

The sufferings of Chinese women over the years are now well recorded. The title of Adeline Yen Mar's early book, *Falling Leaves: The True Story of an Unwanted Chinese Daughter*, speaks for itself. The writer Amy Tan has written the story of her family, including that of her grandmother whose misery in early 20th century China led her to commit suicide. Amy describes looking at a photo of her grandmother and of comparing her life of being constantly downtrodden with her own happy life in America. Her parents went to America after World War Two and she was born there in 1951. [20]

Wild Swans [21] is a powerful study of three generations of Chinese women. It was written by Jung Chang, about her grandmother, her mother and herself in the context of the history of China from the beginning of the Twentieth Century. The writer herself was fortunate to be born in 1952, and although she worked in the fields and in a steelworks she did go to university and was able to leave China to live in the UK in 1978.

Jung Chang's grandmother was the concubine of a warlord in the 1920s and 30s and represents thousands of

20 *The Opposite of Fate*, Amy Tan, Flamingo, 2003.
21 *Wild Swans: Three Daughters of China*, Jung Chang, Harper Collins, 1991.

Photo by John Pritchard

Chinese mothers and children.

women. She had had her feet bound when she was 2 years old and always remembered screaming with agony when this was done. She suffered pain for the rest of her life. When she was 15 her father arranged for her to become a concubine and received great wealth in return. She lived a life of loneliness and fear until in 1931 she gave birth to a daughter who became Jung Chan's mother. Her life improved when the warlord died and she married a doctor. As part of her new life she tried to un-bind her feet and partly succeeded. She was a brave woman who gave her granddaughter and her other grand-children the love and care their own parents had no time to give because they were working for the Communist Party.

It was Jung Chang's mother who perhaps suffered most, growing up during the years of the Long March. She was a brave Communist before the revolution took place, working against the Kuomintang until their defeat in 1949. She married an educated Communist official who always put the party first and even felt that it would be a betrayal of the party to consider his own wife at all. She took part in gruelling long marches, walking and climbing more than thirty miles a day in pouring rain. She searched for food for hungry and starving people and gave birth in the most gruelling circumstances.

Mao Tse-Tung did recognise and bring in equality for women in many spheres of life. After the 1949 revolution there was a crackdown on bigamy, concubinage, child betrothal and the forcing of gifts. The marriage law of 1950 stipulated free choice of partner, the full consent of both partners to marriage and full equality within the home. Divorce had to be by mutual agreement. Changes after the revolution also meant that women began to own land and that there was equal pay for equal work, supported by child care and maternity leave. Women now appear in almost every occupation in China and are powerful in local government, though not yet at the top table of national government.

India and Bangladesh

In India it is estimated that a bride-burning takes place once in every two hours. Girl children are 50% more likely to die between birth and five years than boys.

It is Dalit girls and women who suffer most in India today. Dalits are those who used to be called outcaste before India gained independence. In 2009 India's Central Bureau of Investigation estimated that there were three million prostitutes, including children in the country, and they are probably Dalits, because they are the poorest. The figure of three million is likely to be much higher, because much of the prostitution and internal trafficking are hidden. Forced marriages and forced labour add to the great dangers facing many women of all backgrounds in today's India. Also it is estimated that up to 50 million girls have disappeared over the past hundred years due to the killing of female foetuses and babies.

A fortunate Dalit woman may be one who is employed, perhaps as a maid in an Indian family. However, because she has a husband, children and extended family her earnings will soon disappear. She may also be subject to threats.

Bangladesh has suffered from poverty for longer than the forty years of its official existence but the gradual increase in education is making a very real difference to the lives of the people. Ken Ford-Powell, a teacher who lives and works in Dinajpur in Bangladesh has written about the traditionally low status of women in Bangladesh.

Bangladesh has never had a good educational record. A survey in 1992 found that only 35% of its people were literate. Amongst women, that figure fell to 22% – much lower than other poor income countries. Both the Bangladesh government and non-government organisations made a lot of steps to change this situation such as making it illegal for children to be working, and subsidising the education of all primary age children so that now, nearly 20 years later, over 55% of the population is literate.

But this statistic masks the fact that girls continue to obtain less education. Why? Because, traditionally, a girl is a burden who must be married off as soon as possible. Although that view is changing, girls are still often married as young as thirteen having babies before their bodies can cope with it. If a girl survives giving birth she may have to suffer years of abuse from her husband and his parents, starving to allow the rest of the family to eat the food she has cooked.

NGOs like LAMB[22] working in Northwest Bangladesh work to change this perception. LAMB has worked in the area of development of the poor

---

22 www.lambproject.org.

(especially women) for nearly thirty years and, though primarily a healthcare project, education has been a core tool in this work. Women are educated in the community in the areas of healthcare, nutrition, childcare and hygiene. Furthermore, LAMB established a school for staff and local children from the villages about 15 years ago. This school has grown both in numbers of children and in range of education having just recently begun O levels. Though primarily English Medium, the school educates boys and girls in equal numbers, using Bangla as well as English, and all students have been able to transition successfully into the state system at any stage.

The result is increasing numbers of boys *and* girls who are educated to tertiary level, obtaining work in medicine, engineering, science, law and other high income careers. Families that would have earned around 80 taka per day (below the international poverty line) as farmers or cleaning maids now see their sons and daughters earn much more. Some even go abroad to earn even higher wages before sending the money back to support their village.

In a country where flooding can destroy a harvest one moment, drought prevent the second in the year from growing at all and disease can ravage entire villages at any time, education becomes a real lifesaver both for the health of a community locally and for its long term development, with new income paying for better medicines, farming tools and nutrition. Women marry later having healthier babies that are better cared for and, being wage earners too, or even running their own business, they have much greater respect in the village and amongst their family.

To say that education helps poor families is demonstrably an understatement in Bangladesh but the challenge is still there despite the success of organisations like LAMB. Most of those who are literate today come from higher earning

Above, *photos from LAMB projects.* Below, *flooding is a major problem affecting parts of Bangaladesh.*

families. Reaching the majority of low income families, still without at least one educated person earning a wage, continues to be a major concern for the country. The hope is that it won't take another forty years to achieve this.

Ethiopia

Ethiopia is one of Britian's largest aid recipients. Rachel Stephens visits Ethiopia regularly: As I write there is the sword of Damocles hanging over Ethiopia and all countries involved in achieving the eight Millennium Development Goals.

United Nations reports assert that the Empowerment of Women and Gender Equality remains the most challenging of the MDGs because of the deep rooted nature of the challenge to change attitudes and cultural values. Can you really have a quantifiable target for the much needed change in cultural practice and understanding? By what precise indicators can you measure such a thing as parity of esteem?

MDG 3 seeks to improve Women's situations and is a key goal for Ethiopia but can Ethiopia reach a measurable level of gender parity by December 31st 2015? Some of the chosen indicators for this Goal are clear, for example Gender Parity can be seen in percentages of female school students, of women in parliament and public office, enactment of laws for women's property rights, gender equality in employment. In these ways we already see that the objective is achieving for women equal access to education, health care, adequate food, water, employment, and public services as well as sexual and reproductive health rights.

In 2005 the Ethiopian government upgraded Women's Affairs to a full Ministry and updated the constitution to include these rights. But enacting laws does not ensure the good practice or, in rural Ethiopia, even the knowledge that such provision exists. Yet these are the settings in which Christians Aware member **Ebise Ashana** works.

About six times a year, under the auspices of the DASSC (Development and Social Service Commission) of the Ethiopian Evangelical Lutheran Church Mekane Yesus (EECMY), she initiates Synod gatherings to work towards the understanding of gender parity and the empowerment of women. Most gatherings are in the rural areas and often remote. A few extracts from recent reports by Ebise may illustrate the process.

Gender Perception and Training in rural Ethiopia

I have just been to Illubabor, SW Ethiopia to give training on issues arising from women's treatment and position in Church, Home and Society …. Most participants had had no gender concept training and it was challenging to bring them to the level where they understood such things as their legal position in Ethiopian law, women's rights, practical equality in decision making at home or in the community. Among the participants some could

Ebise Ashana.

speak neither Amharic nor English and their local languages differed. We needed a common experience to begin our Consultation so we had a day visit to a local Church Development Project which had initiated a savings and credit scheme, vegetable gardening, nutrition and bee keeping. Even so, translation took much of our time.

But afterwards the women said:

> ...here in our area we have everything, forest, rain, land but we lacked the knowledge of how to use our resources. Thanks be to God and the project, now we have gained the skill in vegetable gardening and nutrition. We can have, in our hands, money that we have gained in business, whereas in the past it was only our husbands who had

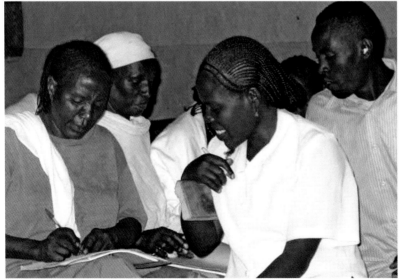

www.eecmy.org

that access. They value education highly and said 'We will transfer the skills we gained to the next generation'.

In another consultation in Tegello the women said '...*this helped us to come out of the tomb. Now it not only provides us with money but we got psychological resurrection.*' What a telling image of their situation!

Women have accepted being second class. How can that culture be changed?

Many cultural changes can be easily observed even if not easily measured. For example one of the biggest problems in rural Ethiopia is violence towards girls and women, which is culturally accepted but not talked about openly. From birth it begins. Many female infants undergo **Female Genital Mutilation** (FGM) or circumcision, which is accepted by their mothers and local women.

In adolescence or earlier they all become the wood carriers and water carriers for the family, carrying as much as their own weight on their heads. It stunts their growth and together with under-nourishment can lead later to painful and difficult childbirth and often to fistula.[23] Lack of even basic education has meant that cause and effect have not been connected and harmful traditional practices continue to blight the lives of women to an extent that is difficult to discover, as women are afraid to talk about it.

Fistula is an abnormal connection between two organs that normally do not connect. If labour in childbirth is obstructed this leads to pain and long and dangerous labour, which the baby will not survive. The woman may leak bodily fluids and be shunned. The condition is treatable.

Again, Ebise wrote in a report in January 2011: 'Talking about gender issues is a recent phenomenon in our country. Gender inequality is exercised

Carrying heavy loads can cause Fistula. Photos by Rachel Stephens.

---

23 See The Fistula Foundation – info@fistulafoundation.org

in Ethiopia and women are given a subordinate position. This has resulted in lack of access to education and health services, lack of self confidence because of lack of involvement in decision making and access to property. Gender division of labour is put in place by the society and gender has its roots in the culture, ie beliefs, customs, attitudes etc. It can be manifested in language, food and physical or verbal abuse.' Ebise tries to distinguish for the women between gender (God given), where, in God's sight, all are of equal value, and gender differentiation, which is a cultural manifestation, through which society gives different status to men and women. In making the distinction Ebise herself experiences opposition even within the Church. But, she affirms, 'Culture can be changed over time and therefore gender differentiation is not static either.' When men and women work together on development and economic empowerment progress can be made. **Education is the key**.

What could MDG3 Achieve?

The required process of deep social change and transformation for both men and women, will need much time and deep appreciation of the differing gifts and roles of men and women. There is still a gap in understanding between the existence of legal prerogatives and entitlements in favour of women and the knowledge leading to the enforcement, the implementation and the claiming of those rights by women. **Again education is the key!**

Adapting an early UK Trades Union slogan we can say *'Knowledge is power and knowledge in the hands of women and men is the power that can change Society and the world.'*

The first big challenge is to get both women and men to see the importance of girls' education. Ebise's Synod Consultations include some men as well as women, often Church officials, and she hopes to get them all to commit themselves to supporting all girls going to school and having time to study and do homework after class; and finally to involve boys in doing their share of the domestic carrying and other work with their sisters.

Empowering Ethiopian women through education would not only go a long way to bringing about social and economic development, but is, in fact, a precondition and indispensible catalyst for the achievement of the entire Millennium Development Agenda in the country. This must challenge the Church and community first to value such work in their own structures. Secondly they need to encourage the Ethiopian Government to support those programmes and strategies leading to implementation of policies which will achieve their Millennium development Goals by 2015. We should pray for this outcome and for the work of the Ethiopian Evangelical Church Mekane Yesus.

Ethiopian Christian pilgrim awaits the start of the Holy fire ceremony at the Ethiopian section of the Holy Sepulchre in Jerusalm, April 14 2012.

Kobby Dagan/shutterstock.com

The Challenge and Joy of Leadership as a Woman in the Philippines, by The Revd. Juanita Doromal Paniamogan

Perhaps, the Philippines is one the of few countries (if not the only one so far) which had two women presidents already: President Corazon Cojuangco Aquino (1986–92) and President Gloria Macapagal Arroyo(1994–2010).

Aquino

Airman Gerald B. Johnson

Both of them were swept to power by unusual events. President Aquino took over from President Ferdinand Marcos after more than 20 years in power including martial law in 1972–86. The famous 'People Power' in 1986 forced President Marcos to step down and he was brought to Hawaii by the benefactor country of the Philippines, the USA. President Gloria Macapagal Arroyo took over the presidency after the elected president, Joseph Estrada was forced to step down after the impeachment process was cut short because of the demand to open the controversial 'envelope' that would confirm or deny his involvement in gambling which enriched him and several cohorts and deprived many. He chose not to open it and the prosecutors walked out and people thronged through the streets and the People Power 2 came about. Gloria Macapagal Arroyo as vice president took over the remaining years of Joseph Estrada and during the regular election got 'elected' but with 'anomalous'dealings.

Arroya

© World Economic Forum

Unfortunately, these women presidents have not brought substantial changes and development to the poverty-stricken Filipinos. Of course a few presidential actions were worth remembering such as the passing of the Family Code which has improved the status of women. In this Code, women are given equal opportunities to be educated, to be employed, to develop a career; to own properties and even retain a maiden name. This happened during the reign of President Aquino. The second president was not good enough. I myself remember her as the one who said 'I'm sorry' when she was linked with election anomaly and the one who authored the Mining Act of 1995 which sells the whole country to foreign investors as if it's the only way to progress. The effects of that law has brought tremendous damage to our natural resources, deprived many farmers and indigenous peoples of their space and contributed to the calamities that are now becoming frequent like landslides and floods, and water becoming scarce, with siltation in seas and destruction to marine life.

The United Church of Christ in the Philippines was established on May 25, 1948. It is now 63 years old. It was a product of five churches or denominations which came when the Americans took over from the Spaniards in colonizing the Philippines. Their motive may have been noble but it came with the imperialists who wanted to add more colonies to their already widening tentacles. The missionaries came mostly as couples. They opened schools and hospitals and established churches.

The UCCP is also a product of patriarchal efforts even if many church members were women and remain so today. The first officers and leaders were men and a few women along the way. The new constitution though in the 80's enshrined women's equal participation and representation in all levels of the life and work of the church. In 1998, the General Assembly (the highest policy making body of the UCCP, composed of representatives from the 46 conferences all over the country) elected its first woman bishop. In 2002, UCCP elected its second woman bishop and in 2010, she was re-elected. This is a concrete manifestation of a church which acknowledges the worth and essence of women.

The UCCP is known for its strong commitment to social justice including women's empowerment, peace and human and environmental rights. This dimension of faith expression has resulted in more than 20 of its ministers and lay leaders being unjustly tortured and even killed. In June 16, 2011, the UCCP filed a class suit against the former President, Gloria Macapagal Arroyo being the chief executive and commanding officer of the military tagged to be the main perpetrator of such crimes. But while the leadership is so firm and aggressive in these social issues, many of the people in the pew still retain the vestiges of patriarchy. A number still prefer to have their children married or baptized by male ministers A number still question why its leaders tackle such 'worldly' issues like mining, corruption, lottery and gambling. They prefer to focus on 'spiritual' concerns.

The UCCP engages with the secular world.

The Surigao District Conference is one of the 46 conferences of the UCCP. It has 110 local churches, worshipping congregations and outreaches; it has 81 church workers including 15 retired and 8 students. It has elected two women conference ministers (equivalent to bishops in the Roman Catholic or Episcopal church or superintendents for the Methodists), one in the mid 70's and another in 2008. The Rev. Ramona Loyola became a moderator (the term then for conference minister now) but her stint was only for four months and a half; she met a vehicular accident on one of her church visits. But her local church experience though showed more of her leadership not only within the four walls of the church but included becoming the president of the Parents-Teachers' Association in the school and the first woman Barangay Captain level government unit; she pioneered ecumenical linkages with Roman Catholic priests for joint concerns and actions.

After more than 30 years, the Surigao District Conference elected another woman conference minister. But this is no longer uncommon for the UCCP. In fact out of 6 conferences within the Southeast Mindanao Jurisdiction,

So strong like Gabriela Silang
Empowerment for the future passing the baton
These other lame gentlemen really gotta see
When we fight for freedom, men and women gotta be free

Above left: *A 1970 stamp printed in Philippines shows Gabriela Silang, a Philippine heroine, who died at the age of 32 in 1763. Her spirit is echoed in the contemporay world by the lyrics written by Lorena Barros for a song called* Intellect *(above right) in honour of the 100th anniversary of International Women's Day on March 8th, 2011.*

four are headed by women. But as a national church, out of 46 conferences, only ten are 'managed' by women. That is still way behind the ideal 50/50 ratio. But is there really a difference with women leaders? That remains to be seen and only 'herstory' will tell if indeed women made a difference. But I do believe there are differences, but perhaps just new and different ways of doing things.

The yearly **women's study course, celebration and production of 16 days reflection** continues to empower women and assist them in their quest for meaning, for domestic peace and equality, for equal opportunities in education and work. Women's leadership can be an opportunity for another way of doing things. But it is not always true in all circumstances. Some women in the UCCP have accepted the challenge and joy of leadership and many good things have been conceived, nourished embraced and cared for. Jesus despite living in a patriarchal society lifted the women and gave them back 'God's image'. So he had women disciples who worked with him, supported him and became core members of the early church. Jesus cared for all and encouraged every one to follow His call and take the challenge of a leadership that gives birth to something new and different; a leadership that serves, cares, and loves. Jesus is our example, our guide and inspiration.

Neneng Paniamogan.

Nepal

Maureen Hawksworth writes about her work with Emmanuel Crafts in Nepal. Started in July 2007, Emmanuel Crafts supports fifteen women and their families by making beaded jewellery and cards. One young girl, Jenuka, is leprosy affected and works for spending money only, as she is sponsored by the Leprosy Mission for schooling and accommodation. Because of her deformed hands, she is unable to make delicate necklaces but can manage one style of bracelet in wood. It was a joy to learn on this visit that she has now got married to a teacher, a love marriage. This is especially good news as it is very rare for anyone to marry someone who has had leprosy. She is very attractive but her hands and feet are very damaged. Two other young girls work to support their siblings and the other ladies are either deserted wives or widows left to bring up children on their own. There is no equivalent of our NHS in Nepal and provision for such people is not made by the state. Life for them is very tough. Working for Emmanuel Crafts means rice on the table and money for schooling for their children. We also help with medical costs and any other emergencies brought to our attention by the women.

Emmanuel Crafts is owned and run by the women themselves and they make all the decisions. The intention of the project is to give work to as many as possible, not to make a few rich. All the women are Christians and each day begins with a small act of worship. It is a joy to hear them singing and praising God. They give thanks every day for the opportunity to work. They have now started a provident fund to ensure a small income when they are no longer able to work. The love and care they have for each other is so apparent.

Having started and supported the project whilst serving as a Methodist Mission Partner in Nepal, I feel I can best help them now by marketing their goods. The jewellery is very well made and reasonably priced. **Everything used by the project is bought in Kathmandu to ensure that it is sustainable and environmentally friendly.** I buy from the women and sell for a small profit which, in turn, helps to support a village school in Nepal for which we raised funds to build. The school is in Palpa district, about 15kms from Tansen on the Pokhara road. There are now over 200 children at this remote

Photos: Maureen Hawksworth

village school and about 80 of them are on scholarships. The school also runs non formal education classes in an evening for the ladies of the village and surrounding area. Last year 180 ladies took advantage of these classes, the oldest lady being 70 years old. The hope and prayer is that they in turn will make sure that their children and grandchildren get an education. It is not compulsory to send your child to school in Nepal. The income from the sale of the beads is the main source of funding for the school.

The work of the women has far reaching effects. It provides them with a fair income enabling them to feed and educate their children; it funds scholarships for the children at Gyanjyoti School and helps pay the teachers' salaries. It funds classes for the ladies of the village as these are provided free and it brings pleasure to all who wear their products. I am very proud of them and thank God every day for their skills, faith and love.

Glimpses of women in Paraguay

Estela is someone who was introduced to a Christians Aware group in Paraguay. She has lived a hard life and has overcome many difficulties. She now works with poor people in her country. As a child she had a vocation to the religious life in the Roman Catholic Church, but was advised by her priest to go to university, where she became a political activist. This was dangerous because it was at the time when General Stroessner's despotic regime was in power. She also met a radical Jewish student, married him

Estela

John Pritchard

and went to Argentina, which was no safer than Paraguay. She told the visiting group that at a time when many people were disappearing the police came to her aunt's house to look for her and her husband. She was alone and told the police that she was the maid. When the police had gone she fled with her husband and the new baby. They made their way to England and then went to Mexico. When it was safe to do so they returned to Paraguay where Estela taught in the university and also set up her own school. She now gives a great deal of her time to working with the poorest people in Asuncion. She is a wonderful example to the women she works with, always encouraging them to believe that they can improve not only their own lives but the lives of those around them.

Santa Maria is a small and neglected town with a glorious past when it was home to one of the many 17th and 18th century Jesuit mission settlements or 'reductions' for the Guarani, the local indigenous people. The gifts of the people, art, music and community worship, kindled by the Jesuits, are still there. There is a craft workshop next door to the Santa Maria hotel, enabled by Margaret Hebblethwaite, who started the hotel as an environmentally friendly opportunity for travellers and to offer employment to local people. The sisters of the Company of Mary are also working with the local very poor women. The women work together to create beautiful embroideries of the lives of the people: the ploughing, sowing, carrying of water and milling. The creations hang in homes and in the church on the town square. They are worked into vestments and have recently been included on Paraguayan postage stamps. The women's work is impressive as is the way they support each other in their work and in their sometimes traumatic family lives.

Gender equality in Burma

Mar Mar Wilson has written about women in Burma, her home country

I am a Burmese woman who is now married and settled in the UK. I grew up in Northern Shan State in Burma and my parents lived in the small mining town of Namtu approximately 100 miles from Yunnan province in China.

Both of my parents were professional people: my father was a mining official in the town and my mother was a nurse at the local hospital. Together with my older sister, brother and two younger twin brothers we enjoyed a wonderful childhood. I know by Burmese standards we were very privileged. We lived in a government house, with large garden to play in and I played tennis in the courts directly opposite our house. Our parents regarded education as the key to success in later life and they encouraged us all in our studies. Both my two older siblings went on to university and I attended nursing college. The twins also found professional jobs in the government.

I realise now that we were so fortunate in having parents who were so far-sighted and who were keen that their two daughters should be given an equal chance in life.

Photos: George Wilson

The gender gap in my country is still very wide with men still dominating most management roles. It is certainly true that women play a major part in family life in Burma and over the last 50 years due to the poor economic conditions they are often forced to stay at home or undertake manual work either on the land or in construction. This is to allow the male members of their families the opportunities to seek the limited number of better-paid jobs. This is certainly the case in poor rural areas where 70 percent of the population live. In urban areas women are already forming a larger part of the business community at managerial level but a considerable number of females work in factories with wages set below those paid to men. Now that the government has allowed workers to form themselves into unions I hope their status will be recognised.

I am writing this just a few days after the recent elections in Burma (April 2012), and I have been very moved not only to witness the election of mother Suu (Aung San Suu Kyi), but also because she will be one of the few females who will be sitting in the Lower Chamber of the new Parliament and will be a guiding light for all Burmese women. Male politicians, many of whom are ex military, dominate this nominally elected parliament. At the elections of 7 November 2010 less than eight percent of those taking part were women and in the recent by-elections out of 3071 approved candidates only 114, or less than 4 percent, were female.

As economic growth is established I feel confidant that Burmese women will take up the many leadership opportunities both in politics and business life. Daw Aung San Suu Kyi has been quoted as saying: "Sometimes I think that the only real 'men' in Burma are the women!" (And that… "Burma's women are Burma's Future.")

I hope and pray that women will be allowed to participate at every level as the country looks to its future with true freedom and democracy.

The Akha are an indigenous hill tribe that live in small villages at high altitudes in the mountains of Thailand, Burma, Laos, and Yunnan Province in China

Aung San Suu Kyi[1] is a Buddhist who has become an icon of peaceful resistance in the face of oppression in Burma. She is someone who has been inspired by the non-violent campaigns of US civil rights leader Martin Luther King and India's Mahatma Gandhi. She is the daughter of the country's independence hero, General Aung San who was assassinated in July 1947, just six months before independence. Aung San Suu Kyi was only two years old at the time.

She studied philosophy, politics and economics at Oxford where she met Michael Aris, her future husband. After living and working in Japan and Bhutan she settled in the UK to raise their two children, Alexander and Kim.

She arrived back in Rangoon in 1988 - to look after her critically ill mother. Burma was in the midst of major political upheaval. Thousands of students, office workers and monks took to the streets demanding democratic reform. She had to join the protestors. The demonstrators were cruelly suppressed, killed and imprisoned. Aung San Suu Kyi has spent most of the last 20 years in some form of detention, mostly under house arrest

Whilst she was in detention she was normally isolated, and unable to see her sons or her husband, who died in 1999. She studied, improved her French and Japanese, played the piano, practised meditation and kept herself fit.

In 1991, a year after her National League for Democracy won an overwhelming victory in an election which the military junta later nullified, she was awarded the Nobel Peace Prize. She was called an example of the power of the powerless.

She was still in house detention during Burma's first elections in two decades on 7 November 2010, but she was released from house arrest six days later. Thousands of supporters gathered to hear her call for Burmese people to work together for change.

Her life is an inspiration for people who work for justice and peace everywhere in the world.

---

1 *The Lady and the Peacock. The Life of Aung San Suu Kyi*, Peter Popham. Ryder, Random House, 2011.

Jesus and the Woman of Samaria – John 4.5–26

The context of this story is that hostility between Jews and Samaritans had gone on for about seven centuries by the time Jesus was alive. The well in the story is near Sychar and is called Jacob's well – the legend being that it was a gift to the people of the region from Jacob. Jacob had, according to the legend, given the local field to Joseph. The well could represent wisdom, or the law or simply the gift of life from God. Wells were always places of meeting, talking, and arguing. Today wells of all kinds in the Middle East simply represent life in the form of water – and are a major reason for quarrels between Israel and Palestine. There is a section on this issue in Chapter 7.

When Jesus spoke to the woman of Samaria at the well he was speaking to someone who was seen as unclean. He should not, according to the traditions of his people, have spoken to her, let alone have asked her for a drink of the polluted water. But he did speak, he focused his full attention on her, seeing her as a real, true person, even though she had had five husbands. It is sometimes said that the five husbands could represent the five gods the Samaritans worshipped in their five groups. The one who is not the husband could be the Yaweh, whom she does not yet fully know.

Jesus asked the woman to help him, to give him water to drink. Jyoti Sahi has painted many pictures of the woman at the well. The image opposite is the first painting he did for the ashram of the Sacred Heart sisters in northern India, on the banks of the Ganges.

Jyoti has painted Jesus sitting by the well with the water of life flowing from the cave of his heart. Hindus sometimes paint Siva with the water of the Ganges flowing out from his hair. In this painting the woman is part of the river. In a way the woman at the well is like the holy river of life which represents wisdom in India. Jean Vanier, the founder of the L'Arche communities, said of the story of the woman at the well meeting Jesus, '*I am begs for water from one of the most despised.*'

The people of India perhaps understand the story of the woman of Samaria best. The Dalit people of India were called the untouchables, until this was made illegal at the time of independence. The word 'untouchable' emerged from the belief that the outcaste people would pollute the high caste Hindu people and therefore they could not be touched, could not read the sacred scriptures and had to live and eat in separate areas, using separate wells. There are many examples of the Dalit people being beaten for using the wells reserved for the high caste people.

There is mutuality in the new relationship between Jesus and the woman – 'Misery and Mercy Meet'. One of Jesus' gifts to the woman is the gift of giving. The good news to the poor, and especially to poor women, is not that others will help them but that God is with them and that they too have dignity and can be givers.

Jesus and the Woman of Samaria, by Jyoti Sahi.

Madonna and Child, by Greg Tricker, from *The Christ Journey*, St Paul's, 2011.

Goal 4
Reduce Child Mortality

A baby girl not six years old
Dwells in the distant hills;
Her timid eyes already hold
Their share of human ills

Of sweets she hardly knows the taste,
No toy she'll ever see;
A scanty rag about her waist
Is her sole finery

And once I saw her stagger home
Beneath a load of wood
Laid on her head, so burdened that
I thought upon the Rood.

Before that little child
I saw the form of one who bowed
Beneath another load, and walked
Amidst an angry crowd.

Verrier Elwin[1]

The poem by Verrier Elwin was written a long time ago, about a child in India in the first half of the twentieth century. Today, according to UNICEF, India is one of 50 countries in the world with the highest under- five child mortality rate. The child in the poem is a little girl, and in the Twenty First Century India is still the most dangerous place in the world to be born a girl.

TARGET - to reduce the under fives mortality rate by two thirds by 2015

Some Reasons for Child Deaths

General Poverty

Infants from the poorest families are obviously the most vulnerable. They are most likely to be part of a large family, where for economic, cultural or religious reasons their parents do not use contraception. Short birth

---

1 Verrier Elwin lived in India in the first half of the 20th century. He died in 1964.

intervals are very likely to leave mothers in poor health, and the babies are likely to be smaller than when there are longer gaps between births. I have looked at the issue of contraception and family planning in Chapter Five. Poor children are also often hungry and are less likely to receive vaccinations than children from better off families. Poor children struggle to survive dirty water and lack of sanitation.

The Boom in Premature Births

The numbers of premature babies are going up almost everywhere, including the developing world. In the West the reasons include women choosing to have their babies at a time to suit them, so many of them become older mothers.

In poor countries the reasons for the babies being premature include infections, malaria, HIV and the high number of adolescent girls who are becoming pregnant.

'Being born too soon is an unrecognised killer.'[2]

Dr. Joy Lawn of Save the Children has led a team from Save the Children, the World Health Organisation, the US March of Dimes Foundation and the Partnership for Maternal, New Born and Child Health.

The high percentage of infant deaths in the first months of life in the developing world is shocking and Dr. Lawn's team states that the reason is very simple. The babies are not expected to survive and are therefore often just left to die.

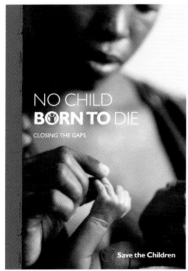

NO CHILD BORN TO DIE

CLOSING THE GAPS

Save the Children

Courtesy Save the Children

Many premature babies who do not die are disabled. It is true that intensive care for premature babies is expensive, but now the good news is that there is another very low cost way forward. **Kangaroo Mother Care** involves the tiny baby being placed on the mother's chest, skin to skin, and staying there for many weeks, until the time comes when the baby would have been born naturally. The trials have shown that this care halves the death rate for small babies. They gain more weight and also feed better than when they are in an incubator. [3]

Steroid injections given to mothers in premature labour cost 60p each and are helpful in developing the babies' lungs so that they can breathe at birth. This injection is readily available in the developed world,

2 Dr. Joy Lawn, Save the Children – see www.savethechildren.org.uk.
3 Kangaroo Mother Care – *The Guardian*, May 3rd, 2012.

Courtesy Save the Children

Kangaroo Mother Care (skin to skin care)

but is only there for 10% of mothers in the developing world. Antibiotics can also help to prevent and treat infection. The simple use of antiseptic cream can ensure that the cord is not infected.

Even in the developed world the pre-term baby deaths are high in some communities and groups, including ethnic minorities and amongst adolescent and older mothers. There is a need for high quality ante-natal care for all women, everywhere in the world, who are high risk.

General Illness

The World Health Organisation has stated that the main causes of death in young children are neo-natal causes, pneumonia, diarrhoea, malaria, measles, and HIV/AIDS. I have looked at these in Chapters Five and Six. Key interventions will be necessary for these dreadful conditions to be reduced in young children. There is some encouragement in the reduction in deaths from measles due to vaccination.

Maternal deaths will also have to be reduced, and this is a long way away.

Another issue is that of **baby milk powder**. Although it is sometimes necessary for baby milk powder to be used there is no doubt that mother's milk is best. This is particularly true in the developing world where it is usually hard to clean the baby bottles properly. There is also the temptation for mothers to mix the milk powder with water which has not been boiled and also to dilute the powdered milk so that it lasts longer. The companies which promote the use of baby milk powder must ask whether their profits are worth more than the lives of the babies.

Rising Food Prices

I have written about the hunger caused by rising food prices in Chapter One. This is a main cause of the suffering of the children, but the lack of will to do anything adds greatly to the scandal. Why do countries not do more to help their children? Why do the people themselves not do more?

The World Bank has issued a strong warning about the impact of the rising cost of food prices on millions of poor people around the world who are being pushed into poverty. Wheat and maize prices have gone up dramatically. It is estimated that the rise in food prices has resulted in roughly a quarter of a billion parents actually reducing their children's food. They can never afford meat, milk or vegetables. They are also taking children out of school and sending them to work. The parents are in fact themselves malnourished, feeble and unable to do much work.

In 2012 the world has seen a food crisis in West Africa and it is estimated that more than a million children could face life threatening malnutrition there.[4] Crops have failed across the region and food prices are rising every day. The lives of hundreds of thousands of children and of whole families are at risk. The situation is made worse because the Sahel region of West Africa is landlocked so that it is not easy to take supplies in. This region already has one of the highest mortality rates in the world: one in five children die before the age of five years

Malnutrition

The UN World Food Programme has predicted that 24 million more children will be malnourished by 2050

I lived and worked in Zambia in the 1970s and then 1 in 5 children died before they reached the age of 5 years. It is sad to reflect that the figure given today is that 1 in 7 children die before they reach the age of 5 years in most of sub-Saharan Africa. Progress is poor. I have a memory of travelling to a mission station in very rural Zambia when our baby was taken ill and was diagnosed by the mission nurse as suffering from tonsillitis. An African mother brought her baby in whilst we were there and he was also diagnosed as having tonsillitis. Both children were given the same medicine. Our child was much better the next day and I can still remember our horror when we learnt from the nurse that the African child had died in the night. He was malnourished and therefore had no strength when he was faced with illness.

---

4 UNICEF.

In February 2012 Save the Children produced a report arising from their survey of children in the developing world. The report, 'A Life Free from Hunger ~ Tackling Child Malnutrition,' estimates that 1 in 4 children are stunted because of malnutrition. In India 48% of the children are stunted. In Nigeria and in Tanzania the number of children who are malnourished is rising particularly rapidly.

Justin Forsyth, the chief executive of Save the Children, has written,

Courtesy Save the Children

> **'This is a hidden hunger crisis that could destroy the lives of nearly half a billion children unless world leaders act to stop it. Every hour of everyday 300 children die from malnutrition related causes simply because they don't get to eat the basic nutritious foods we take for granted in the UK. Yet solutions are clear, cheap and necessary. Not only will tackling hunger save children's lives, but, at a time of economic meltdown, it will help reboot the global economy.'** [5]

What is needed is for governments to organise good, cheap food for the children who are the future for their countries. Why does a country like India have half its children stunted from malnutrition? What is the point of being a rising power if this is the case? What has happened to the very cheap high protein milk biscuits from Australia which I used to promote in the Lusaka Nutrition Group in the 1970s?

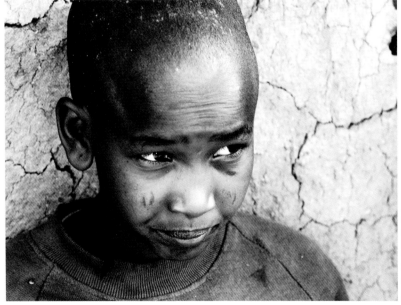

Anna Omelchenko/shutterstock.com

---

5 *The Guardian*, 15th February, 2012.

Stunted children who do not die do not have a very productive or happy life. They are small and listless and, because their brains cannot develop, have low IQs.

Cecil Rajendra, a Malaysian poet, has described hungry children as having saucer eyes, pumpkin bellies, bamboo limbs. He sees all hungry children as having a passport to what he calls the 'dominion of disease,' the world of kwashiorkor, beri beri, cholera, malaria, rickets, scurvey, TB.[6]

Child Oppression

Street Children

It is estimated that the world has at least 100 million street children,[7] but this figure is obviously very approximate because it is impossible to count accurately the thousands of children who hide away in the cities of the developing world. It is estimated that the numbers of street children are growing in China and also in India. Street children are vulnerable and many of them die, especially the little ones.

Children are driven onto the streets for many reasons but violence, war and general poverty are the main reasons they are there. Sometimes girls who have been raped are driven out of their homes because they are seen by their families as no longer respectable. Some children are on the streets to earn money for their families. Many studies have shown that a high percentage of street children take drugs regularly.

Many street children have lost both their parents, either through separation in war or through death. These children are likely to live and die on the streets. The children who do survive are likely to be the older ones and also the most resourceful and quick witted. Some of the children survive by begging, collecting rubbish and performing menial tasks like shoe shining. Many of the girls become sex workers. It is estimated for example that there are 400,000 street children in Bangladesh and that nearly 10% have been forced into prostitution to survive. A high percentage of street children in Phnom Penh, Cambodia, have had sexual relations with tourists.

The street children everywhere often face violence and other abuse. Human Rights Watch found that in Bulgaria, police harassed and beat street children, chasing them away from their shelters. They also sprayed the children with gas, and demanded sex from girls.

Many groups work for and with street children around the world. There is a consortium which is based in the UK and which does campaigning work and research.[8] I have included something on the work of the South Asia Council for Community and Children in Crisis in the section on progress as an example and because it is work I know well.

---

6 Cecil Rajendra, *Songs for the Unsung*, Risk Books, World Council of Churches, 1985.
7 UNICEF.
8 www.streetchildren.org.uk.

A child collects garbage in the street of a suburb in Mumbai (India).

Alberto Loyo/shutterstock.com

Child Labour

It is impossible to find correct statistics about child labourers but one estimate is that there are 250 million in the world.[9] Most of the children who work, and some of them are as young as 4 years, have no real life. They work for long hours, normally in bad conditions. Some of the children work on scrap heaps, some make carpets, some are in factories and shops, some are selling things on the streets. Child workers are likely to be unhealthy and to have no education. UNICEF has produced a series of leaflets to help British businesses by giving them information on child labour and also to enable them to challenge the countries they work with to end child labour. So far there has been little success. UNICEF has focused on 10 countries: India, Bangladesh, the United Kingdom, Brasil, Nepal, Thailand, El Salvador, Pakistan, Costa Rica and Tanzania.

Mark Thomas includes an important section on child labour in a book about his travels in search of the story of Coca-Cola.[10] Mark points out that harvesting in sugar cane fields is regarded as one of the worst forms of labour by the United Nations. The children are vulnerable to being cut by machetes, the cane sap can cause rashes and many children develop breathing problems. In El Salvador the children get up at 4.30 am and work until 1.00 pm by which time they are exhausted and therefore don't attend school. There are estimated to be about 30,000 children working on the cane harvests in El Salvador.

Child Labour in India

It is estimated that there are 280 million child labourers in the world and that 35 million of them are in India.[11] Estimates of numbers do vary and none of them take into account the many hidden labouring children. What is clear is that India is the country with the highest number of child labourers in the world and some of them are very young.

There are different kinds of child labour. Many children in India work simply because they can do no other, because their families are poor and would otherwise not survive. It is important to realise that if many of the children were immediately prevented from working there would not necessarily be a good outcome for them or their families. The task ahead is to tackle poverty: benefits to children would then follow. Most families obviously love their children and are not happy to see them working.

However, sometimes the horrendous situation arises of families selling their children to do work for others. The families may do this out of desperation but it means that the children who are sold have to work in very

9 UNICEF.

10 *Belching Out the Devil, Global Adventures with Coca Cola.* Mark Thomas, Ebury Press, 2008. See also *Turning a Blind Eye, Hazardous Child Labour in El Salvador's Sugar Cane Cultivation*, Human Rights Watch, 2004.

11 Figures from UNICEF.

Above, *a young boy working in a Delhi textile factory.* Left, *A child laborer working with bricks in Peru.*

unhealthy conditions, and for very little or no pay. They are sometimes forced to live in the place where they work, away from their families and parents, and their lives are usually very short. This type of work is known as 'bonded labour'. Examples of bonded labour may be found in the diamond industry, making fireworks, the silk industry, building work and making bricks. Dangerous bonded labour was made illegal in India in 1986: it is against the human rights of adults and children. The sad situation is that it is still common and must be rooted out.

One example suffices to illustrate the nature of bonded labour. This is in the silk industry, which provides the beautiful cloth which so many people all over the world enjoy. In this industry it is not unusual for 4 and 5 year old children work for 12 hours a day and for 6 or 7 days a week for less than 10 rupees a day. The children are obliged to put their hands into very hot water to touch and check the cocoons.[12]

Christians Aware has a link with Trinita in Calcutta. This charity was started to raise and educate the poor child labourers in the slum areas of the city. Some of the work the children do is general labour, commodity selling, rag-picking, van and rickshaw pulling and being servants in many places. The literacy rate is very low, health is poor and there is a lack of awareness by the people of their basic needs. The people are vulnerable in every area of life. Trinita works to help child labourers, especially in the fields of health and education.[13] They are included as a sign of hope towards the end of the chapter.

Some Promising Work – and Good News for Children

Recent help includes:

- ○ Vitamin A;
- ○ Treated mosquito nets;
- ○ More breast feeding;
- ○ Immunisation – especially against measles;
- ○ Antiretroviral treatment for pregnant mothers who are HIV positive.

The progress that has been made in reducing child deaths is largely in the field of medical facilities. For instance, child deaths from malaria have been cut by a third since 2000, largely due to the increase in bed nets. I look further at malaria in Chapter Six.

In 2011 world leaders pledged to vaccinate 250 million children by 2015 which it is estimated will save 4 million lives. Forty countries are committed to increasing their number of health workers.

---

12 Human Rights Watch estimates that 350,000 bonded children work in the silk industry
13 Trinita01@rediffmail.com.

Mother's milk is best

Janice Clark, a Methodist Mission Partner, has written: Giving birth to our two sons in Papua New Guinea in the 1970s was an exciting time as the newly independent country passed the Baby Feed Supplies Control Act which restricted the sale of baby bottles and prohibited the promotion of baby milk products. Being a firm advocate of breastfeeding, I applauded this decision, made to address increased child mortality as a result of the introduction of formula feeding. This law still exists today, and breastfeeding is almost universal. PNG has one of the lowest incidences of diaorrhea among children. If every baby was exclusively breastfed for their first six months, an estimate 1.3 million additional lives would be saved and millions more enhanced every year.

In recent years I lived in Southern Africa where breastfeeding again became an issue because of HIV virus transmission in some poverty-stricken countries. However, breastfeeding is now thought to be the best method of feeding even if you are HIV positive. The risk of passing the virus is less than 5%, the baby will be healthier, and even an infected baby will take longer to develop AIDS than will a formula fed baby.

Janice, along with Rosemary Wass of the Methodist Church, believes that: '...So many lives are saved by a simple, natural method of feeding babies. The valuable immune-building ingredients and antibodies in the mother's milk reduce the vulnerability to diahoerea and pneumonia. As the slogan says, **Breast is best**.'

 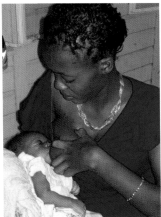 

Photos by Janice Clark.

Exclusive breastfeeding is recommended for the first six months of a baby's life....Breastfed babies are less likely than formula fed babies to get infections and sickness, and less likely to develop health problems such as asthma, diabetes, obesity and SIDS [sudden infant death syndrome]. To breastfeed successfully, women need support from their doctors, hospitals, families and communities.[14]

14   Dr. Thomas Farley, New York City Health Commissioner, 2009.

Some Work of 'Muslim Hands'

Muslim Hands is a UK registered charity which started in 1993 in Nottingham with the conflict in the Balkans. A small group sent aid out to Bosnia and the response was so encouraging that the charity was formed. Today the work covers forty countries and includes help for regions suffering disasters, conflict and poverty. The mission statement of the charity is:

> **To be at the forefront in delivering relief from poverty, sickness and the provision of education worldwide. To provide an ethical service for the collection and distribution of funds in an efficient and transparent, wholly effective manner.**

An important project organised by Muslim Hands is the school feeding project in many countries and especially in refugee areas. In the Sudan there are feeding centres in schools, giving children an early morning meal and one other nutritious meal every day. Therapy is provided for children who have gone through trauma and disaster. This work includes care for children whose are in prison with their mothers.

New Hope in Burundi

Groups all over the world are working to improve the lives of the children. I recently met Mathilde Nkwinkiye, a lawyer who lives and works in Burundi, one of the poorest countries in the world, affected badly by its own war and also by the genocide in Rwanda, which lies immediately to the north.

The war is over now, but the problems are enormous, with malaria, TB and a life expectancy of 39 years. There are hundreds or orphans, some whose parents have died from AIDS related illness and some whose parents died in the war or from poverty.

The Rainbow Centre is in Bujumbura, the capital city of Burundi. It was inspired in 1999 during the war, when an orphaned girl was taken in and at the same time a rainbow appeared in the sky.

> 'And the bow shall be in the cloud; and I will look upon it, that I may remember the everlasting covenant between God and every living creature of all flesh that is upon the earth.'[15]

The story of the beginning of the centre is told by community members.

Our story began in September of 1999 when God gave us a 4th orphaned baby girl, six-day-old Cindy Marie. Perfect in every way, we couldn't believe she could test HIV positive 5 days later. The day God placed her in our home he put a vibrant double rainbow in the sky radiating its glory into our yard, like a promise and blessing on this little life. We named her Munywamazi, which means Rainbow in Kirundi, and we hung rainbows everywhere to remind us of the promise of God. The rest of the story is still going on. Cindy is now HIV negative and a delightful

---

15 Genesis 9.16.

Mathilde and members of the 'Arms of Love' Babies Home.

healthy child. Because of her we wanted to help other babies. We joined with Mrs. Mathilde Nkwirikiye, Lawyer and Childrens' Rights Advocate, to begin the Rainbow Centre. God provided the vision, the property, and the people to help. We are working with a wonderful team of Burundian colleagues to oversee the whole Rainbow Centre project. We want to show the love of Jesus and through Christ-like caring and compassion, to give hope. This is the true meaning of the rainbow...'hope'.

> To give unto them beauty for ashes, the oil of joy for mourning, the garment of praise for the spirit of heaviness; that they might be called trees of righteousness, the planting of the Lord, that he might be glorified.[16]

Mathilde and others became more aware of the number of abandoned children and offered day by day compassion, following the way of Mother Theresa of Calcutta who said that:

> When a life comes into my hands all my love, all my energy, goes to support that life, to help that life to grow to its fullness, because that person has been created in the image of God.[17]

Mathilde and her group founded the 'Arms of Love' babies home in 2002. This home has taken over from day-by-day compassion and offers a real home, with trained staff and also volunteers.

---

16 Isaiah 61.3.
17 From 'My brother, My sister.' A conversation between Mother Theresa and Jean Vanier.

At the heart of the work in the babies home is the enormous effort made to give each child a story, by gathering snippets of information. The babies are found a home and the baby home supports them and their families with food and also with practical and spiritual guidance.

The Rainbow Centre has a clinic and also a community centre which serves more than 500 community babies. The community centre offers spiritual and practical support and hope to people who are not only very poor but also traumatised. There is also a playground, a meeting area and a hostel for the volunteers. Through a grant from the United States Defence Department there is an office/clinic building at the Rainbow Centre. There is a paediatrician who oversees the babies at the Baby Home and at TWIZERE.

TWIZERE, meaning 'Let's have faith and hope', brings together care-givers for the over 500 community babies. Care-givers are impoverished, HIV+ widows, grandmothers, aunts, young sisters, even neighbours of the malnourished or orphaned babies. These care-givers take responsibility for the orphaned or abandoned babies. Care-givers are referred by AIDS organizations, clinics, hospitals, and word of mouth. The centre sees babies throughout the week, making sure they are receiving milk and porridge. The centre also helps the families of the care-givers with medical, legal, emotional and spiritual counselling, food, and monetary support, so they can have small businesses to generate income. Often they will sell bananas or fish but it's hard going. When care-givers are AIDS infected themselves, they often are too weak to think past survival. The centre offers encouragement, love and acceptance in an atmosphere of trust, without judgmental prejudices. Our goal is to strengthen the whole family, many of whom are now or soon will be headed by children because of parents dying of AIDS.

Work to help child labourers

I mentioned Trinita earlier in this chapter. Trinita is one of many NGOs working with child labourers in India which began to work with child leather workers in Kolkata in 2004. The work has quickly been extended to include rag pickers, domestic servants, restaurant and factory workers, rickshaw pullers and others. Anthony Das is the founder of Trinita and he was urged on by his burning sense of the injustice which drove poverty stricken parents to put their children to hard work at a time in life when they should learn, play and be happy. Trinita has tried to be realistic and not to ask parents to stop their children working, because it is realised that the alternative might lead to hunger and even death for some. Trinita raises awareness of the rights of the children both with the parents and with the employers, organising awareness classes twice a month. They work to give the child workers a better life by working to offer them some release and play time, and also some education and access to health care. They

Photos of activities at Trinita by Anthony Das.

try to ensure that the children have one full day off every week. They also monitor the living and working conditions of the children.

Trinita has set up a home for the poorest and most deprived children and otherwise tries to make sure that children do go home at night time. In January 2011 a night shelter was opened with the aim of providing a welcoming place for the homeless children but also to curtail late night work and other forms of exploitation. Education is offered for child workers, including special coaching for those who have never been to school and classes in English. Health check-up camps are arranged regularly and free medicines are given where needed. Common illnesses include skin diseases, malnutrition, fevers, coughs and colds.

Efforts are also made to educate mothers in basic nutrition and lessons in cooking hot meals are given. A mid-day meal has been made compulsory for the children. Meals include egg and fish curry, vegetables, milk, rice and bread. At the end of the day the children are given biscuits or bread and fruit.

One of the main aims of Trinita is for the child workers to be as happy as possible in their circumstances. They try to make sure that the children have some physical education every day and also games at least twice a week.

The achievements of Trinita have been great, and there are now 960 children who are being helped, but the achievements have not been reached easily. There has been a lot of opposition to the work from both employers and parents but also from the children themselves, who did not like going into the night shelters at first. Trinita members held many public meetings and also visited parents and spent time with the employers, basing their arguments on the rights of the children and challenging both parents and employers to see them as real people. Attitudes have changed, especially amongst the parents, who want to work with Trinita for the well being of their children.

Sakil is a typical child who has been helped by Trinita. He was found working in a leather factory with his father when he was nine. He worked for between 15 and 17 hours a day and the slept on a drainage bank. He was sickly and suffering from a skin disease. Trinita persuaded Sakil's parents to let him attend their school and to receive health care. Today he lives in the night shelter, is a healthy child and is in Class 5 of the Islamic high school. He has friends and 'loves going for a picnic.'

Work to help street children in India

The South Asia Council for Community and Children in Crisis is 19 years old. It is based in Bangalore and works throughout South India for the poorest of the poor. Children, mostly boys, are picked up in the city, usually at night time. They are taken to night shelters, where they are offered good food and care. A variety of educational opportunities have been developed, including vocational training.

I have visited the Mar Thoma Ashram at Mulayam in Kerala twice now. It is a home for 45 boys who are orphans or whose parents are very poor. The ashram is a real home for the boys, who would otherwise be on the streets, and they attend schools nearby. The boys take a lot of responsibility in the running of the ashram, guided by the staff. They grow and plan the food, clean the buildings, look after the library, care for the sick children, and lead the devotions. When they leave school the boys are offered suitable further education or training. Every effort is made to give the boys not only a home, education and health care, but also opportunities to develop wider skills and to enjoy relaxation. I was taken to see the rubber tapping and we were also entertained with songs and drama. An expedition is organised once a year.

Mar Thoma Ashram. Photos, by Samuel Issmer, show the children making coconut matts for sale, as well as bananas and yams that they have grown. There are many opportunities for the children to play and relax.

The Lister Girls' Home

The Lister Girls' Home is run by SAC-CCC and the Church of South India. The girls are well fed, spiritually nurtured and well taught. They are given good health care and are encouraged to pay attention to their appearance, to be neat and tidy and to be active. The hope is that they will be future leaders in a country which has few female leaders at the local level. Photographs show the girls at school, and joining in festivals and special dances.

And the daughter of Pharaoh came down to wash herself at the river; and her maidens walked along by the river's side; and when she saw the ark among the flags she sent her maid to fetch it. And when she had opened it, she saw the child: and, behold the babe wept. And she had compassion on him and said, 'This is one of the Hebrews' children.' Then said his sister to Pharaoh's daughter, 'Shall I go and call to thee a nurse of the Hebrew women, that she may nurse the child for thee.' And Pharaoh's daughter said to her 'Go.' And the maid went and called the child's mother. And Pharaoh's daughter said unto her, 'Take this child away, and nurse it for me, and I will give thee thy wages.' And the woman took the child and nursed it.[18]

Prayer

God, our parent, source of goodness, through our actions may we work for what is best for your children. Keep us alert to the dangers your children face, especially those that we can change through our determination to consume that which promotes healthy living, and is life enhancing. Amen. (Janice Clark)

Statue in St Martin-the-Fields Church of the death of Hector Pieterson in South Africa, during the 1976 Soweto uprising.

---

18 Exodus 2.5–9.

Drawing by Jane Walton-Loxton.

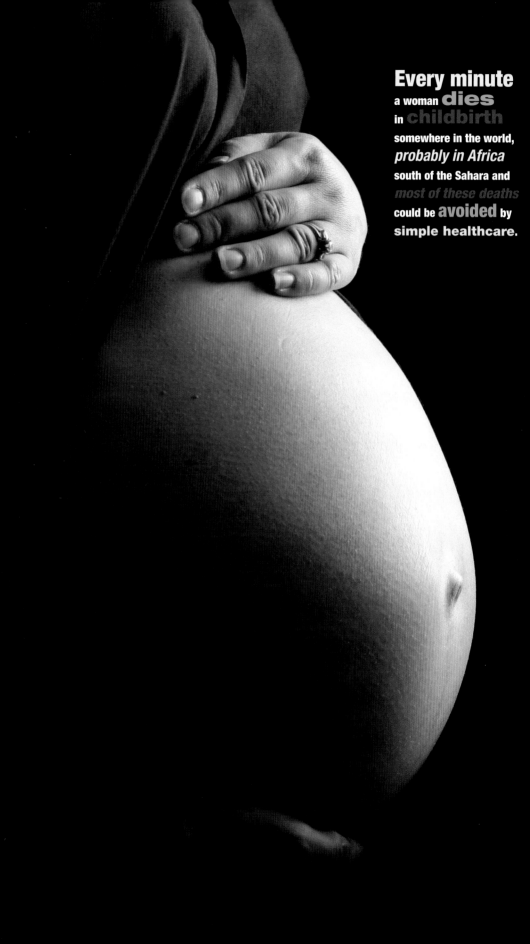

Every minute
a woman **dies**
in childbirth
somewhere in the world,
probably in Africa
south of the Sahara and
most of these deaths
could be avoided by
simple healthcare.

Goal 5

Improve Maternal Health

This goal is the one in which least progress has been made. A poem by Malawian writer Jack Mapanje brings home in a very harsh way the conditions many women in the developing world face when they give birth.

I was out of bounds, they insisted, outside
the wards, where iron roof crumble under

Rotting mlombwa leaves, green paint rusts
the wards, where iron roof crumble under

Rotting mlombwa leaves, green paint rusts
To two decades of dust, windows are

Covered in threads of matting (to stop our
Scorpion pneumonia of June?) Inside some

Sixty inmates of spasming women top and tail
on thirty beds, ninety others with infants

Scramble over the cracked, cold cement floor –
A family under each bed, most in between.

On a slab, a cramped enamel plate (with
a piece of tripe she could not chew) labours.

But this is no asylum and no one is fighting
the desert war here. These are refugees only.

Jack Mapanje[1]

Mary in the Storm –
Jyoti Sahi woodcut.

Barbara Tonge writes: Little did I know when I was in the Labour Ward in the hospital in Linlongwe that I would later meet Jack Mapanje who wrote this poem.

The time was exactly at the time of 9/11, but we knew nothing of this on that day. On the shores of Lake Malawi, life and death come everyday and we only knew of 9/11 on reaching the Bishops House in Muzuzu – it was very unreal, just something like a science fiction film on a screen.

---

1 *The Chattering Wagtails of Mikuyu Prison* (African Writers Series), 1993, Heinemann Educational, Oxford.

The small bare Labour Ward held three beds, two against the walls and just 18" between them. All three beds were occupied with women giving birth, and another woman waited on a chair, a small plastic bag round her wrist holding the necessities – a cloth to clean herself and a wrap for the baby. She could wait no longer – so a plastic mac was put on the floor, one woman moved off on to it and the fourth woman gave birth.

60 babies are delivered in that unit every 24 hours, forty of them at night with just two staff. The maternal and neonatal mortality rates are high, not because of the lack of skill on the part of the nurses, but because of the mothers' state of health and the added burden of HIV Aids transmitted to the babies.

Jack Mapanje is now a good friend of mine living in the UK, having suffered imprisonment in Malawi for 3 years 9 months and 4 days. He wrote this poem with the experience of his wife in mind – before I ever knew him.

TARGET – to reduce the maternal mortality ratio by three quarters

The World Health Organisation's estimate is that more than 500,000 women a year die as a result of complications in pregnancy and childbirth.

> **We may imagine that every four hours, every day, a plane crashes and every time all 250 passengers are killed. The passengers are all women, most are from the developing world, very young and many still in their teens. They are all pregnant or have just given birth. Many of them have other children who depend on them.**

Maternal health is a major global health challenge. The aim of this MDG, to reduce maternal mortality by three quarters by 2015, is not possible. Some progress has been made. There has been a 34% decline in maternal mortality since 1990 but much more needs to be done. The average annual percentage decline in the global maternal mortality ratio has been 2.3%.[2] A 5.5 % annual decline would be necessary to meet the MDG target. The target can only be reached when there is access to reproductive health for every woman.

The countries which have made good progress so far include Sri Lanka, Egypt, Thailand, Nepal and Honduras. Some of the ways forward, examined later, include the obvious one of education, including sex education and knowledge of family planning, and free community health services. The world religions vary in their attitudes to family planning and the Christian world is divided. Free access to abortion is very controversial and most

---

2 United Nations MDG report 2010.

religions are against it, though some accept it in cases of rape and when the mother's life is in danger. I discuss abortion later in this chapter.

It is obvious that if real progress is to be made in this goal, the goal of gender equality must also be reached, and, as I pointed out in Chapter 3, gender equality is extremely hard to measure and even harder to achieve.

Some Reasons for High Maternal Mortality in the Developing World

Of all the issues and problems women face in the developing world the issue of giving birth is the most urgent and is linked directly to continuing poverty, the lack of water and sanitation, the lack of rural health systems, the lack of trained people and the lack of will to do anything about it by most of us.

There are also the cultural and social obstacles which people need to face in their own families, communities and countries. When we approach women's health we touch the tip of an iceberg which goes very deeply into history, culture and current circumstances and points ever downwards to a deep ocean of uncertainty and suffering.

The Lives Many Women Lead

Women are injured and disfigured and go on to die in childbirth because of the lives they lead and the work they do, which is normally informal and is therefore unprotected. Women's paid work may include heavy manual labour. I have seen women digging roads and working on building sites in many areas of India. They look very small, weak and unhealthy. As I wrote in Chapter Three, a major part of a woman's day in many areas of the developing world, pregnant or not, working elsewhere or not, is spent collecting water and fuel for the family. These basic requirements are in short supply now, often due to drought and deforestation which means that the women have to walk for longer and longer distances. Often little girls are also

Collecing water.

helping their mothers, and themselves carrying huge burdens. Shortage of wood often leads to women using animal dung as fuel and to build houses, causing noxious gases to be emitted which may lead to bronchitis, heart failure and lung cancer.

Rape

Rape is a type of sexual assault which damages women irreparably and if it does not end in their deaths it is likely to lead to them giving birth to babies in the most horrendous and dangerous circumstances. It is impossible to find any reliable statistics for rape, often it is unreported and even hidden, because it is deemed to bring disgrace on the woman who has been raped. Parents are often reluctant to tell anyone if one of their children is raped. South Africa is known to have a very high rate of rape against children.

Rape is recognised by the United Nations as an element in the crime of genocide when it is committed with the deliberate intention of destroying a whole community of people. Secretary-General Boutros-Ghali told

the Beijing Conference that more women were suffering directly from the effects of war and conflict than ever before in history. *"There is a deplorable trend towards the organized humiliation of women, including the crime of mass rape"*, the Secretary-General said. *"We will press for international legal action against those who perpetrate organized violence against women in time of conflict."*

In January 2012 a team from Christian Solidarity Worldwide[3] visited Kachin State in Burma and received many reports of the rape of women by Burmese troops. On May 1st a woman sheltering in a church was attacked and gang raped over a period of three days.

In our world, where rape and other forms of abuse are very evident, a letter written by the United States President on May 15th 2012 is very encouraging. It shows a clear commitment to work against rape and other forms of abuse in the world today.

---

3 www.csw.org.uk.

Thank you for sharing your thoughts with me. Many Americans have written to me about human rights around the world, and I appreciate your perspective.

The United States was founded on the principles of freedom and equality, and our history is marked with triumphs and struggles in fulfilling these timeless ideals. Our task is not finished, and protecting these core values is a shared obligation and a priority for my Administration. No nation should be silent in the fight against human rights violations. When innocents in places like Sudan, Syria, and the Democratic Republic of Congo are raped, murdered, or tortured, it is a stain on our collective conscience. I am committed to reinvigorating America's leadership on a range of international human rights issues.[4]

Women's Illnesses

There are the many illnesses which beset every person in developing situations and which I consider at in Chapter 6. The lack of water often leads to the spread of disease including diarrhoea. I have also written about food shortages which affect pregnant and nursing women very badly

The poverty of women in the developing world is exacerbated in the twenty first century by HIV/AIDs related illness, the spread of which is clearly linked to poverty; and women are much more vulnerable than men, and continue to give birth to children who are HIV positive. The reduction in HIV/AIDS related illnesses and deaths is examined in Chapter 6.

A doctor consults with mother and children about HIV/AIDS.

4 Letter to David Pitts from Barack Obama, May 15th, 2012.

However, the vicious circle still goes on and is in danger of spiralling out of control in some areas of Africa.

Fistula

There was reference to the development of fistula through the carrying of burdens in Chapter 3. Rape is also a cause of fistula because it is normally carried out by physical force. Fistula mainly results from lack of competent help during the giving of birth. A fistula develops when the blood supply to the tissues of the vagina, rectum and bladder is cut off, most often during labour, leaving a hole through which urine and faeces pass uncontrollably.

Fistula leads to obstructed labour, and to the deaths of mothers and babies in countries where there are very few caesarean operations. There are many more surgical deliveries in the growing developing economies including much of Latin America and China, but these deliveries are not always as safe as they are in the developed world.

Tanzania is the largest provider of fistula surgery, working through mobile phones, which makes it possible to receive information and to transfer patients to hospital quickly.

Between 1999 and 2004 mobile phone subscribers in Africa jumped from 7.5m to 76.8m. Most people use pay as you go cards and travel to the nearest store for the phones to be charged up The users of mobile phones are not just the middle classes, they are used in villages and shanty towns, by nomads and street vendors, for business and to demand ransoms. Sierra Leone offers rural women the opportunity to ring a hotline for advice about fistulas and for practical help.

Fistula Hospital, Addis Ababa.

The leading fistula hospital in the world is in Addis Ababa. It was founded in 1974 by doctors Catherine and Reginald Hamlin, and Catherine continues the work now that her husband has died. The hospital provides treatment and rehabilitation for fistula patients, providing free treatment for 2,500 women every year. Most fistulas can be repaired. There are 50 long term patients in the Addis Ababa hospital. There is also a programme for the prevention of fistula and another for the training of health professionals from all over the world.

There is a global campaign organised by the United Nations Population Fund, which is working in 45 countries to end fistula. Fistulas are particularly common in adolescent mothers.

An x-ray reveals an incidence of fistula.

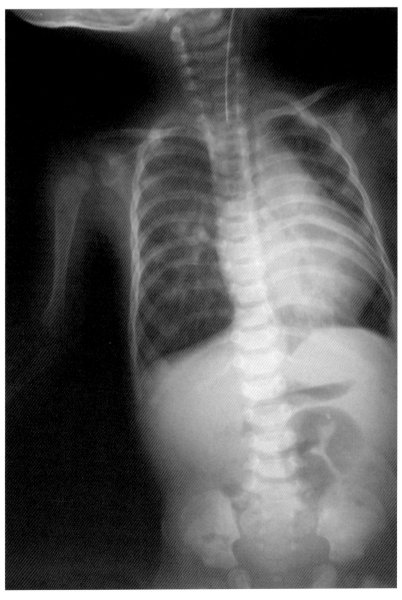

LIVING TESTIMONY
Obstetric Fistula and
Inequities in Maternal Health

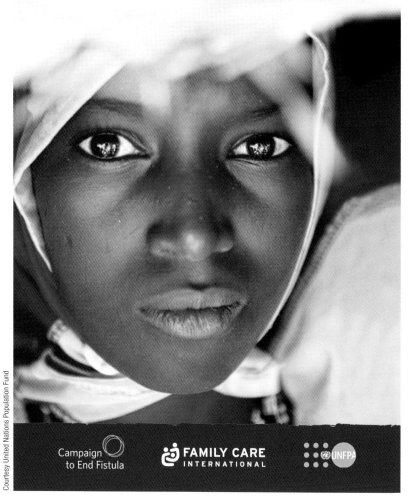

Campaign to End Fistula   FAMILY CARE INTERNATIONAL   UNFPA

Maternal deaths amongst adolescents

Risks are higher amongst younger mothers, aged 15–19 years – there are 70,000 maternal deaths every year in this age group. Babies also have a higher risk of dying when the mothers are in this age group. The adolescent birth rate is highest in sub-Saharan Africa

Childbirth is harder for adolescent girls than for older women because normally the adolescent pelvis is not wide enough to take the baby's head. The baby often gets stuck in the birth passage and unless there is immediate attention the baby dies and the bodily tissues begin to rot. A common result of this is that fistula develops and girls lose control of their bladders and bowels and thus become 'unclean' and are often rejected by their families. There are hospitals, like the one in Addis Ababa, which treat fistula, but treatment depends on the sufferers reaching them and many do not. Many girls hide their condition until it is too late for them to receive treatment.

Abortion and maternal mortality

Unsafe abortion is responsible for 13% of maternal mortality in developing countries. There are 70,000 deaths a year worldwide from unsafe abortions. 99% of these deaths occur in sub –Saharan Africa, Central and South-East Asia and Latin America and the Caribbean.

Approaches to abortion are difficult to assess. Some individuals and groups would want to say that legal and safe abortion is the only possible answer to unwanted pregnancies and that the alternative is driving women to resort to illegal, unsafe and secret operations, often resulting in their deaths. Other individuals and groups, including some of the world religions, are adamant that abortion is wrong under any circumstance because it is the deliberate killing of the unborn child. Many countries have severe restrictions on abortion. Ireland is one example. The Roman Catholic Church teaches that abortion is always wrong because it is the taking of a life. This teaching holds firm even when the foetus is in its early stage of development and also when the mother's life may be in danger. Even when abortions are legal of course they may be mis-managed, leading to complications and deaths.

From a practical and humanitarian point of view what is needed is the prevention of unwanted pregnancies. The lack of the availability of safe contraception to prevent unwanted pregnancies contributes greatly to deaths from abortion. Prevention of pregnancy may be achieved by strict religious discipline as advocated by the Roman Catholic Church, although even members of this church often find this either difficult or impossible. When I visited the Philippines I was bombarded by Roman Catholic women who were campaigning in vain for their church to allow them to practice contraception. Many of the women I met were quite bitter about the lack of willingness of their church to engage with them in any discussion.

I would want to say that contraception for men and women has to be efficient and more readily available. Failing this safe abortion and post-abortion care have to be considered, but are far from desirable options.

Giving birth without the help of trained people

Every development organisation agrees that the availability of skilled birth attendants is vital and also very difficult to achieve. There is first of all the challenge of training the attendants, and many countries are working hard to achieve this. It is estimated that 700,000 new midwives are needed worldwide. Midwives not only deal with most complications during birth, but they also know when to take the future mother to hospital. Further, they are also there to make sure that the environment for the birth is clean.

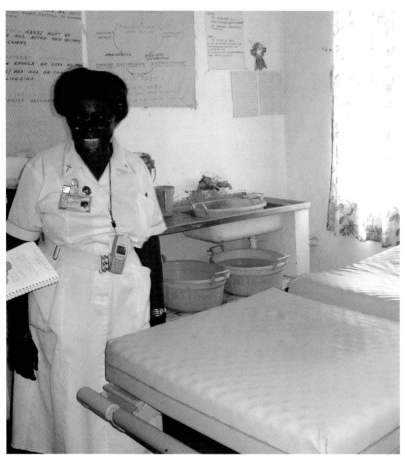

There is however the huge issue of what happens to medical personnel once they are trained. The temptation for people with any training in the developing world is that they apply to work in other countries where they think they will enjoy a good lifestyle and where their children will go to good schools. This is understandable but does not help the developing world.

Some countries are seeking to introduce a temporary plan to train and use community health workers who are not sufficiently qualified to go to work in other countries and are supervised by fully trained midwives in health centres. Surgery is also undertaken by under qualified people.

Giving birth alone

Many rural women still have no choice but to give birth at home, often with unqualified help or with no help at all.

Little has so far been done to help women who prefer to have their babies at home. In Papua New Guinea for example the health centres are normally staffed by men and women refuse to go there – Nancy Garland, who was a midwife for many years in Papua New Guinea, relates her experiences there. Papua New Guinea is a land of very rugged terrain, high mountains, rivers, swamps, jungle and tropical sandy beaches.

Under these conditions women have given birth according to local culture and customs and because of the fear of contamination of the issue of blood the women had to deliver outside their village homes, often in the 'garden house'. In the Managalas area a woman was considered to be strong if she could deliver herself! This led to all sorts of complications and included infant and maternal deaths.

Traditionally a woman would deliver in a shelter with a rope hanging from the ceiling, squatting and holding on to the rope to enable her to bear down with her contractions, the coastal women usually had another woman or two helping them and the baby was wrapped in a clean piece of tapa cloth. I understand the cord was cut with a sharp piece of bamboo. The infant would be placed in a clean, newly made string bag which was hung from the head of the woman.

On one occasion I was walking from village to village to conduct the maternal child health clinic with my nurse assistant (villages were between 2 to 8 hours walk apart and we would stay overnight in the village), when a man came running up to me to say, 'Sister, come quickly my wife is trying to give birth and baby not coming!' We followed him to a clearing in the garden where the food was grown and found his wife alone clutching on to a banana tree and pushing as hard as she could! I encouraged her to lie down so that I could examine her and of course the contractions were early labour pains – we insisted that she came back to the village with us so that we could help her as it was becoming dark and cold in the mountain air. On arrival at the village we were told that it was not their custom to deliver in the village, so I explained that the woman would deliver in the rest house with us as the rest house was usually at the end of the village. After sedating and settling the woman for the night we tried to get some rest and just before daybreak we delivered a healthy baby boy.

An hour or so later I found the woman with the baby in the string bag sweeping under the rest house with her palm frond broom in case any blood may have fallen through the slatted floor during the delivery!

Naturally, I used this opportunity to educate the husband about not allowing his wife to be alone during childbirth and that there must be at least two others present in order to fetch help if needed. The number of deliveries at our little health centre increased following this experience, thank the Lord.

Improved health care in the rural areas, mainly by the many Christian health workers, has helped, through improved ante-natal and post-natal care, to reduce the infant and maternal mortality rate although I haven't any facts or figures to verify this.

Village midwives have been trained by different church health workers and women having their first infants have been encouraged to deliver at the nearest health centre and also for the fourth. Most women in PNG are

anaemic due to malaria and lack of iron in their diet. It is pleasing to note that male health workers were being accepted by the women to help in deliveries as education and improvement of health facilities have taken place. *Families in PNG. Photos by Nancy Garland and John Daniels.*

Difficulties faced by the national health workers are transport from village to village and lack of respect for the female nurses if they need to stay overnight. The boys can cause problems so the girls do not want to go on long patrols but prefer to return to the health centre each night.

In the 1960's we would have a ward at the hospital/health centre for motherless babies (mothers had died for various reasons) who needed to be fed with milk. Health services have improved the general health of the population and family planning where accepted has improved the health of the mother and child.

Human Rights

One of the underlying reasons for so many maternal deaths is that women's human rights are not as respected as they should be in much of the developing world, because women are generally not regarded as equal in status and value with men and because sometimes they and their lack of rights are hidden from public view. I noted the 1981 'Convention against all forms of discrimination against women' in Chapter 3, but there is a very long way to go in achieving this. Women have to speak up for themselves and to develop the understanding in their communities that their issues, including childbirth, are not marginal but central to the future of the communities.

The dire situations of suffering women find themselves in when they are pregnant and giving birth are treatable, but there seems to be a lack of will to do enough to bring change and to save lives. Women's education will improve things but I want to reiterate that all women will have to struggle to overcome many cultural practises. Women have to feel a burning sense of injustice, for themselves and for other women, and they have to be prepared to take risks in working for new life, for women's right to choose their ways of life and of health. Above all women have to work hard for justice.

Most recommendations for post-2015 work are very clear in stating that the poor, and above all poor women, must find a voice. The UN Secretary General has committed himself to a listening approach towards future action.

Maternal Health in India

India is an emerging global economy but has very high maternal mortality levels. Of every seventy Indian girls who reach reproductive age, one will die from pregnancy, childbirth or unsafe abortion. This statistic may be compared with one death in 7,300 in the developed world. Girls in India will die from injuries, infections and disabilities which could be prevented.

The statistics hide the disparity between states and also between caste and class. Haryana and the Punjab actually show an increase in maternal deaths. Maternal health is very poor amongst the Dalit and tribal people of India.

UNICEF and Johns Hopkins University have conducted interviews with families in six high risk areas with the support of the Indian Government

Indian children on their way to school.

PavelSvoboda/Shuttertock.com

and the World Bank, and have identified clear sources of maternal death from anaemia, obstructed labour and unsafe abortion. They also identify hidden causes, including the low social status of the women. A 2007 study in six northern states of India revealed that 61% of maternal deaths were in the Dalit and tribal communities. Hidden causes include inadequate facilities and general lack of awareness of distances involved in travel to rural health centres.

The Indian Government is aware of the need to provide more public health facilities and some monitoring of health including an annual health survey in some key states. There is also the need to provide more midwives, to give girls more confidence and to work against child marriage.

A Human Rights Watch report[5] on maternal health care in India has pointed out that maternal mortality will only improve when health care and facilities are in place for every woman and girl in the country regardless of class, caste, income, religion and home. There must also be health care accountability.

Human Rights Watch carried out research in Uttar Pradesh between 2008 and 2009, where maternal mortality is high. The researchers came to the conclusion that the high mortality rate was due to gaps in care, demands for payment for safe delivery, barriers to emergency care and poor referral practices. The monitoring of the system was deemed to be poor as was the failure to gather information.

No Tally of the Anguish
Accountability in Maternal Health Care in India

HUMAN RIGHTS WATCH

Courtesy Humans Right Watch

Already the National Rural Health Mission provides services to the rural poor but there is little monitoring of how the services work. There are also huge gaps in medical teams and especially in emergency health services. In Uttar Pradesh only 1 in 20 referral centres offers caesarean sections and only one in a hundred centres have blood banks. Sometimes blood transfusions are a hundred miles away. Sometimes women are shuttled from one place to another until they finally die. Other women lack the confidence to seek help in the first place.

It is often the case that women with two children and girls under 19 years of age are refused free care. Further, in a culture of bribery money is demanded everywhere and for every stage of birth. There is the typical story of the man who took his wife into a health centre for the delivery of their child, carrying with him the 300 rupees he had gathered from the sale of wheat, only to be asked for 500 rupees. He was asked for a further 50 rupees for the cord to be cut and then for 50 rupees for the sweeper to clear up. He had to beg for the extra money he needed.

---

5 *No Tally of the Anguish*, Human Rights Watch: www.hrw.org.

The Human Rights Watch report makes it clear that much better monitoring of maternal deaths is needed. This is hard to achieve because there is no real will to achieve it, especially at the local level. Further, the death of a woman is not regarded as maternal if it is eight hours after the delivery. There is also fear of reprisals against health workers if there are too many deaths. Often health workers exclude women of Dalit and tribal communities from either monitoring or care. Monitoring of maternal deaths is improving in Tamil Nadu where there are regular awareness campaigns right across the communities and special training in recording for health workers.

Women themselves have no easy way to report harm done to them. There is ignorance and fear.

Human Rights Watch has issued recommendations for both the national Indian government and for state governments, so that the country may work towards no longer being the country with the highest number of maternal

Outside a clinic in Calcutta.

deaths in the world. The recommendations include much more rigour in the monitoring of maternal deaths, including the reasons. They suggest more staff, including recorders and ombudsmen to record grievances and to pursue redress. There should be a telephone hotline for pregnant women facing emergencies. Donor countries and international agencies should be ready with necessary equipment and money.

These recommendations towards clarity about what faces many pregnant women in India will inevitably lead to improvements in the worst areas of inefficiency and neglect, and thus to a reduction in maternal deaths. The recommendations must also be useful in other countries.

Maternal health in the drylands of Kenya

A 2011 visit to Kenya gave me the opportunity to find out about the lives of women in the dry lands. The insights I was given offer a valuable opportunity for understanding some of the difficulties inherent in the struggle to reach Goal Five in many rural areas of the developing world.

In Kenya there is a new health programme for mothers and children amongst the nomadic pastoralists of the north. The aim is to give them access to health services. The programme is organised by several Anglican dioceses and in many ways is a sign of hope. At the same time the work towards the programme has brought out the incredible difficulties the health workers are facing.

Painting by Petra Röhr-Rouendaal

The plan is that the government will also help by providing the infrastructure for the programme and by offering necessary drugs. The current government is supportive and very keen that the country should meet the Millennium Development Goals. The main stumbling block in the dry lands is that pastoralists do not stay in one place, they move.

It is vital that people in the communities themselves are trained to deal with illness and childbirth, so that when the people are on the move there is always someone to care, even if it is not a formally qualified person. It is important for those working with community trainees to be aware of good things the communities are already doing as part of their tradition and to move on from there in what may be described as a bottom up approach.

However, even when local community members are trained to care for people and to deliver babies they do not qualify to meet Goal Five, because they are rarely certificated. The MDG requirement is that a skilled and qualified person must deliver babies. The only way this can be achieved is for the mothers to have their babies in a hospital. In 2012 ninety per cent of deliveries in the Kenyan dry lands are at home.

Painting by Petra Röhr-Rouendaal

One of the traditional practices which stops mothers from going to hospital is that when a baby is born the elders of the tribe kill a goat and perform rituals for the new child. Baby boys also receive snake venom from the elders. The question being asked by health workers is whether the practise may continue but at a later date, or even in the hospital.

Another suggestion is that there should be 'waiting hostels' where mothers to be can live until their babies are born, so that they are safer when the people move on.

It is believed that mothers-to-be will wish to remain behind if there is a reliable source of water. They might then keep animals and grow crops to help their families. The children might also go to school and receive the appropriate vaccinations from time to time. Family planning might also be an option.

One way of working for the survival and continuing health of mothers and their babies is obviously to provide reliable water, through water catchment and other schemes. It is currently being suggested that underground reservoirs would be the best way forward.

The United Nations figures for maternal deaths are given for the developing world in general and also for sub Saharan Africa. It is almost impossible to find out what is happening in the dry lands where people don't talk about the dead. It is not possible to know who has died, adult or child. People are buried on the day they die.

The issue of family planning is sometimes hard to face in the developing world. When I first visited Kenya in the 1980s most of the families had between six and ten children, but some were larger. The educated middle classes were the exception, often having about four children.

Bocman1973/shutterstock.com

Today the families are generally smaller and the Anglican Church is committed to family planning. It is still hard to talk about sex, but perhaps this is true in many cultures, not just in the developing world.

I have already touched on the difficulties of family planning in relation to the Roman Catholic Church. The Roman Catholic hospitals do train nurses, and those nurses have to go to other hospitals, usually government hospitals, to be trained in family planning. The Roman Catholic hospitals and clinics offer natural family planning, but do send people to other clinics for contraception, including condoms.

Traditional culture often raises difficulties for health workers

Difficulties are compounded when community members are made aware by outsiders that practices such as female genital mutilation are harmful. Community members are not likely to take kindly to being told that their old cultural practises are not only unhealthy but positively dangerous. I have looked at FGM in Chapter Three. Its eradication is an on-going challenge.

Safe delivery is improving in most refugee camps

The most obvious reason for safer delivery in refugee camps is that monitoring and care are easier in refugee camps than in many more normal situations in the developing world, although the will to help has also to be there.

A woman in the Dadaab refugee camp receives pre-natal care from a Red Cross docter.
I looked at Dadaab Camp in north eastern Kenya in Chapter One. Over half the people in the camp are women and children. The annual recorded delivery is 8,000 babies.[6] This figure does not include the many Somali women who choose to have their babies indoors and then to stay there for

homeros/shutterstock.com

---

6 From UNHCR.

forty days. UNHCR has introduced an audit of maternal deaths and the reasons for them, including anaemia, delays in seeking help and delays in reaching help. Recent improvements include a new maternity hospital, more midwives, improved transport and the education and the involvement of the community. The creative plan of UNHCR is to share the experiences of Dadaab with other countries with refugee populations. This plan makes the work in Dadaab a great contribution to the refugees of the world.

TARGET - universal access to reproductive health

Ante-natal and post-natal care / Contraception and family planning

It is clear that many women do not want to be continually pregnant in the developing world, but most of them do not manage to do anything to prevent it. The reasons women give include total lack of knowledge about contraception, and fear that contraception may be dangerous or expensive. Family planning programmes are obviously important and where they do exist they help people, preferably couples together, to choose the way forward for them, so long as the way chosen is one they can afford. Family planning is obviously much better than unwanted pregnancies and the resulting unwanted abortions. It is important however that there are follow up programmes and counselling.

There is clear need for funding by partners in the western world to enable good family planning in the developing world. The United States has been the largest funder of family planning, but since 1995 the funding has been much reduced, partly through the influence of the far-right under George W. Bush. Barack Obama has increased funding, though not to its former levels, and the Gates Foundation includes funding for family planning as one of its projects.

Family planning in Iran

This is an interesting example of what may be achieved in a short time. The policy of the country following the 1979 revolution was to encourage families to have more children, but this changed in 1989 when the Muslim religious leaders accepted family planning as the way forward for the country. Family planning classes were given with free contraception for all. Men and women were issued with condoms. The family planning programme coincided with the expansion of education for women who quickly accepted the challenge to plan their families. In 1970 the average woman had 6.6 children, whilst today the average woman has 1.9 children.

The education of women is the first step towards the acceptance of family planning everywhere in the world. In 1984 the Women's Global Network of Reproductive Rights was set up. In 1985, at the UN Women's conference in Nairobi a statement that women had the basic right to control their own fertility was accepted. It was also stated that this was the basis for all other human rights. The message was firmly that family planning was a human right and not in any way part of population control. In 1994 the UN conference on population and development in Cairo focused on women's empowerment. Today this is clearly a key to the lowering of the dreadful maternal death rate in many parts of the world.

FOR REFLECTION

Homage to Thee, Buddha Mother of Courage!
Born from the tear-filled Eye of Compassion:
Ferrying all beings across the sea of suffering
to the other Shore;
Fearlessness in doing what needs to be done:
Surpassing all obstacles as green grass
pushing up through stony ground;
Avalokitehvara who never abandons
training or sentient beings!
We will enter Thy Abode, our True Home!
I pray thee enter into our hearts!

Homage to Thee, Buddha Mother of Giving!
Of Abundant Dharma Jewel Offerings,
Seeing with the Wisdom Eye of True Equality
all beings as our own children:
Dissolving the delusions of pride and self hate
as the warmth of the sun in splendour
dispels the clinging mists and dews:
Thy Thousand hands and eyes are
eternally giving!
We will enter Thy abode, our True Home!
I pray thee, enter into our hearts!

Meeting Buddhists

From 'The Mandala of the Buddha Mothers, Refuge of all Beings.' Rev. Master Kōten Benson, 2004, Lions Gate Buddhist Priory 'The Buddha Mother Mamaki is She who regards all Beings as her own children, which is the very basis of metta, of loving kindness.'

Cosmic
Mother,
by Jyoti Sahi.

The Handmaid of God

(Liberation from Social Predjuices)

Why are women counted
some times as humble creatures?
Why is a woman likened
to Mother Earth –
taking upon herself all burdens
silently bearing much abuse?

Is she not also
a consuming fire
a conquering goddess?

For all that we know
when God decided to become incarnate
He chose to enter
the womb of a woman.

Solomon Raj, a reflection on Luke 1.48

Woodblock print by Solomom Raj

Goal 6

Combat HIV/AIDS, Malaria and Other Diseases

They that wait upon the Lord shall renew their strength; they shall mount up with wings as eagles; they shall run and not be weary; and they shall walk and not faint.[1]

It was as long ago as 1978 that the World Health Organisation and the United Nations Children's Fund, meeting in the USSR, issued the Alma Ata Declaration and called for 'Health for all by the Year 2000'. This has very obviously not been achieved and, with the awareness of and increase in HIV/AIDS infections, has gone into reverse. The way forward, for tackling HIV, malaria and many other diseases is through education in primary health care. This, with all the necessary associated actions, remains the only way for people all over the world to take control of their lives, to improve their health, general well-being and life opportunities.

The 1978 declaration defined primary health care as:

> '...essential health care based on scientifically sound and socially acceptable methods and technology made universally accessible to individuals and families in the community, through their full participation and at a cost that the community and the country can afford to maintain at every stage of development, in the spirit of self-reliance and self-determination.'

At its best primary health care takes into account all the factors affecting the health of individuals and communities. It aims to tackle the underlying and root causes of ill health, and it recognises that improved health is dependent on improved knowledge and choice for every person.

Improved health is thus dependent on other MDGs being realised, especially release from poverty, better education and a rise in the status of women. There is still a lot of ignorance about HIV/AIDS, especially amongst the young in developing countries. Communities need to come together to organise themselves to improve the education and health of their members.

Opposite: Turmoil, Anne Gregson

---

1 Isaiah 40.31.

A big step towards Goal 6 was taken at a meeting held at the United Nations in New York in October 2010 when $11.7 billion in new funding was pledged for three years to add to the global fund to fight AIDS, tuberculosis and malaria.

TARGET – to have halted by 2015 and begun to reverse the spread of HIV/AIDS

New trends in the 2010 AIDS epidemic report show that there is a change of course as the number of people being infected is declining, and AIDS related deaths are decreasing.

> **'We have finally reached the first part of Millennium Development Goal 6 – by halting and beginning to reverse the spread of HIV.'**
>
> Ban Ki-moon. World Aids Day, December 1st, 2010

HIV stands for human immunodeficiency virus. It is passed on from person to person through bodily fluids. The virus depletes the immune system so that those infected can no longer protect themselves against a whole variety of illnesses. AIDS stands for acquired immune deficiency syndrome which covers these illnesses.

Work in the area of HIV/AIDS, continues to be hard and often depressing. Progress seems to be slow partly because there is the constant battle against prejudice, superstition, shame and fear on the part of those suffering from the illnesses, and also from their families and communities.

There is a shining and encouraging story of hard work, perseverance and finally some success in the battle against another disease however, which,

Aids virus

rather like HIV/AIDS, has aroused fear in many people. **Over thousands of years leprosy was feared,** and still is in the developing world, where new cases arise every year. The worst thing people can do is to hide their infection, but many still do this, until it is too late to prevent suffering, including disfigurement.

We read in Leviticus,[2] '…as the leprosy appeareth in the skin of the flesh, he is a leprous man, he is unclean and the priest shall pronounce him utterly unclean… And the leper in whom the plague is, his clothes shall be rent and his head bare and he shall put a covering upon his upper lip and shall cry "Unclean, Unclean". All the days wherein the plague shall be in him he shall be defiled; he is unclean: he shall dwell alone; without the camp shall his habitation be.'

2 Leviticus 13.43–46.

Leprosy is an infectious disease of the nerves and skin.[3] It is caused by a germ very similar to the germ causing tuberculosis. It attacks the nerves of the feet, hands and face. If it is untreated it destroys movement in fingers and toes and leads to disfigurement, including stunted limbs. Sometimes it destroys the ability to feel pain which is very dangerous as patients may easily burn.

Leprosy has now mercifully disappeared from Europe, though the work of the Leprosy Mission has only recently, in early 2012, resulted in the UK Home Office stipulating that no person may be refused entry to the country on the grounds of having leprosy. Leprosy is still a problem in the developing world but it can be treated and even cured if it is caught early enough.

A leper in historical re-enactment festival near the Saint Jean Castle in Nogent le Rotrou, France.

Radu Razvan/shutterstock.com

---

3 www.leprosymission.org / www.leprahealthinaction.org.

In 2004 400,000 new cases were identified, 70 per cent of them in India. Treatment includes a course of pills, known as multi-drug therapy, which can bring speedy relief, and, when taken over about two years, can result in complete cure. Many patients are cured within six months or a year, but this depends on early diagnosis which is very often not possible when people who fear they have the disease hide away.

In *The Island*[4] Victoria Hislop tells the story of the small island of Spinalonga off the coast of Crete, which owed its reputation to its role as the main Greek leper colony from 1903 until the leprosy patients were allowed to leave in 1957 when the development of drugs was advanced enough to stop the development of leprosy. The story of the leprosy patients is focused on the Petrakis family. Eleni is the mother of the family. She becomes a 'leper' through contact with one of her pupils in the village school. Her journey from her loving home on the Cretan coast to Spinalonga with Dimitri, her pupil, is short in the time taken and the distance covered in the small fishing boat plied by Georgiou, her husband, but it is very long in terms of her move from home to a leper colony.

rook76/shutterstock.com

> **'Now that they were on Spinalonga it seemed to both Eleni and Dimitri that they had crossed a wide ocean and that their old lives were already a million miles away.'**[5]

The tunnel she has to walk through when she leaves the boat takes her to the heart of Spinalonga. It is symbolical of the huge crossing she has made from normal family life to isolation as an infected person.

Spinalonga

---

4 *The Island*, Victoria Hislop, Review/ Headline Book Publishing, 2005.
5 *The Island*, page 65.

As I read Eleni's story, and later the story of her daughter Maria, who also made the same journey, I thought also of those who suffer from leprosy today, who are still seen as 'unclean' so that they often try to hide their condition. I have visited villages created specially for leprosy patients in Haryana, to the north of Delhi. Like the people of Spinalonga in the past most of them work, mainly at farming and crafts. There are also schools and health centres. Sadly the taint of the disease never leaves them, even though, in twentyfirst-century India, visitors are allowed into the 'leprosy villages,' and treated patients are allowed to leave.

Perhaps the worst aspect of being a leper was, and is, the fear it engendered in those who did not have it. Many medieval European churches had a hole in the wall where lepers could peep in to see the elevation of the host during the Mass. There is such a squint in the church in Harbledown near Canterbury in Kent. It is on the route medieval pilgrims would have taken on their way to Canterbury. Modern pilgrims tread the same path and will find the squint and also realise that the floor of the church slopes, so that it could be washed down to prevent the spread of the disease. In *The Island* one of Eleni's daughters marries a man from an 'important' family and feels that she has to keep her mother's condition a secret. When the other daughter, Maria, contracts the disease the 'important' family is very fearful and also angry because of the disgrace.

Leprosy is spread by water droplets from the nose and mouth and by coughing and sneezing. The fear of people who have leprosy is a reminder of the fear shown towards those who are HIV positive in the world today and especially in the developing world. HIV positive people are not infectious, they can enter normal life, work, enjoy a meal with others and shake hands.

HIV in Sub-Saharan Africa

Two thirds of those living with HIV are in sub-Saharan Africa, most of them are women. The tragedy is that they are those most responsible for their families.

HIV can be contracted through infected blood transfusions and through intravenous drug injections. It can also be passed on to babies by HIV positive mothers. The main way however in which HIV is contracted is through unprotected sex . It follows that the main age group affected is young heterosexual adults, and young women are more vulnerable than young men.

Sadly the joy of sex is not the main reason for the spread of HIV/AIDS. Poverty is still one of the main reasons, including hunger and lack of basic knowledge about protection, especially amongst young people. Sometimes there is no sex education at all. Lack of food may lead women into prostitution. Lack of work may mean that men are likely to migrate to urban areas and to other countries, thus becoming more vulnerable to extra-marital sexual contacts. Unemployment can also lead to feelings of hopelessness amongst young people, leading to risky sexual encounters in which they may live or die, and often they don't care. Some traditions lead young girls to have dangerous sexual encounters at puberty, to show that they are mature women. Further, when women have low status in a community they are likely to be abused.

I have already referred to a recent Christian Aid report[6] which points to a glaring omission in the MDGs and which badly affects efforts towards Goal 3, achieving gender equality and also towards Goal 6. This omission is gender based violence. The work of the Irish Joint Consortium on gender based violence is quoted in the report.

Gender based violence is an abuse of human rights and failure to address it amounts to complicity...the cost of not addressing gender based violence is significant both socially and economically. The current economic crisis threatens to undermine hard-won advances in human rights and accelerate an increase in gender based violence in countries most seriously affected by the downturn.[7]

Gender based violence is largely responsible for the high number of women who are HIV positive.

The Anglican diocese of Namirembe in Uganda is working hard to combat gender based violence which they understand very clearly as leading to the high numbers of women who are HIV positive.

The photographs overleaf were taken during a session in Maganjo Parish in Namirembe Diocese, where 6 congregations from the Anglican and Roman Catholic Churches are working on gender violence. They take turns to host the

6 'Poverty. We're All in this together', a Christian Aid report, 2010.

7 An issues paper from the Irish joint consortium on gender based violence. Realising Rights: the Ethical Globalization Initiative, New York, Feb. 2010.

workshops. They have to produce a play, a poem, a dance and music to tell the story of how gender based violence manifests itself in the communities and how it is being tackled. It manifests itself in many forms – verbal, physical and psychological. Each of these forms is damaging in so many ways. It is sometimes tackled by identifying violence in the Bible like the 'Rape of Tamar'.[8] Amnon was King David's eldest son and his heir. He raped his half-sister Tamar and was later killed by Absalom, Tamar's full brother. The workshop groups follow their bible studies by looking at their own family homes, and work and worship places for examples of abuse and infection.

Some of the solutions suggested try to bring the spiritual and the practical together. One play performed by the young people teaches that prayer is not enough to combat violence, the police should also be called.

Pictures of sessions in Maganjo Parish by James Claude Mutyaba.

8 Rape of Tamar – Samuel 2.13.

The groups offer advice and write poetry. At the heart of the advice given to the communities by the young people is that everyone must pull together and be together. The worst possible action is to segregate people who are HIV positive. They should be normal members of the community, sharing meals, shaking hands and also being employed.

> **All in all, AIDS is a disaster avoidable and yet unavoidable**
> **Let's play our role, being good citizens is enough**
> **We should not discriminate the victims**
> **We should be friendly and helping**
> **Employ them if qualified**
> **Eat, play and worship with them.**
> **In a nutshell, love your neighbour like you love yourself.**

AIDS and children

The number of AIDS orphans is growing and there are fewer and fewer people to care for them so that many live alone or join the growing ranks of street children. Traditionally African orphans would have been taken into the extended family, but this is more and more impossible as the numbers of orphans continues to grow and the parents continue to die.

> The plight of children affected by AIDS is great. In *2007 – 15 million* children worldwide had lost one or both parents to AIDS. This figure has now increased to more than 16 million. **12** million are in sub-Saharan Africa.

Sometimes children are cared for by the elderly but more often the little ones are looked after by the older children, who don't have the energy or ability to offer the love a parent would offer. The children are often excluded from school because of their poverty. Their parents are likely to be buried in the family garden.

Benson is nine years old and lives in Zambia with his disabled grandmother. His parents are both dead and he cries a lot. He does go to school but his grandmother is afraid that if she dies he will join the growing ranks of the street children.

> **It is estimated that more than 2 and a half million children worldwide are HIV positive. 80% of these children are living in Africa.**

Children may be infected by HIV because their mothers are HIV positive. They are infected during birth or because they are breast fed. Since 2004 some mothers have access to antiretroviral treatment, but many do not have this opportunity to safeguard their unborn children. More than half infected children die before they reach two years and 80% die before they reach 5 years. Children develop AIDs related illnesses more quickly than adults and have less resistance to being hungry and to living in unhealthy conditions. A typically poor housing area in many African countries will include broken down homes where the children are crowded in and where they share water and sanitation with hundreds of other people. Animals and chickens run around in such areas, obviously spreading dirt and disease. An urban slum is likely to be much worse than a rural slum. Urban slums are described in Chapter Seven.

The plight of HIV positive children is exacerbated because Africa's health systems have been in decline since the 1980s. This was at first partly due to countries struggling unsuccessfully to pay off their debts. Often now rural health services have disappeared and if a clinic does exist people have to queue for a very long time before they reach it.

In the twentyfirst century most countries are developing programmes for the orphans and other vulnerable children – whatever the cause of their condition. The aim is to keep children fed, sheltered and in school.

In Uganda the Hope Institute for Transformational Leadership and Development, in partnership with Oxford Friends of Canon Gideon Byamugisha and Health Serve Australia, is making a big contribution towards breaking the hopelessness and despair of many HIV positive children by sponsoring them for education and vocational training. The principal goal of the Ambassador Life and Peace Project is to train and graduate AIDS competent, spiritually empowered and gainfully skilled youths that are able to fend for themselves and their families. This project has managed to sponsor 62 older children in different vocational courses like hairdressing, tailoring and catering. There are also motor vehicle mechanics, and 35 have graduated and gone into work.

James Claude

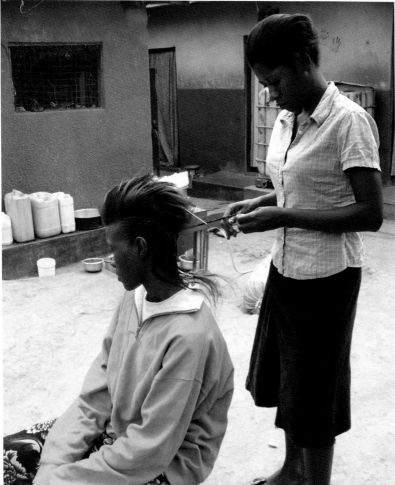

Senoga Viola Grace earns herself a living from her hair dressing course as she plaits ladies from their homes.

James Claude

One success story from the 2009/2010 sponsorship is about Senoga Viola Grace who is 18 years old, has successfully completed her one year course in hairdressing and is already earning a living from it. When she was interviewed about her new career, she said that she likes it because it brings in quick BUT clean money.

"You don't have to wait for the month to end, you earn every day as long as you get a customer every day. I am now able to sustain myself and support my mother in looking after our family", says Grace, busy plaiting 'pencil' – one of the complicated hair fashions in Uganda

Gideon Byamugisha

Gideon Byamugisha's personal story is encouraging and also hopeful. His life experience points to the need for every person living with HIV to access love, care, acceptance and treatment. Social acceptance is very important and may lead to self acceptance which is essential for any progress towards healing to be made. The worst situation to deal with is one when people have

to live with stigma imposed on them by communities who should be offering care and love. Gideon is sure that his long life has been possible because his family and the wider community accepted him unconditionally as an HIV positive person.

When people who are positive are loved and cared for not only are they enabled to live longer and productive lives but they may also become resources in the community efforts to prevent new HIV transmission.

One of the saddest outcomes for those who are HIV positive is the tendency for many of them to sink into despair, apathy and terrible poverty. The psychological damage inflicted through the disease can be more harmful than the disease itself. Many HIV positive people are known to lose all interest in life and to simply wait for death.

Gideon was born and brought up in Uganda, where he attended Makerere University and then, after marriage to Hellen, he went to Mukono Theological College. Before he was ordained into the Anglican Church his wife died leaving him with a baby daughter to care for. The bombshell came six months later when Gideon learnt that his wife had been HIV positive and had died from an AIDS related illness. He has written of the shock he felt:

> **Two months before graduation, my wife Hellen died after a very short illness, leaving me with baby Patience who was nine months old baby then. Six months later in October, I learnt from one of my sister-in laws that my wife died of an HIV and AIDS related illness.**

He went on to write of the terrible trauma he felt when the revelation came:

This was a great shock to me since we had been erroneously told in AIDS awareness seminars of the then period that 'Aids attacks prostitutes, homosexuals, drug addicts and other people of very loose and unfaithful behaviour.' I have since learnt that actually HIV attacks anyone who lacks appropriate information, attitude, skills and services for self-protection irrespective of his/her moral, spiritual or socio-economic status!

He went ahead and was ordained, but with a big burden of guilt and worry that he himself might be HIV positive. A year later, in 1992, he offered himself for a test and proved to be HIV positive. He struggled with whether to announce his condition or to keep quiet. As he struggled he asked himself, *'What about the stigma, the shame, the rejection that I could face?'*

He decided to announce his status, to work for other HIV positive people and to face whatever came to him.

How would I be an honest practicing faith leader if I was living a double identity – smiling to the public but hurting and fearful in private? How would I get courage and support if I did not own up to my problem? How would the religious faithful offer specific prayers on my behalf if they did not know what was going on in my life? I decided to disclose; to share about my HIV positive status, the pain, agony and confusion that has created, and the hope I had in God to transform my pain and suffering into an opportunity to help others. I did not know that by making that tough decision I was making history as the first HIV positive religious leader in Africa to become publicly open about his or her HIV status.

He later married an HIV positive woman and together they decided not to have children until they could do so without passing the virus on to them. They now have two healthy children, born after the introduction of the mother to child transmission programme. Their eldest daughter is called Hope.

Progress in the treatment of HIV/AIDS

Recently there has been great progress in treatment which may also become prevention. Treatment should be seen as a window into expanding and doing HIV prevention better. This development will mean that children and other members of the population will be better protected because the risk of transmission will be much reduced.

The research has revealed that successful treatment can be successful prevention – given that new transmission is reduced by 96% amongst HIV positive people who have undergone anti-retroviral treatment and had their virus almost knocked out from their bodily fluids.

What is now needed is the spiritual and political conviction to put the new knowledge to good use in every country. Uganda is working on this, and at least half of those who need treatement are receiving it. Brasil, Rwanda and Botswana are doing very well in giving treatment.

Ways Forward in Combatting HIV/AIDS

Gideon Byamugishu suggests a **SAVE** approach:

Safer Practices

Access to treatment and nutrition

Voluntary, routine and stigma free counselling and testing

Empowerment of children, young people, women, men, families, communities and nations living with or vulnerable to HIV/AIDS

The Malawi Council of Churches has given a strong lead in ways forward by running ecumenical workshops and by committing themselves to:

'...promote behaviour change; provide care to orphans, the sick, widows and widowers; to be open and talk and teach about AIDS; to promote the creation of hope and to ensure economic empowerment.'

In Southern Malawi the synod has committed the diocese to several steps:

○ Breaking the silence, removing the stigma and being open about HIV/AIDS;

○ Seeing sexuality as a gift from God;

○ Promoting pre-marriage testing;

○ Empowering girls to refuse unwanted sex;

○ Influencing cultural practices that contribute to the spread of AIDS;

○ Recognising that there is a role for condoms;

○ Affirming that God loves, and especially, sinners;

○ Teaching that nothing, even death, can separate us from the love of God.

Many local and international groups are now working hard to combat HIV/AIDS. One of the most valuable pieces of work has come from the Strategies for Hope Trust.[9] The trust has produced 'Call to Care' toolkits which are very practical handbooks on issues related to HIV/AIDS. They are designed for use by church leaders, especially in sub-Saharan Africa.

The materials have provided information in a simple form and have led to increased understanding and changes in attitudes.

---

9 www.stratshope.org.

The real-life personal testimonies are very powerful and have helped to reduce the terrible fear surrounding positive people and the virus itself. There is new hope for people living with HIV, including understanding of and hope in a suffering and loving God

One of the toolkits is designed to help those living with HIV/AIDS in sub-Saharan Africa to grow more good food for themselves and their families.[10] The foreword to this book points out that the antiretroviral treatment now available, and making such a contribution towards longer and better quality lives in the Western World, is of little use without good nutrition. The food insecurity I have written about in Chapter One is a major hindrance to HIV positive people who seek to live healthier lives, because without good food the drugs are of little use. Communities must face the challenge to grow their own organic and

Rachel Stephens

10 *More and Better Food. Farming, Climate Change, Health and the AIDS epidemic,* Anne Bayley and Mugove Waltewr Nyika.

sustainable food, promoting bio-diversity and giving all their people good nutrition and the strength their bodies need to resist illness and, when needed, for drugs to work well.

The toolkit 'More and Better Food' points out that it is hard but not impossible for people to achieve good health. When Nelson Mandela was in prison he grew his own food. For better health people should not overcook their food. They should eat a variety of foods, including bright red, orange, yellow and purple fruits and vegetables and green leaves every day. Seeds and nuts should be eaten several times a week.

The 2012 One World Calendar focuses on food and the picture for April is of a woman feeding a child in her home in a village on the Middle Atrato, in the Department of Choco, Columbia. We learn that the Choco rainforest provides all the food the woman and her family need to survive. There are green bananas, freshwater fish, rice and animals.[11]

There is new hope now that several networks have recently come together to form the Alliance for Food Sovereignty in Africa. Any community can link in with this organisation. One way in which food sovereignty can be achieved is through permaculture, when farmers work with nature rather than fighting against nature. Soil, water, energy, plants and animals are all needed and work together to provide a healthy eco-system. Agro-forestry and intercropping are an excellent way forward, and are good for people, for the environment and for the future generations. They provide shade and shelter, they use carbon dioxide and they store water.

As I mentioned earlier Gideon has established 'The Friends of Canon Gideon Foundation', through which he equips faith leaders to help to break the stigma facing people who are HIV positive. He also works to give people tools to be brave and themselves to work for changed attitudes and for help, especially for the children.

11 The New Internationalist publishes the calendar. www.newint.org.

Gideon's foundation works, through the Hope Institute, to give people new life and hope by offering vocational and health training for adults and children. In 2002 ANERELA was formed. It is the Africa Network of Religious Leaders Living with HIV/AIDS. It started with 8 people and now has a membership of 1500 leaders of the world faiths in 113 countries of Africa. The international network was started in 2006. The main aim of ANERELA is to get rid of stigma and to act voluntarily, and with governments when possible, to bring change.

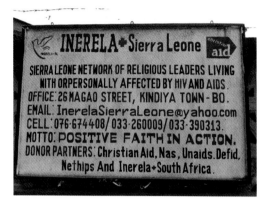

Archbishop Desmond Tutu accepts an ANERELA SAVE toolkit.

Gideon's work continues to offer hope of new life for those who are HIV positive and for the orphans of those who have died.

'Love in any language
Straight from the heart
Bonds us together – never apart
Once we learn to speak it
Everyone can hear
Love in any language
When fluently spoken – heals.'
Song from an unknown author

"Also in this (vision) he showed me a little thing, the quantity of a hazel nut, in the palm of my hand; and it was as round as a ball. I looked thereupon with the eye of my understanding, and thought: 'What may this be?' And it was generally answered thus: 'It is all that is made.' I marvelled how it might last, for methought it might suddenly have fallen to naught for littleness. And I was answered in my understanding: 'It lasteth and ever shall last for that God loveth it.' And so all thing hath being by the love of God. In this Little Thing I saw three properties. The first is that God made it: the second is that God loveth it: the third that God keepeth it."

Revelations of Divine Love, Mother Julian of Norwich, 1373

TARGET – by 2015 to have halted and begun to reverse the incidence of malaria and other diseases

Malaria

> He loves the haggard frame, the shattered mind,
> Gloats with delight upon the glazing eye,
> Yet, in one thing his cruelty is kind,
> He sends them lovely dreams before they die.[12]

A Christians Aware group in Uganda went to a health centre run by the Church of Uganda where there was no electricity, running water or even a single doctor. The group met Rose, a widow who had six children who were often ill with malaria. Scovia was also a widow with eight children who suffered regularly from malaria. Jane had eight children. Jill, a widow with ten children, is so poor that she can't afford mosquito nets for the children and they are often ill. The children who are under five years old often die.

A mother in Mozambique, who had lost one child to malaria, said, '*I fear for my surviving children every single day. I have to balance between farming and looking after my sick children. Every two weeks I have to rush to the health centre with one of my children, praying that I don't end up losing them, as has so often happened to other people around here.*' [13]

Here are some facts about malaria:

○ Very recently we thought that approximately 655,000 people die each year from malaria. We also thought that deaths were mostly of young children in sub-Saharan Africa. A 2012 study shows that 1.2 million people die every year, including not only children but also adults.[14]

○ The report reveals that 42% of victims are older children and adults.

○ While malaria accounts for 11% of overall deaths and a similar proportion of illness in Africa, it is an even more serious problem in the continent's impoverished rural areas. Recent research has found that those with malaria are more likely to acquire HIV/AIDS

The Global Fund to fight AIDS, TB and malaria has provided the funds for the battle against malaria so far, including the bed nets and drugs, but it is now in financial crisis and has had to cancel round eleven of funding.

---

12 'Malaria', from *India's Love Lyrics*. Trans. Laurence Hope. New York: John Lane Co., 1906.

13 Story from World Vision.

14 The research comes from the Institute for Health Metrics and Evaluation, IHME, based in Seattle. This work has taken place over a 5 year period, funded by the Bill and Melinda Gates Foundation, and is published in the lancet.

The first thing to realise about malaria is that it is a preventable and treatable infectious disease transmitted by mosquitoes. Today malaria can be prevented, diagnosed and treated with a variety of tools.

Malaria is caused by a parasite called plasmodium, which is transmitted via the bites of infected mosquitoes. In the human body, the parasites multiply in the liver, and then infect red blood cells. Symptoms of malaria include fever, headache, diarrhoea and vomiting, and usually appear between 10 and 15 days after the mosquito bite. If not treated, malaria can quickly become life-threatening by disrupting the blood supply to vital organs. In many parts of the world, the parasites have developed, and are developing resistance to a number of malaria medicines.

In those parts of Africa where malaria is common, someone dies of malaria every 30 seconds and that person is still likely to be a young child. The affected regions include the parts of South Africa bordering Zimbabwe and Mozambique and parts of several other Southern African countries. The incidence of malaria is increasing and it is worsening the poverty of already disadvantaged populations. The poverty cycle means that as people become poorer they become increasingly incapable of fighting any illness, including malaria.

The countries with most malaria deaths are Nigeria, Democratic Republic of Congo, Uganda, Ethiopia and Tanzania.[15]

malariainomore.org.uk

---

15 From the Global Malaria Action Plan.

The IHME report published in March 2012, has revealed 'the hidden toll of malaria deaths'. The report shows up a terrible situation; that twice as many people die from malaria every year as the official figures have so far shown. This must mean that a new approach to eliminating malaria is needed and that it is very unlikely that this will be achieved by the UN target date of 2015. Further, because most deaths are still children it is very unlikely that Goal Four of cutting child mortality by two thirds will be reached.

There is a little good news in that the downward trend for malaria deaths, reported by WHO, is confirmed, but this comes from a high peak of 1.8 million deaths in 2004 to 1.2 million deaths in 2010, and is the result of huge inputs of money and effort. By the end of 2011 235 million bed nets had been distributed. Now that the global fund has cancelled round eleven of funding it is very possible that progress made will not be sustained, though money is coming in, and the hope is that the funding may continue before too long.

So what can be done?

Anton Alexander's paper, included at the end of this section, explains how malaria was eradicated in Palestine/Israel. We learn of dedicated research, strict discipline and hard work in a number of associated areas. This story brings home the fact that the most important key to getting rid of malaria is education, and that this must include the teaching of simple facts; sometimes people are not even aware that mosquito bites cause malaria. There is also the need for the raising of awareness and the putting into practise of an orderly and strict regime by every member of every community.

The fight against malaria must be a community effort or it will never be successful. One member of the Mozambican Christian Council said, 'The mosquitoes of my neighbour can visit me at any time…...We must work together.'

Key interventions to control malaria include prompt and effective treatment with combination therapies. Unfortunately, despite much research and real hope for success in the future, as yet there is no safe and effective vaccine against malaria. The only anti-malarial drugs that local people can afford to take regularly have lost their potency. It is vital that research work is continued to fight parasite resistance to drugs.

There is also the need for people at risk to sleep under insecticide treated nets and to spray their homes with insecticide to control the vector mosquitoes. Window and door screens may also help to exclude mosquitoes

For 150 million children in Africa, a 1$ treatment can make the difference between health and handicap.

FOR A MALARIA-FREE WORLD
Work with the Roll Back Malaria Partnership: www.rollbackmalaria.org

ROLL BACK MALARIA PARTNERSHIP

from homes, but they are not cheap. People should realize the need to wear long sleeves at night and also strive to get rid of the unsanitary conditions that may provide breeding grounds for the insects.

Reducing the number of mosquitoes is essential. Mosquito breeding areas are mostly in damp and dirty places, in sluggish, swampy, vegetation clogged water, and in standing water. The first challenge is to clean up the areas around houses, and then the bush, surrounding and in standing water, can be cleared. The breeding areas can thus be reduced or even eliminated.

There is a big rise in the use of bed nets to protect children from malaria. However, the IHME report now recommends that every member of every household should have nets.

There is good research evidence that sleeping under bed nets impregnated with insecticide is the most cost-effective way to combat malaria. Nets halve the number of attacks of malaria and reduce the deaths in young children due to this cause by about a fifth. Insecticide can be incorporated in the net at manufacture so that it retains its effectiveness for two or more years.

One of the big advantages of bed nets is that even the poorest and most illiterate family can come to understand the importance of having nets for everyone and particularly for the young children. The presence of the nets in poor homes largely depends on governments or churches introducing them. There are many places where there are still no nets at all. There are other places where people have been given nets and use them for fishing. I have however seen nets in the simplest homes in Africa. Sometimes families may have only one net, and this is not always given to the children. I stayed in a mud walled house in Tanzania, where I did in fact suffer from malaria and was given the only net available in the whole compound.

Bishop Dinis Sengulane of Mozambique is a champion of the introduction of bed nets. He is chair of the World Advisory Council and also of the 'Roll Back Malaria' initiative. Dinis says, *'Prevention must be the norm. We must succeed in our efforts to have every Mozambican child sleep under a bed net.'*

The 'Roll Back Malaria' initiative was launched in 1998 to work for a malaria free world, and operates from WHO in Geneva. It has 500 partners, including malaria endemic countries, 'ngos' and research groups. Partners work together to raise malaria control efforts at country level. The Global Malaria Action Plan is in two parts. First of all the plan is to scale up the preventative interventions, and secondly to sustain malaria control over time.

Long term commitment by governments and community leaders is essential for combating and eradicating malaria. Communities should practice as many preventive methods as possible Village health workers have an important role in ensuring the proper use of nets and in keeping up the many other measures which reduce the number of mosquitoes. If there is a will to bring change the mosquitoes will be eradicated.

I will now include what Anton Alexander has written about malaria in Palestine 100 years ago, and about the eradication of the disease there.

'A desolation is here that not even imagination can grace with the pomp of life and action. We never saw a human being on the whole route.' So wrote Mark Twain in "Innocents Abroad" on his visit to Palestine in 1867.

And this sets the tone of the state and condition of Palestine all those years ago. Several factors explain the constant diminished population of Palestine over the centuries. In the 18th, 19th, and early 20th centuries, Bedouin raids were a common occurrence. Palestine also hosted several epidemic diseases. The Black Plague

made appearances all the way up to the 20th century. Typhus fever, smallpox and cholera made their rounds. Dysentery and tuberculosis were rampant. And above all, malaria was there for centuries. These diseases drastically cut down the population.

> **'Malaria stands out as by far the most important disease in Palestine. For centuries it has decimated the population and it is an effective bar to the development and settlement of large tracts of fertile lands... There are few regions actually free from it.'** [16]

> **'... the experts of 1918 ... (prophesied) that the future of this country (Palestine) might be considered to be almost hopeless from the malarial standpoint...'** [17]

Attempts were made by the Zionists to establish settlements. In 1878, the settlement at Petach Tikvah was started, and four years later it was abandoned after recurrent bouts of malaria had devastated the workers. (It was eventually resettled but only after the local swamps had been drained.) In 1890 a settlement was started in Hadera: by 1910 the majority of workers had died from malaria (out of a population of 540, 210 died of malaria) [18]– only an idealistic commitment to overcome such destructive conditions avoided abandonment. The pioneers' exposure to malaria was further heightened by the fact that the Jews were usually able to purchase land for settlement only in highly infected areas.

---

16 1926 – First Annual Report of the British Mandate Department of Health.

17 *A Review of the Control of Malaria in Palestine 1918-1941*, Department of Health.

18 Khan Museum, Hadera.

Because the Jews had often fled from persecution, this malarious situation was a preferable alternative. They were intent on creating a place for themselves where they might eventually enjoy self-determination, and there was a resignation with which these terrible conditions were accepted by all engaged in the Zionist enterprise. However, the motto of the Zionists was simple: 'Palestine must be settled, malaria or no malaria.'

Malaria presented the Jews with a practical problem, and either they remained with the conditions as they were, and became martyrs to the cause, or they had to consider practical methods for the reconstruction of Palestine by practical economics, practical sanitation etc. Simply put, unless malaria was eradicated, a Jewish homeland was unlikely to be physically possible.

Dr Israel Kligler was already a Zionist and a respected bacteriologist in the USA when in 1920, he was requested to go to Palestine to assist with malaria control.

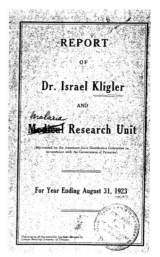

In the early 1920s, the Haifa Malaria Research Unit, under the control of Dr Israel Kligler, and acting in co-operation with the Health Department of the British Mandate in Palestine, was formed to assist with the control of malaria in Palestine.

Before Kligler came and reorganised the methods of malaria eradication, attempts to eradicate by drainage alone had had little effect. Kligler demonstrated through the Haifa Malaria Research Unit that drainage of the swamps alone would have had little effect on the malaria, because mosquitoes breed in little, out-of-the-way unsuspected places, which even the most elaborate system of drainage would not have reached. Kligler pointed out that at least half of the malaria could be ascribed simply to human carelessness and neglect.

Dr Kligler brought about a change in the attitude towards the disease of malaria, and he caused people to realize that malaria was a preventable disease. Thereafter, it was no longer inevitable, it was no longer a matter of chance if malaria was contracted.

The main idea of the Malaria Research Unit was to establish malaria control on an extensive scale at low cost. Collection of data regarding the prevalence of the disease, types and breeding places of the mosquitoes concerned went hand in hand with the education of the public in regard to controlling the disease, and the value of this education was probably as important as the immediately practical results obtained.

In order to reduce the incidence of malaria, it was necessary to reduce relapses of chronic malaria patients and eliminate the dangerous parasite carriers. This necessitated an examination of the entire population, and a systemized and carefully controlled form of treatment in charge of the local malaria inspector or local nurse.

Malaria control involved many questions requiring investigation for each site. The methods used to control were based on sound

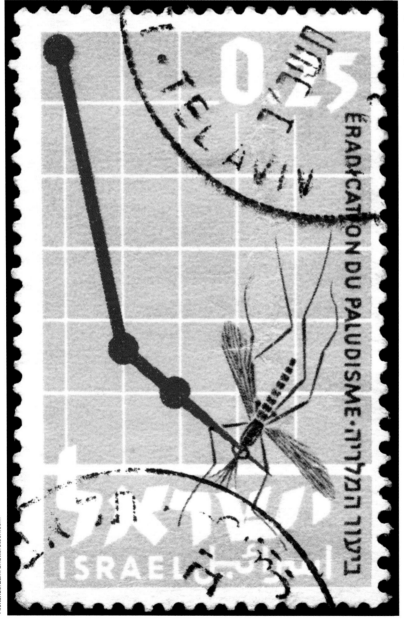

A stamp shows the Anopheles Maculipennis and chart showing decline of malaria in Israel, c.1962.

principles, and while not novel in practice, were unique in many of their details. Such questions included:

1. Did malarial infection exist throughout the year?
2. What types of mosquitoes were present?
3. How and where and when do they breed?
4. What role did they play in malaria transmission?
5. Could malaria be controlled with a small expenditure where no money was available for drainage?

An essential part played in the eradication was the role of the British authorities. Their administrative experience enabled them to oblige co-operation from the Jews and Arabs. Whilst the British Mandate Health Department retained certain powers to oblige co-operation with the anti-malaria procedures, and whilst there was at first, a certain amount of feeling engendered owing to adoption of radical measures for the destruction of the causative factors of malaria, the benefits of the anti-malaria procedures were eventually understood, and co-operation was generally provided. This was a necessary partnership – the British authorities arranging the co-operation of the population and the Zionists providing the scientific eradication methods.

The Malaria Research Unit was specially active in the permanent elimination of breeding places. First the swamp areas were methodically surveyed and then cheap and effective methods were devised for their eradication. The chief methods employed were drying by intermittent damming of streams and cleaning pools with or without larvicides. The statistical tables show that there was a marked decrease in malaria incidence following the application of these measures.

And by 1941, progress could be reported –

'An interesting recent feature has been noticed. In a number of areas where intense endemic malaria had resulted in **no** *population for generations, recent schemes (of malaria control) have created large tracts of cultivatable land.'*

and...

'That very large areas of what is recognised by all as some of the most fertile land in the country have been reclaimed, after centuries of waste, by the anti-malaria measures undertaken, it is now obvious. ...... Many large tracts which until recently **meant nothing but death to those venturing into them,** *have now been reduced into rich and fertile land free from all danger to health.'* [19]

---

19 Department of Health. *British Mandate, A Review of the control of Malaria in Palestine 1918–1941.*

But it was only by 1967 that malaria had become virtually eradicated in Israel. However, monitoring and anti-malaria activities continue to this day, and for the time being, Israel remains relatively free from malaria, except for a small number of imported cases.

It may be constructive to quote from the Hebrew University Hadassah Newsletter of 1944 writing of Dr Kligler's death and of his contribution towards malaria eradication in Palestine:

> *It made the country habitable, made settlements possible, encouraged immigration and economic development and conserved life and health. This malaria program which he conducted was an enterprise for the responsibility and budget of a government. All the more wonder at its accomplishment with relatively small sums ….. In a country where 'malaria' was not considered an illness and was, indeed, taken for granted, **intensive educational campaigning had to be conducted**. …… He realized and consistently stressed the paramount importance of constant vigilance in malaria control.*

In his own words ***'Daily vigilance and labour of man subdues nature and harnesses her to his purposes. The moment, however, that man slackens, nature asserts herself and in a few years she can undo the labour of a century.'*** [20]

Other Diseases

Tuberculosis

Tuberculosis (TB) is said to be second only to HIV/AIDS as the greatest killer worldwide due to a single infectious agent. TB usually attacks the lungs and is spread through coughs and sneezes. Symptoms of the disease are coughs, fever, night sweats and weight loss. Treatment is difficult, including courses of multiple antibiotics. The BCG vaccine was first used in the 1920s but it was not until 1946 that cure became possible.

John Keats died from TB, or consumption as it was known, in Italy in 1821. He wrote 'La Belle Dame Sans Merci' when he knew that he was dying from TB.

TB in sputum.

O What can ail thee, knight at arms,
Alone and palely loitering?
The sedge has withered from the lake,
And no birds sing.

O what can ail thee, knight at arms!
So haggard and so woe-begone?
The squirrel's granary is full,
And the harvest's done.

---

20 See www.eradication-of-malaria.com.

Stamp printed by Burkina Faso, shows Robert Koch, c.1977.

Model of the streptomycin molecule.

Rook76/Shutterstock.com

There is now a growing problem of antibiotic resistance to TB. Prevention relies on screening programmes and BCG vaccination.

○ **In 2010, 8.8 million people fell ill with TB and 1.4 million died.** [21]

○ Over 95% of TB deaths occur in low- and middle-income countries, and it is among the top three causes of death for women aged 15 to 44.

○ In 2009, there were about 10 million orphan children as a result of TB deaths among parents.

○ TB is a leading killer of people living with HIV, causing one quarter of all deaths. There is a special problem in sub-Saharan Africa, where rates of HIV are high. However, India has the highest number of cases worldwide.

○ TB is linked to overcrowding and malnutrition. Smoking, alcoholism and silicosis also increase the risk. It can also be spread by mammals.

○ Multi-drug resistant TB (MDR-TB) is present in virtually all countries surveyed.

○ The estimated number of people falling ill with TB each year is declining, although very slowly. The TB death rate dropped 40% between 1990 and 2010, largely due to World Health Organisation programmes.

This means that the world is on track to achieve the Millennium Development Goal to reverse the spread of TB by 2015.

---

21 World Health Organisation.

Most mammals, including bats, may carry rabies.

Rabies is killing more than 55,000 people a year [22]

When I spent some time in a Kenyan primary boarding school in 2011 there was a terrible uproar when it was discovered that a pack of wild dogs had managed to get into one of the dormitories and a boy had been bitten. Teachers were galvanised into action and the boy was rushed to hospital for the necessary injections to save his life. After that the police had to be called in to kill the dogs.

Rabies is a viral disease that causes acute encephalitis or inflammation of the brain. It is transmissible from infected animals to humans, normally by bite, though scratching can also be lethal. A woman was scratched by a bat in an African game park and was told by the game warden in charge of the party that bats didn't carry rabies so there was no need to go for injections. She died.

The first effective vaccine was invented by Louis Pasteur in 1885.

Rabies is fatal for humans if the prophylaxis is not given before the onset of symptoms. The virus infects the central nervous system, and death comes when the brain is diseased. The incubation period varies, it can be a few months, but once symptoms begin to show the infection is untreatable and fatal within a few days.

REPUBLIQUE CENTRAFRICAINE

PASTEUR
Centenaire du premier vaccin contre la Rage

POSTES 1985

150F

Rook76/Shutterstock.com

---

22 World Health Organisation.

*Members of the
ABC INDIA team
on a search for
free-roaming dogs
to vaccinate them
against rabies.*
abcindia.org.in

Symptoms of rabies are head-ache and fever, followed by acute pain, violent movements, excitement and depression, difficulty in breathing, followed by coma. People infected with the disease need to start a post-exposure vaccination course within 24 hours of being bitten. In 2011 stray dogs attacked an American soldier in the mountains of Afghanistan and he was given only given half the injections because the second half of the treatment was out of date. It was months later that his arm began to tingle, and then he struggled to breathe and finally he died.

The island of Bali unknowingly imported a rabid dog in 2008 and now has hundreds of infected animals and has suffered 132 deaths.

- ○ Approximately 100 children worldwide are killed every day, most often because their parents can't afford the injections.

- ○ India also reports deaths due to rabies. However, as the cost of the vaccine is high (Rs. 400), it is unaffordable for the poor.

- ○ It is estimated that it would cost $1 per head to eliminate rabies in Africa.[23]

Diarrhoea

Diarrhoea is not named as an illness to be tackled and reduced in the MDGs, pernaps because it is often a symptom of other diseases, including malaria and AIDS/HIV related illnesses. However, diarrhoea very sadly exists in its own right and it is one of the main killers, of children. It is estimated that it is the second most common cause of infant deaths worldwide. The loss of fluids through diarrhoea can cause dehydration, which is fatal in young children.

---

23 Global Alliance for Rabies Control.

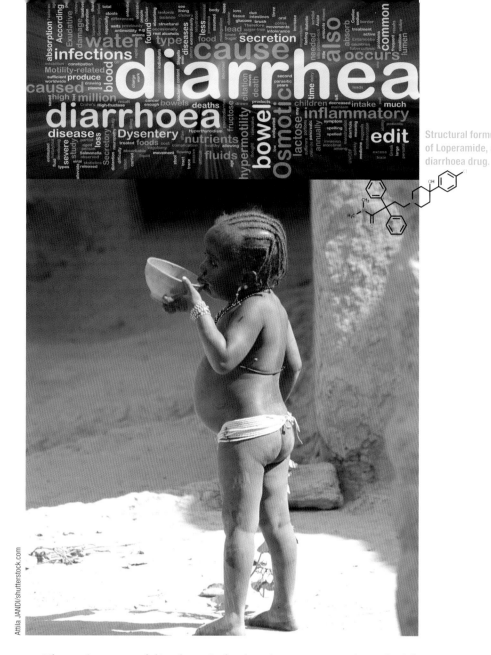

Attila JANDI/shutterstock.com

Structural formula of Loperamide, a diarrhoea drug.

The main cause of diarrhoea is food and water contaminated with human waste. There has been a huge increase in the availability of clean drinking water since the Millennium. However, as I show in Chapter 7, one in four people in the developing world use no form of sanitation. Seventy percent of those without sanitation are in rural areas. This is a scandalous situation which may be so easily remedied.

It is estimated that diarrhoea causes approximately 1.1 million deaths in people aged 5 years and over and 1.5 million deaths in children under the age of 5 years.

The best treatment is the oral rehydration solution and zinc tablets. A homemade rehydration solution can be made by adding one and a half to one teaspoon of salt and six teaspoons of sugar to one litre of water. The solution should have the taste of tears. It is estimated that 50 million children have been saved in the past 25 years.

Again, education is the main solution to deaths from diarrhoea as it is the key to ending to so many of the illnesses which disable people in the developing world. The oral rehydration solution is obviously very cheap. All that is needed is the will to teach the people and by doing so to save the people.

FOR REFLECTION

So many of us flee from people crying out in pain,
People who are broken.
We hide in a world of distraction and pleasure
Or in 'things to do.'
We can even hide in various groups of prayer
And spiritual exercises,
Not knowing that a light is shining
In the poor, the weak, the lonely and oppressed.
Or, if we do not flee from suffering
Perhaps we revolt in anger,
And this, too, blinds us to the light of Jesus
Glowing in people who are in pain.

Jean Vanier, from *The Broken Body: Journey to Wholeness*, Darton, Longman & Todd Ltd, 1988

Luke Chapter 17, verses 11–17

This is a story which took place on the border between Samaria and Galilee. As Jesus walked along and was about to enter a village he encountered ten men who suffered a dreadful and dreaded skin disease. They asked Jesus to help them and he suggested that they go to be examined by the priests. On their way they realised that they had been healed and one of them, from Samaria, returned to thank Jesus and to praise God for his healing and new health. Jesus pointed out that he had healed ten men and wondered what had happened to the other nine.

Eden Project, Cornwall, UK.

Goal 7

Ensure Environmental Sustainability

The environment is shared by everyone and determines the quality of all life. The growth of the world population, wars and natural disasters have largely caused the degradation of the environment and the problems we now face.

It is possible to argue that although all the Millennium Development Goals are linked together in a permanent knot, so that they all depend on each other, it is environmental sustainability which is first and foremost essential for the achievement of all the other goals. There have been a number of critical agreements established over the last thirty years. The **1985 Vienna Convention** for the Protection of the Ozone Layer outlined states' responsibilities for protecting human health and the environment against the adverse effects of ozone depletion. This convention established the framework under which the **Montreal Protocol** was negotiated in 1992, stipulating that substances that deplete the ozone layer in the stratosphere must be gradually phased out.

'Our natural environment underpins our economic prosperity, our health and our wellbeing.' Department for Environment, Food and Rural Affairs, UK

Also in 1992, in Rio de Janeiro a landmark United Nations conference on the Environment and Development, known as the **Earth Summit**, led to the Framework Convention on Climate Change. This conference also led to the Convention on Biological Diversity, which looked at the potential for the exploitation or care of biological resources. **Agenda 21**, the programme for action, arose from the Rio conference. It provides options for combating degradation of the land, air and water, conserving forests and the diversity of species of life. It deals with poverty and excessive consumption, health and education, cities and farmers. It includes everyone: governments, business people, trade unions, scientists, teachers, indigenous people, women, youth and children. A special children's challenge was produced. Agenda 21 does not avoid business. It says that sustainable development is the way to reverse both poverty and environmental destruction. Ten years later, in 2002, another conference in Johannesburg, sometimes dubbed **Rio + 10** aimed to adopt concrete targets and steps towards achieving the Agenda 21 programme.

The European Union has worked for high standards for the environment for many years. The action programme for 2001–10 called for action on:

- ○ Air pollution;
- ○ Waste Recycling;
- ○ Management of resources;
- ○ Soil protection is vitally important. Soil pollution and erosion and building on farm land are some main problems;
- ○ Urban environment includes better urban planning, mobility and waste management;
- ○ Sustainable use of safer pesticides;
- ○ Marine environment is under threat from overuse and pollution'

TARGET – to integrate the principles of sustainable development into country policies and programmes and reverse the loss of environmental resources

The MDG monitor for this goal states that a decisive response to climate change is urgently needed. The challenge is that, due to climate change, the melting of water from glaciers, in both Greenland and Antarctica, causes a 1mm a year rise in the sea levels. This could be calamitous because 71% of the earth consists of its oceans. The Arctic Sea has lost half its summer thickness of ice since 1950 and the ice could totally disappear in the summer time by the middle of the 21st Century. Climate change could kill about one third of the plant and animal species of the world by 2050. The success of the Montreal Protocol shows that action on climate change is now within reach if the will to do it is there.

The will to do things is the great problem and challenge we all face, governments and individuals alike. When the Climate Change Summit in Copenhagen took place in 2010 it proved to be a disappointment and certainly not a decisive response. As I write this in 2012, the Kyoto agreement will expire without any binding agreement set to follow it. The Copenhagen conference stated that global emissions must be reduced so that the global temperature increase remains below 2 degrees centigrade, but nothing was said about how this would be achieved. The developed countries did promise to give money to help the developing world to cope with climate change, but similar promises made in the past have not always been honoured.

In 2008 the then Labour Government enacted the Climate Change Act, making the UK the first country in the world to have a legally binding long-term framework to cut carbon emissions. It also created a framework for building the UK's ability to adapt to climate change. The current Coalition Government has also set out its commitment to action. Advice is easily available from DEFRA[1] and relevant committees, and a climate change risk assessment is planned.[2]

Climate change will hit the world's poorest people hardest. In fact, poor people in the Global South, and poor farmers in particular, are already suffering its effects. 70% of the world's poor depend on small-scale farming to feed their families and earn a living.[3] The majority of these rely on rain-fed agriculture, therefore changes in rainfall patterns can cause real problems.

In countries like Ecuador, the effects of extreme weather events such as drought or torrential downpours are being felt more and more acutely. For poor farmers, climate change means the availability of water resources is unpredictable – they can no longer count on stable weather patterns to guide their planting regimes. Carlos Ruiz lives in El Cristal – a community within a protected nature reserve in Intag, Ecuador. Carlos depends on farming to make a living, and has been directly affected by changes in rainfall and the regularity of the seasons:

> Now, everything has changed completely. We don't really know when it's going to rain, or even be cold or hot. It's hard because we aren't used to it, we are used to seasons that tell us when to plant.
>
> Of course, we have to adapt to these changes in the climate. The rivers have lower levels, but flood when there is torrential rain. We have been planting trees to prevent erosion when this happens – but it's still very unpredictable. Right now we have too much water – but that could change, because a few months ago we had a drought.

Adapting to unpredictable water resources is key to adapting to climate change. In order to tackle the effects of climate change along with its causes, water cannot be forgotten. Understanding how to manage our water resources in a changing climate, in a sustainable and equitable way, needs to be at the top of the agenda.

---

1 In the United Kingdom, the Department for Environment, Food and Rural Affairs, DEFRA, publishes a handbook every year, *The environment in your pocket*.
2 United Nations Framework Convention on Climate Change – gives information on what different countries are doing.
3 *Unheard Voices*, Concern Worldwide, http://www.concern.net.

Bangladesh

With a current population of over 145 million living in an area the size of England and Wales, Bangladesh is one of the most densely populated agricultural countries in the world. The majority of the country is a vast flood plain, with land often only a little way above sea level. This makes it extremely vulnerable to changes in the climate.

Flooding and erosion have always been part of life in Bangladesh and are vital for the renewal of land. However, severe floods with devastating effects on people's livelihoods used to happen once every 20 years. They now occur every 5–7 years. In 2007 the country suffered two major floods and a cyclone.

Each year the river banks erode around 7 times faster than land is gained, thus forcing riverbank communities to keep moving. River erosion has been called Bangladesh's slow, silent disaster. Each year 1 million people are affected by river erosion and 100,000 more people lose their homes and land. If you're poor, you often have no choice but to live on flood-prone land because safe land is expensive.

Poverty makes it very hard for people to adapt. Natural disasters, on a small and large scale obviously make poverty far worse. Despite warnings by scientists that a rise of two degrees centigrade could push the planet and human society to the tipping point of catastrophe, a rise of only 0.6 degrees centigrade so far is already pushing many of Bangladesh's poorest people beyond the tipping point.

Attempts are being made to adapt to the changing scene. For example, the Bangladesh Centre for Advanced Studies[4] aims to build a 'climate resilient society'. Cyclone shelters are being built and already they have reduced the number of lives lost. The poorest communities are being helped to adapt by learning new skills and ways of living, including breeding crabs

Cyclone shelter in Bangladesh by Tahsin R Hossain.

4 Bangladesh Centre for Advanced Studies is a Christian Aid Partner.

and ducks. People are also encouraged to have 'floating allotments.' The floating allotments are not new to Bangladesh but they are now spreading across the country.

The Pacific

The peoples of the Pacific Region are those most immediately threatened with losing their homes through climate change. Julia Edwards[5] has written about her visit to the Carteret Islands in Papua New Guinea where the first man-made climate change evacuees still await resettlement.

Dubbed by many as the world's first climate change refugees, the people of the six low-lying Carteret Islands in Papua New Guinea have welcomed more than their fair share of curious but well-meaning researchers, journalists and film crew over the past few years. With rising sea levels and the threat to the islands from storm surges (the so-called king tides), their regional government made world news back in 2007 when it took the decision to relocate the islands' 2,700 population to the larger Papua New Guinea island of Bougainville. At the end of 2010, and when government representatives and environmental lobbyists converged on Cancun to debate a new climate deal, only two Carteret families had successfully relocated the 100 km (62 miles) to the 'mainland'; the rest of the population remain on the islands, afraid of the encroaching seas.

They have much to fear. The highest point of this atoll chain is just 1.2m (less than 5ft) above sea level and data collected for the South Pacific Sea Level and Climate Monitoring Project indicates that this part of the Pacific has recorded some of the largest year-on-year increases in sea levels over the last two decades. The last king tide to affect the Carteret Islands in 2008 completely inundated the main island of Han, home to more than 1500 people. Its community with nowhere to escape could only watch from the centre of the island as the seas washed away their homes. Rufina Moi, a retired teacher, and a spokesperson for the community, expressed her fears: *"I am really afraid of the ocean because when strong storms come you can see the waves and the island is very small now."*

Storm surges are not the only threat to the community's day-to-day survival. Over the last twenty years or so the invasion of salt water from the rising seas has destroyed the islanders' crops. Previously they were able to grow beans, greens, yams and swampy taro. Today there are no kitchen gardens, the breadfruit trees are dying and the islanders' diet consists almost entirely of coconuts and fish. Last month the community received its first emergency shipment of food supplies since June. Each person received only one and a half bags of flour. No one knows when the next aid will arrive.

---

5 Julia Edwards is a Mission Partner with the Methodist Church UK, and will be serving as a researcher for the Pacific Conference of Churches on climate change and resettlement within the Pacific region. She wishes to thank Bread for the World, Germany for the opportunity to accompany them to the Carteret Islands in November 2010.

Lynette Roberts, an island resident, confided: '*We appear happy, but we were starving before last week's supplies arrived.*'

Two agencies, the Bougainville Autonomous Regional Government and Tulele Peisa, a local community-based organisation dedicated to the relocation, are working independently in the resettlement process. For both organisations, land ownership issues and accessing suitable finances have proved critical factors in the relocation.

The Bougainville authority has received 2 million kina (about £575,000) from the national government and they are close to securing 600 hectares of land at Karoola, an hour's drive west of the town of Buka on Buka Island. The first 40 Carteret families have been selected and will move as soon as houses have been constructed, hopefully sometime soon. Ephraim Eminioni, the co-ordinator of the resettlement programme for the regional government, pointed out: '*The resettlement process is not just about what we [the government] can put in, but also about what we can assist the Carteret people in bringing along*'.

Tulele Peisa, working on a smaller scale, was given 71-hectares by the Catholic Church at Tinputz on the larger island of Bougainville. The community-based organisation has to raise funds locally for the construction of homes, and to date, only two houses have been built at a cost of 27,000 kina (£7,500) each. A third house is nearing completion. Ursula Rasoka, the Executive Director of the organisation, argued: '*Tulele Peisa should receive a share of the resettlement funds provided by the national government*'. At the moment the organisation is entirely reliant on local donations, which means that the development of the Tinputz site is slow.

The majority of Carteret islanders, therefore, still await an opportunity to leave their island homes, and they are frustrated with their situation. In the past visitors to the Carteret atolls were welcomed by the community as the islanders believed that publicising their plight to the outside world would bring much needed help. No assistance has so far appeared and the islanders no longer welcome casual onlookers.

Thomas Hirsch, Senior Climate Change Policy Advisor for Bread for the World, the development arm of the German Protestant Church, comments:

> As yet the issue of climate-induced migration has not received the serious attention it deserves. By not assisting the Carteret island-ers, we might be denying them their most fundamental human right, to survive. Their lives are threatened by the next king tide. We call on state authorities to address this issue urgently in order to avoid a human catastrophe, not just on the Carteret islands but also on many more low-lying atolls.

The people of the Carteret Islands may be the first entire population to move because of man-made climate change, but they will not be the last, assuming that future sea level rise predictions prove accurate. Over the coming years the populations of entire island nations, such as Tuvalu, Kiri-bati and the Maldives, will be under threat from the rising seas.

As Fei Tevi, General Secretary of the Pacific Conference of Churches, puts it:

> The number of people affected in the Pacific is 'a drop in the ocean' compared with the estimated 250 million people globally who will face climate-induced resettlement by 2050. Nevertheless, we as publicists and perpetrators of their plight have a responsibility and duty of care to those communities already making our climate-change headlines. This is more than a story, and we are more than story tellers; this is reality for the people of the Carteret Islands, a community who are awaiting our help.

Cape Farewell

Many organisations are working in education to change lifestyles in the field of climate change. One such is Operation Noah, an educational charity inspired by the biblical story of Noah, who protected all creation and not just the human race. The main focus for the work of this charity is the reduction of carbon emissions, based on the conviction of its members that the climate crisis is not simply environmental but also moral and spiritual. The charity states that it *'aims to change hearts and minds and not just light bulbs.'*

With similar conviction, Cape Farewell was formed by David Buck-land, who saw it as the bridge between climate science and people in the communities in the UK and beyond. The hope has been that the message of the urgent need to deal with climate change will be communicated in a variety of ways. The programme has faced the huge task of seeking to change cultural values and thus to halt climate change and the degradation of the environment. Artists, writers and others are brought together to produce creative works which will stimulate the imaginations of enough people to change climates of opinion and to bring real change for a future of hope. In 2001, when Cape Farewell was beginning, David Buckland wrote:

> **The Arctic is an extraordinary place to visit. It is a place in which to be inspired, a place which urges us to face up to what it is we stand to lose.**

The programme works by artists, writers and scientists being sent on expeditions to areas where the environment is threatened. There have been 8 expeditions to the Arctic and one to the Andes and a wonderful collection of art, exhibitions, writings and educational materials has resulted.

Yann Martell, author of *Life of Pi*, who joined the expedition to the Andes in 2009, wrote about the importance of the focus on the Arctic by Cape Farewell:

> **The Arctic is like a canary in a coalmine when it comes to climate change.**

Ian McEwan went to the Arctic in 2005 with Cape Farewell, and later wrote his brilliantly researched and best-selling book *Solar*.[6] This entertaining book touches on the huge issues relating to climate change. McEwan points to the awful frustration of the fact that the challenge at the core of the struggle to combat climate change is not whether change can be tackled but rather whether selfish and self-absorbed human beings are even capable of beginning the task in any meaningful way. On the ship in the Arctic in *Solar* the gathered artists and writers were there to save the world, through their depiction of climate change, but they could not even keep the boot room tidy.

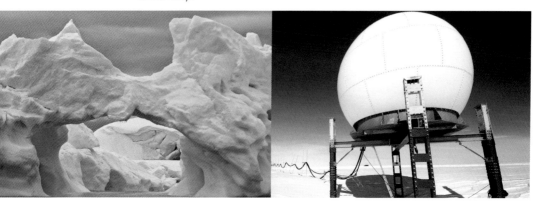

6 Ian McEwan, *Solar*, Jonathon Cape, 2010.

The main character in *Solar* has fine hopes and even resolutions, his 'ocean of dreams', but always ends by saying 'not today'. He works to make photosynthesis happen artificially, but he has stolen the idea from one of his students who has died. His whole professional life, which began with great promise, is marred by his love of himself at the expense of everyone around him, including his family.

Solar points to the need to start small, and to start at home, with the realisation that every little action is either for or against a good future for the planet. There is the need for laws, as there was the need for laws when taxation towards social security and the health service were developed in the UK in the twentieth century. Weak human beings were not, and are not, capable of giving adequately in any other way than through taxation. Human beings will never save the earth unless there are laws in place.

TARGET – to reduce biodiversity loss, achieving, by 2010, a significant reduction in the rate of loss

The world has missed the 2010 target for biodiversity conservation, with potentially grave consequences.

Forests

Trees are essential to life. They stabilise the soil, they generate oxygen, they store carbon, they provide a home for many varieties of wildlife. They provide raw materials and shelter. They provide food, timber and medicines. They provide fertility for the soil.

Tree planting is one of the most cost effective ways of tackling climate change

Forests are also magical places, they are the inspiration for poetry and stories, and also favourite places for walking and relaxation. A world without trees and woods would be a sad place, barren and bare.

> For there is hope of a tree,
> if it be cut down,
> that it will sprout again,
> And that the tender branch thereof will not cease.
>
> Though the root thereof wax old in the earth,
> And the stock thereof die in the ground;
> Yet, through the scent of water it will bud,
> And bring forth boughs like a plant. Job 14.7–9

In 2009 Yan Martell went to the Andes with Cape Farewell. He joined an 18 day trek, beginning near depleted glaciers close to Cuzco and walking through more shrinking glaciers, cloud forests, lower forests, deforested areas and the Amazon River basin. He wrote about the Amazon, and was

enthused by the variety of trees and of the species who have their home there. One tree may be home to more than a hundred species of termites for example. If climate change is to be slowed down trees must be added and not taken away.

Nostell Priory is an eighteenth-century house in West Yorkshire. It is built on the site of the Medieval home of Augustinian Canons. The house is now owned by the National Trust. It is surrounded by 300 acres of wonderful gardens and parkland. The poem below was inspired by a fallen tree in the grounds of Nostell Priory. It brings out some of the goodness the tree gives to its surroundings. There is even something to give when the tree has fallen.

Turkish Oak felled by floods [7]

Kath Osgerby

I was a stranger here,
Handpicked, my waxen leaves
A safety mask against
The penetrating fumes of northern industry.

I fitted in,
my lead black bark a worthy match
for pit-head props and
landscape smothered with the dust of smoke.

I lasted well;
slight stoop of age but strong -
I outlived cast-off coal
till floored by rain's earth-loosening grind.

---

7 Poem by Kath Osgerby taken from *Poetry Walks*, a National Trust collection, August 2009.

Lifeless now,
redundant as the mines,
no purpose but
to feed these coppered frills of velvet fungus.

In the United Kingdom the '**Big Tree Plant**'
aims to encourage people and communities to
plant more trees in urban and residential places. Local
community groups are encouraged to plant and care for
trees, especially where there are not many of them. This project brings
together conservation organisations, DEFRA and the Forestry Commission.

The **Plant for the Planet Billion Tree Campaign** is a World Agroforestry
Centre and United Nations Environment Programme initiative for the whole
world. Organisations, governments and individuals are asked to commit
themselves on line to planting trees, particularly indigenous trees. So far the
campaign has had excellent results. In 2009 more than 7.4 billion trees were
planted. An important partner is the Kenya Greenbelt Movement, which
gives a good example of what can be done with vision and commitment.

The Kenya Greenbelt Movement

Community members take action in the Greenbelt Movement
because they understand the linkages between the environment
and poverty – that is the core of it all. Njogu Kahare

The Greenbelt Movement was started in Kenya in 1977 by Wangari Maathai
and the National Council of Women. The vision of the pioneers was to
create a society where people were aware of the need to work to improve
their environment and were committed to work for this.

Their mission is to mobilize community consciousness for equality,
self-determination, better livelihoods, security and environmental
conservation. They challenge people to action, accountability, transparency
and empowerment. The vision and the mission are worked for through
the tree planting. Greenbelt members have expanded their work to include
indigenous tree planting, education, advocacy, food security, change for
women and eco-safaris.

Wangari Maathai,[8] the founder of the Kenya Greenbelt Movement,
died in September 2011. She was an inspirational woman who made a
huge contribution towards improving her country's environment. She also
contributed greatly to African women's health, development and confidence.
When she died Daniel Howden wrote in *The Independent*: 'From a small
village to a global crusader for women, human rights and conservation: an
extraordinary life story has ended.'[9]

Wangari Maathai

8 Wangari Maathai, *Unbowed: A Memoir*, William Heinemann, London, 2007.
9 *The Independent*, 27th September, 2011.

Wangari came from a poor family of small farmers in Kenya but when she began to go to school at seven it was quickly obvious that she was very bright. She went to a convent high school from where she was awarded a US government scholarship to study in Kansas and Pennsylvania for bachelor and master's degrees. She returned to post independent Kenya in 1966 to join the University of Nairobi as a researcher and lecturer in veterinary anatomy. In 1971 she was the first woman in East and Central Africa to earn a PhD. She also became head of her department. She was married and had three children.

She became aware of the ecological crisis Kenya was facing in the mid-1970s. She saw that forests were disappearing as plantations were developed, streams were drying up and the desert was spreading. She began her work for the environment by visiting and listening to rural women through the National Council of Women of Kenya. She decided that part of the answer to the situation was the planting of trees to replenish the soil. The trees would also provide fuel for the women, protect the watersheds and, through growing fruit trees, make better nutrition possible. She set up a tree nursery in Karura Forest on the edge of Nairobi. At first she had little response but in 1977 she gave birth to the Greenbelt Movement of Kenya.

The Greenbelt Movement has worked with women in the community from the beginning and has always taken the needs of the communities into its work, including the planting of nutritious food crops and the introduction of water harvesting schemes. Training programmes in areas of food, farming, business management, health and HIV/AIDs prevention have been central.

In the 1990s Wangari Maathai and the Greenbelt Movement became high profile in Kenya and East Africa when they embarked on a programme of awareness raising to save the forests. One of the areas they saved from a government built tower block was the Nairobi Uhuru Park. This success attracted the wrath of the government and of President Moi, and Wangari Maathai spent time in prison and also suffered ridicule, physical attacks and death threats. She was driven to move around from house to house for a time. Life was made easier when Kenya legalised opposition parties in 1992 and the Greenbelt Movement went from strength to strength. In 1999 there were clashes with the government over Karura Forest and the Greenbelt Movement was successful in preventing development. In the 2002 elections in Kenya a new government and president were chosen and Wangari Maathai became Member of Parliament for Nyeri and then minister for the environment.

I spoke to Wangari in September 2009. She still saw her work as largely educational but recognised that people's immediate needs must be met before they can be expected to work for the environment. A great challenge continues to be to reduce poverty and then people can be asked not to cut down trees to make charcoal for cooking. Another great challenge is to the people themselves not to make excuses for their condition by blaming the institutions and colonialism. Aid, trade and debt are all implicated in what has gone wrong for Africa, and these issues are dealt with in Chapter Eight. Wangari however went back to the people and challenged them to move on from dependency, passivity, fatalism and failure. She also challenged leaders to avoid corruption and selfishness. In her recent book she wrote:

'Charcoal' balls are made of paper rubbish to avoid the use of trees in Kenya.

> Every African, from the head of state to the subsistence farmer, needs to embrace cultures of honesty and hard work, fairness, and justice, as well as the riches – cultural, spiritual and material – of their continent.[10]

Part of the success of the Greenbelt Movement in Kenya is that people right across society see the need to plant trees and work hard to do so. The churches hold tree planting days and the government also now aims for 10% of the land to have trees. People are being encouraged to plant fruit trees including paw paws, mangoes, avocados, bananas and guavas.

Beate Dehnen tree print.

---

10 Wangari Maathai, *The Challenge for Africa: A New Vision*, Heinemann, 2009.

The government is now, due to the pioneering work of the Greenbelt Movement, making efforts to save the existing forests, including the largest, the Mau forest. The Mau forest suffers from timber sawing, charcoal burning and farming. The government has begun to evict people from the forest area. This action will hopefully save the forest but there is a question about what will happen to some of the people who are evicted.

Bolivia

Bolivia provides another example of a social enterprise which is attempting to tackle the problems of deforestation. The following was written by **David Vincent** of the **Cochabamba Project**.

It would be difficult to find another example in the world which illustrates the link between poverty and climate as clearly as Bolivia. Large scale deforestation of the Bolivian Amazon has led to more erratic and violent rainfall causing increased flash flooding. During one of our visits in 2009 eight people were killed in floods which swept across the departments of Cochabamba and Santa Cruz.

Deforestation is the direct result of poverty. For several decades, Bolivia has witnessed the mass migration of impoverished communities from the highlands, enticed by the offer of legal titles to virgin land along the new roads which run along the rim of the Amazon basin beneath the foothills of the Andes. The name of each "communidad" often symbolises the faith and hope of its members; Nueva Esperanza, Israel, Nueva Palestina. Not often farmers by tradition, they are simply left to eke out a living from the jungle as best they can. Without the knowledge or capital to do anything else they employ 'slash and burn' farming methods, depleting the soil with rice and other crops (including coca) as well as cattle grazing.

ArBolivia is a social enterprise, funded partly by revenues from carbon credits and partly from socially conscious investors from the UK and the Netherlands. It builds on the established social structures with a comprehensive programme of economic and practical support for over 1600 smallholders in communities across the tropical lowlands. Firstly it helps them establish parcels of native tree species for future timber production. It also commits smallholders to planting separate areas for conservation, typically along water courses prone to erosion. Finally it provides invaluable help and support for them to develop more sustainable farming practices on the remainder of their land. In this way families get immediate, medium and long term social and financial benefits.

Emma is one such smallholder. Her husband died 8 years ago and she was left to bring up her four children and care for her elderly parents alone. On her smallholding she grows cassava, maize and fruit and raises a few pigs and chickens. Whilst the whole family pulls together on the smallholding Emma works 5 days a week clearing undergrowth with a machete in the new road programme. Emma has planted one hectare of teak (the only non-native tree species used) and looks after it at weekends. The payments for planting and maintaining her trees are welcome but the real benefits will be for her children. The trees are less labour intensive than her crops and the project has taught her how to work more efficiently, with mixed planting of cassava, guava and teak on the same parcel of land. She is also proud to be doing her bit for her community and for the world at large.

Emma

ArBolivia is a true partnership. The land and labour provided by each smallholder is matched by the capital invested by the investor, and future profits from the forestry enterprise will be shared 50/50. The smallholders also benefit from regular maintenance payments in addition to the practical support from their own technical advisor.

To support Arbolivia's invaluable work the Cochabamba Project was established in the UK in March 2009 as an industrial and provident society. To date it has raised over £1.2 million. As a co-operative its shares can be redeemed at face value (or less) but cannot be sold or transferred. This protects the society's aims and values from speculators. As a social enterprise surplus future profits will be reinvested into the communities in Bolivia. However the society can award interest to members on an annual basis in order to attract and retain investment. An interest rate of 7.5% was declared for the financial year ending 31/10/2010. The directors intend to maintain interest in this region in order to attract and retain the capital required to cover operational costs until the timber revenues become self supporting but may not by law exceed 10%.[11]

Photos courtesy www.cochabamba.coop

11 You can find out more about investing in the society and see a video of Emma's story at www.cochabamba.coop

Human rights, land acquisition and environmental degradation in SW Ethiopia

There are worrying developments in Ethiopia which seem to be making matters worse there. The following information has been given by an Ethiopian student who must remain anonymous.

It is reliably reported that the Ethiopian Government is leasing large tracts of land in Gambella, an area in SW Ethiopia near the Sudanese border, to foreign governments 'for agricultural purposes'. It is not absolutely certain which countries are involved but sources suggest India and Saudi Arabia as the two countries concerned. These leases will turn some 45,000 local people off their land and large areas of forest are now being felled. The government claims that the local people are pastoralists, but it appears that they are agriculturalists and have been farming much of the land in question for some time, using traditional farming practices. Already 20,000 people have been ousted from their land. The forest has always been a resource for these people. In hard times it was always possible to go into the forest and find something to eat, but now the forest is being felled and the people are being moved away so both sources of livelihood are being removed. As yet we do not know where they are being resettled, but there is already tribal unrest in the local area, exacerbated by incursions by Sudanese gangs in which cattle are stolen and children kidnapped. There is the fear that the resettlement process will be fraught with difficulties of many kinds. The people have been evicted from their lands and homes by the military. Community elders who have spoken out against the policy and the process have been jailed.

Children selling crafts in Simien mountains, Ethiopia.

In the light of recent assurances by DFID that Ethiopia is one of our largest aid recipients it would seem important that as many people as possible write to their MPs asking them to urge either the Foreign Secretary or DFID Secretary to ask the Ethiopian Ambassador for some explanation of the actions that have been reported.

This policy will not serve to fulfil the MDGs concerning sustainable land use and forest conservation, nor will it help towards halting climate change. It appears to be another Ethiopian Government attempt to relocate small ethnic groups in areas where there has been dissident activity and thus assert their authority by force rather than agreement.

It is instructive to ask ourselves whether the world religions are part of the solution to problems of sustainability or whether they may sometimes add to the problem when it comes to the forests of the world.

No world religion appreciates the tree more than the Jain religion

Jainism emerged in the 6th Century BCE through the witness of Mahavira, a contemporary of the Buddha, who spent most of his life as a wandering ascetic, largely in what is now Bihar. Jains follow Mahavira in living lives of austerity and fasting. They practice non-violence, seeking to go through life without harming any living thing. The three jewels of the faith are right faith, right knowledge and right conduct. Jains are naturally interested in ecological issues and in environmental protection.

Jain praying in Leicester temple.

A story was told in the Jain temple in Leicester, a beautiful place which was designed to appeal to both Eastern and Western tastes. The unique stained glass windows tell the story of Mahavira.

The Jain story is of a very hungry person wandering in a forest and seeking something to eat. He is a Jain and he knows that however hungry he is he must not chop down a tree to reach the fruits. He must not even break a branch of a tree. He must walk until he finds fruits which have fallen to the earth and then eat those. If he is desperate he may pick a fruit, but only if he can reach it without harming the tree.

Vrindavan, eighty miles South of Delhi, is the legendary birthplace of the Lord Krishna. Many of the trees were cut down and the Christian and Hindu Vrindavan Forest Revival Project and the World Wildlife Fund organised a huge tree planting programme with the declaration that:

Nature enjoys being enjoyed but reacts furiously to exploitation.

The number of animal species threatened with extinction is rising

There are many reasons for the dramatic reduction in the numbers of animals in our world, including terrible exploitation, especially hunting, but also climate change and the loss of natural habitats.

The most endangered animals are the tiger, the polar bear and blue fin tuna. They are closely followed by the giant panda, the Javan rhinoceros, the mountain gorilla, the monarch butterfly, the walrus, the Magellanic penguin and the leatherback turtle. Other endangered animals are orang utans and leopards.

A few examples of what is happening to a few creatures from the above list will show clearly why they are reducing in numbers and may point to what can be done to reverse this calamitous trend.

Tiger, painted by Hannah, aged ten.

There are only 3,200 wild tigers left with only 7 per cent of their original land area, largely due to de-forestation and poaching of the tigers for their body parts and skins. The Javan and Balinese tigers are already extinct. The rise in the sea level, due to climate change, has had a part to play, threatening as it does the mangrove swamps in India and Bangladesh.

Polar bears are also victims of climate change in the Arctic and it is said that they may disappear within the next hundred years. There are also threats from shipping and from oil and gas works.

The Pacific walrus normally lives on floating ice, where the babies are born, and is faced with its natural habitat beginning to disappear due to climate change.

Mountain gorillas are herbivores. They are now losing their habitats in Uganda, Rwanda and the Democratic Republic of Congo. There are said to be only 680 left in the wild. A lot of work was done to preserve them in the 1970s and 80s, not least by Diane Fossey who had been encouraged to study the gorillas by Dr. Louis Leakey. She published a book[12] which later became a popular film, Gorillas in the Mist. An important part of her work turned out to be trying to stop the poaching of gorillas, including the organisation of patrols. In December 1985 she was murdered in her cabin in the Virunga Mountains in Rwanda. The last entry in her diary was: 'When you realise the value of all life, you dwell less on what is past and concentrate more on the preservation of the future.'

A mountain gorilla in the cloud forest of Uganda.

---

12 Diane Fossey, *Gorillas in the Mist*, Houghton Mifflin Company, 1983

The mountain gorillas are now losing their habitats partly due to the traditional farming method of slash and burn by the local people, but also due to the use of the forests for firewood for local people and for refugees. War, especially the genocide in Rwanda in the early 1990s, has also destroyed much of the natural environment. The reduction in gorilla numbers continues also to be caused by poaching.

Fish stocks are decreasing

Slowly but surely humans are polluting the water supplies in oceans, rivers and lakes. Most of the rivers of the world are polluted. Groundwater is being used up at such a rate that it cannot be replaced for many years. More than 97% of the water on the earth is sea water and it is now badly overfished and polluted. A report was issued in June 2011 by the International Programme on the State of the Oceans which was described as shocking.

Carbon is being absorbed by the oceans at a great rate. The coral reefs are being killed off, overfishing has reduced many fish stocks by as much as 90%, sea creatures are disappearing, pollutants are being traced in the Polar seas.

Important areas of oceans near to the land are contaminated and sometimes toxic. They have been used as sewers for too long. The waters of the Black Sea are said to be 90% dead.

Overfishing is depleting the oceans all over the world. This has largely happened since World War Two, as sophisticated methods of catching fish have been developed, including the super trawlers. Cod fishing is collapsing in the North Sea, and the Grand Bank off the Eastern Canada coast has been plundered.

In July 2011 *The Sunday Times* included a report of an Icelandic whaling tycoon who has broken international rules to slaughter endangered fin whales. The meat and blubber are sold to Japan. Iceland apparently has a stockpile of frozen whale meat.

Atlantic Cod, one of the most overfished species in the entire world.

TARGET – halve, by 2015, the proportion of the population without sustainable access to safe drinking water and basic sanitation

'Of all our natural resources, water has become the most precious...' Rachel Carson[13]

Water is essential to all of life. It may be taken for granted by many people in the developed world whilst at the same time it is a scarce resource in the rest of the world. I sometimes give school assemblies about water when I ask the pupils what water means to them. The responses include activities like swimming, fishing and boating and sometimes bath-time. When I asked the same question in Africa the responses were very different and included walking a long way to find water, drinking, feeding animals and watering crops.

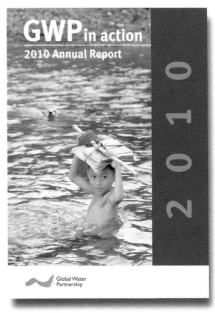

It is said that every time we in the developed world flush a toilet we use more water than most people in the developing world have for their daily needs, including cooking, drinking, cleaning and feeding any animals.

The Global Water Partnership pointed out in 2000 that the fresh water resources of the world are under enormous and increasing pressure due to the growth in population, increasing economic activity and higher standards of living for some people. The exploitation of forests also contributes to the loss of usable water.

Water Aid works in 26 countries in Africa, Asia and the Pacific to improve water, sanitation and hygiene education. Appropriate sustainable technology is used.[14]

Water as a peace and justice issue in the Middle East [15]

As early as 1985, the then UN General Secretary Dr. Boutros Ghali, famously declared that "the next war in the Middle East will be fought over water, not politics". In 1979, King Hussein of Jordan identified water as the only reason that might lead him to war with the Jewish State. Since 1950, global use of water has tripled, and throughout the world, a water crisis prevails in numerous countries, with use far exceeding supply, causing a dramatic increase in the rate of desertification across parts of Africa, and acute shortages in the Middle East.

13 Rachel Carson, *Silent Spring*, Penguin, London, 1964.

14 www.wateraid.org.uk.

15 This piece was written by Anglican priest, Andrew Ashdown, author of *The Stones Cry Out*, Christians Aware, 2006.

> 'All peoples may, for their own ends, freely dispose of their natural wealth and resources without prejudice to any obligations arising out of international economic cooperation, based on the principle of mutual benefit and international law. In no case may a people be deprived of its own means of subsistence.' *Article 1(2) of the 1966 United Nations Human Rights Convention*

Water has now become a political issue, and in few places is this more evident than in Israel and Palestine. As a regular visitor to Israel and Palestine, this issue has been evident on many occasions. We shall consider some facts shortly, but first a few reflections. Walking from Nazareth to Bethlehem across the West Bank and through the Jordan Valley in 2000, it was a privilege to stay in homes in remote Palestinian villages, but the contrast between these villages, and the many Israeli settlements that surround them (which are illegal under international law), could not be greater. Whilst the settlers, whose towns are built on Palestinian land, enjoy well-watered gardens and parks, swimming pools and an unlimited supply of water; Palestinian villagers have to cope with minimal water resources with water availability sometimes being limited to as few as two days a week – for both domestic and agricultural use.

Descending into the Jordan Valley several miles north of Jericho, there is a beautiful gorge called the Wadi Auja. Scrambling for three hours down the gorge from the Wilderness escarpment, we finally reached a wonderful sight – a gushing spring pouring ice-cold crystal clear water out of the rock, creating a small river bordered with palm and fig trees. The Al Auja spring is the largest spring in the West Bank and has biblical associations. There is every possibility that Elijah and John the Baptist, and perhaps even Jesus himself, may have refreshed themselves at this very spot. After days of walking and in the heat of the desert valley, it is blissful to sit in the stream and cover one's head with the cool water. But our exuberance was short-lived, for less than 50 metres down the valley, the river disappears into Israeli water-pipes. It is transported for use in the Israeli settlements, kibbutzim, and army camps in the Jordan valley and in the hills. Whilst local villagers struggle to water their crops and their livestock (the valley below the spring is parched dry), the nearby settlements and kibbutzim have swimming pools and watered lawns. Only 16% of all the water in the West Bank's aquifers is used by Palestinians, and even that is sold back to them by the Israelis at an inflated price which Palestinians find hard to afford. The remaining 84% of the West Bank's water is used to supply Israel and Israeli settlements in the Palestinian territories.

About 20 miles south of Al Auja spring, in a wilderness valley east of Bethlehem, we came across an even more shocking effect of the Israeli occupation of the West Bank that is rarely mentioned. These valleys have been used by shepherds from time immemorial. Ruth and Boaz, David and Jonathan, and the shepherds in the birth of Jesus narratives would have known these valleys well, and still today, as we walked up from the Jordan Valley

towards Bethlehem, we often came across shepherds, some even now playing the simple flute – their haunting tunes drifting in the air, along with the wild birds that migrate across this region from Europe to their seasonal homes in Africa and Asia. Also abundant in these valleys are many ancient cisterns, some dating from Roman times, and all of them crucial for watering the flocks, and providing water for the small villages that are dotted around the desert. But nothing is held sacred under the Occupation. We came across several ancient cisterns that had either been blown up by the Israeli army or sealed with concrete. In one valley, a Bedouin shepherd told us that this was increasingly common; that without the cisterns, they would not be able to water their sheep; that the valleys would become parched, and this would enable the Israelis to plant a new settlement on supposedly 'unused' land.

One of Israel's prides is the country's national water carrier – a pipeline built in 1964 that transports water from the Sea of Galilee down the full length of Israel as far as the Negev Desert, and provides much of the country's drinking water. This pipeline proceeds above ground for much of the way, and for part of the way sits alongside the so-called 'Security Barrier' that separates Israel from the Palestinian territories, a mixture of high walls and electrified fences, much of it built within the West Bank. There are several Palestinian villages that sit alongside the pipeline for which all the Palestinian restrictions apply, whilst neighbouring Israeli settlements and towns receive the full benefit of the pipeline. Worse still is the situation for Palestinian villages whose lands have been taken by Israeli settlements, and whose water supplies are increasingly being deliberately polluted by the settlers. In

Fahmi and Ata Manasra survey a dried up water cistern in the village of Wadi Fouqin near Bethlehem, where the water table has plummeted due to the building of the nearby settlement built on their land.
Photo Andrew Ashdown

the village of Wadi Fouqin, not far from Bethlehem, over two thirds of the village's fertile lands have been expropriated by the huge Israeli settlement of Betar Illit, that is being built above the village. However, sewerage from the settlement has been directed into the village's water supply, and building waste from the building of several thousand homes has been poured into the village's remaining fields, leeching into the water supply as well.

To the average pilgrim to the Holy Land, much of this is invisible. For the average visitor, the nearest hint that there is a problem would be seeing the alarmingly obvious reduction in the level of the Sea of Galilee; the sluggish polluted stream that is now the Jordan River; and the shocking reduction in size of the Dead Sea, which is a consequence both of the reduction in flow of the River Jordan into the Dead Sea, and the very high levels of evaporation that are experienced in that area. It is true that as part of the peace agreements with Jordan, the Kingdom of Jordan receives a share of the Sea of Galilee water supply and of the Jordan River, but the vast majority is used by the State of Israel.

Israelis and Palestinians share two inter-related water systems: the underground system, known as the Mountain Aquifer, which crosses the border between the West Bank and Israel; and the surface system, known as the Jordan Basin, which also belongs to Jordan, Syria and Lebanon.

The Mountain Aquifer is 130km long and 35km wide. It is divided into three sub-aquifers. The first is the Western Aquifer. Most of its recharge area lies in the West Bank, while the entire storage area lies in Israel. Israel uses 95% of the water from this aquifer. The Northern Aquifer has almost all of its recharge and storage areas within the West Bank. However, Israel extracts about 70% of the water from this Aquifer. Finally, the Eastern Aquifer is entirely within the West Bank. 37% of its water is consumed by Israel – mostly by the settlers.

As for the Jordan Basin surface aquifer: Palestinians have no access to this whilst 31% of its water is consumed by Israel.

The World Health Organisation declares that a minimum adequate rate of water consumption should be 100 litres per person per day. B'tselem, the Israeli Human Rights Organisation reports that in 2008 in the northern West Bank, Palestinian daily per capita consumption varies between 37 and 44 litres per person; and Oxfam reports that some Palestinian households are trying to get by on 16 litres of water per person per day. As Michael Williams wrote in the *Church Times* on 2 August 2002: 'We are talking about standards that are usually applied to large refugee populations in tent cities in Africa or on the edge of war.' By contrast, consumption in the settlements that surround the Palestinian villages exceeds 300 litres per person per day – using water mostly from Palestinian aquifers.

The issue of availability of water is only one of the issues that face Palestinians within the West Bank. Mention has been made of the deliberate polluting or even destruction of water supplies, that occasionally happens to Palestinian communities, especially at the hands of settlers. But Israel also actively prevents Palestinians from accessing water resources legally, technically, and physically. Legally, water is classified as Israeli public property, and any request to drill new wells or fix existing ones requires a permit. Permits have to go through eighteen stages of approval in various administrative departments and are unaffordable to most Palestinians. Rarely does an application succeed. Often Palestinians are deprived of access to water supplies simply by being deprived of access to their land or wells. And physically, little effort is made to maintain the water system, either by Israel or the Palestinian municipalities, who lack the financial resources to intervene. The amount of public expenditure in all fields is less than the fiscal revenues Israel collects from the Palestinian population.

Since the 1990's, a number of agreements have been sought between Israel and the Palestinian territories as regards water usage. And since 1995 there has been a Palestinian National Water Policy that seeks to develop and manage the water resources and capacity. However, the political situation has rendered most of these arrangements either dormant or ineffective or both. Given the importance of water for all communities, this issue has the potential to be an opportunity for mutual cooperation. But there is no sign of this at present.

It is possible that International Law and specifically the 1997 UN Convention on the Non-navigational utilisation of international water courses, could play a role in coming to an agreement that could benefit both Israel and Palestine. A starting point would be to agree on the principle that each nation on an international watercourse has a right to a portion of the water, and to establish how much water is needed by each party to meet both domestic needs and those for economic development, then to agree on what represents an equitable and reasonable usage. The difficulties that this issue raises could be unique, in that water usage, production and conservation provide an opportunity to work together to face a mutual problem in a scientific, rather than political way.

However, nothing in Israel and Palestine is equitable, and agreement on anything feels like a distant dream. Most people on both sides of the political divide desire peace, but a peace that is just and equitable is a long way off. Sadly, the situation in Israel and Palestine raises significant questions on human rights, and compared to most other places around the world that highlight issues of human, social and political concern, they are highlighted to a particularly challenging degree in Israel and Palestine. This is no less true of the human and political issues that surround the water crisis that is affecting so much of our planet. The situation in Israel/Palestine reveals just how deeply the issue of water can be connected to issues of justice and peace, and has a lasting impact on political stability.

World religions offer wisdom in our stewardship of water

Water is essential to life and every world religion has inspirational stories relating to it. The Hebrew Bible has many stories of water. 'Moses' means taken from the water. 'O you who are thirsty come to the waters.'[16] Christians know the Gospel story of the woman at the well as a story of the bringing of new life to the woman and also to Jesus (see p. 110 for full story).

Baptism and the Dream City, by Jyoti Sahi.

There is an early Buddhist story of life-giving water which is very similar to the story of Jesus and the woman at the well.

The Buddha taught his disciples to see the One Life in all and to respect the least among the lowly and the lost.

Ananda, passing one day by a well and seeing an 'untouchable' girl drawing water, asks her for water to drink. She humbly says: 'Oh thou of noble birth! I am an untouchable. How can I give thee water to drink?'

Ananda answers: 'Caste matters nothing to me. I ask for water.'

She gives him water to drink. He drinks it with joy. On learning that Ananda is a disciple of Gautama Buddha, she goes to the Blessed One and says to him: 'Master! Teach me the Way of Dhamma.'

---

16 Isaiah 55.1–2.

And the Buddha says to her: 'Blessed art thou! I teach thee the Dhamma of compassion and service.' [17]

'Chandalika' is a play by the Bengali writer Rabindranath Tagore which is a very similar story.[18] In it a young Dalit girl, Prakriti, tells her mother what happened to her at the village well:

> That noontime while I was washing the motherless calf at the well
> a yellow-robed monk came and stood before me and said, 'Give
> me water.' I sprang up and did obeisance. When I found my voice
> I said, 'I am a daughter of the Chandals and the water of this well
> is polluted by my family's use.' He said, 'You and I are of the same
> family. All water that quenches thirst and relieves need is pure.'
> I never heard such words before and with these chandal hands,
> which never before would have dared touch the dust of his feet,
> I poured water for him.

TARGET – to have achieved by 2020 a significant improvement in the lives of at least 100 million slum dwellers

Some academics think that the urban slums of today are the cities of tomorrow, a depressing forecast which must obviously be avoided. Slums are places of illness and of early death. One point being made which is positive is that the slums are the places to which many ordinary people flock to find the hope for the future which they lacked when they lived in the rural areas of their countries. Whether they find hope or not is unclear and variable. What is clear is that people who live in slums do find community support and care.

As long ago as the 1950s Trevor Huddleston wrote about the slums of South Africa:

> Newclare is a struggling suburb separated from
> Sophiatown by the main road... you can walk down a narrow
> alley between houses and discover an open yard, with
> a row of rooms facing it, doors open or half shuttered
> with old packing cases to keep the children in, a single
> latrine, a single tap and twenty families making their own
> community... Moreover they will be laughing as they hang
> out the washing...[19]

Things have not changed much in the new South Africa. The lives of the slum dwellers are worse now in that they are more aware of the wealth of many black and white people in their country.

---

17 From *The Face of the Buddha*, Mira Union.
18 *A Tagore Reader*, edited by Amiya Charkavarty, Beacon Press Boston, 1966.
19 Trevor Huddleston, *Naught For Your Comfort*, Fontana Books, 1958.

I have visited the Mumbai slums in Western India, and was once marooned there when the rains came early and everything was flooded. My group was in a bus and the water came half way up the sides so that we couldn't move. We saw houses floating away and people trying to swim to safety. The squalor of Mumbai was shown in the film 'Slumdog Millionaire' when the filth was not hidden from the hundreds of people who watched from the comfort of cinemas all over the world. Sadly the slums are still there.

I have also visited Calcutta and have spent time in the slum or bustee communities, where most people live in what I would call shocking conditions, with very little space in small cardboard houses with no facilities, and with passageways of filthy slime to walk through.

Slum in Mumbai, India.

M.R./shutterstock.com

The writer Dominic Lapierre was taken to a Calcutta slum where everything was dark and ugly and he stayed there to experience a life of rats and cockroaches, with tracks flooded with sewage. He lived in a small hovel which had no light and he wrote about the place and the people. His book was called *City of Joy*, for in this seeming hell he discovered people he called saints, and beauty and hope for the future.[20]

---

20 Dominic Lapierre, *City of Joy*, Century, 1985.

The month of May ended with a terrible pre-monsoon storm, during which the level of the drains and latrines rose…. The corpses of dogs, rats, scorpions and thousands of cockroaches began to float around in the foul sludge…. Naturally the floodwater invaded most of the hovels, transforming them into cesspools. Yet in the midst of the horror, there was always some kind of miracle…. This one took the form of a little girl in a white dress, with a red flower in her hair, who picked her way through all that dung, with the regal air of a queen.[21]

Based on John Le Carre's book *The Constant Gardener*, Fernando Meirelles' eponymous film was partly filmed in the Kibera Slums in Nairobi in Kenya. It gives a vivid, horrible and accurate view of the largest slum in the whole of Africa, with more than a million people living there.

The government owns the land but most of the shacks, made of mud walls, tin roofs and mud or concrete floors, are owned by individual landlords, most of whom live elsewhere. People pay rent for their rough shacks of mud, twigs and tin. There is some casual work in the area and people can earn enough to buy food, a can of water a day and to pay the rent. The Kenyan countryside is beautiful and much healthier, but there is little work there and little chance of paying for school uniforms.

There is now some clean water but not everywhere and not for everyone. The worst problem is that roughly 50 shacks share one hole in the ground which serves as the only lavatory. The worst temptation is not even to make use of the holes! At least 50,000 of the children are AIDS orphans and a high percentage of people, some sources say at least half, are HIV positive.

There are government plans to gradually move the people into decent housing, and this process has begun. In 2009 the Kenyan government built some new multi-story flats for slum dwellers, but having accepted the flats the people moved back to the slums and rented the new flats out. The reason was not simply the money, needed for food and school uniforms, but also the need people always have to keep their communities together.

In 2002 Bill Bryson went to Kenya with CARE International and his first experience of the country was a visit to the Kibera urban slum in Nairobi. He wrote about his experiences:

To step into Kibera is to be lost at once in a random, seemingly endless warren of rank narrow passageways wandering between rows of frail, dirt-floored hovels…. Each shanty is home to five or six people. Down the centre of each lane runs a shallow trench filled with a trickle of water and things you don't want to see or step in….[22]

---

21 *City of Joy*, p. 273.
22 *Bill Bryson's African Diary*, Doubleday, 2002.

Kibera in Nairobi, Kenya, the largest slum in Africa. About 270,000 people were living there in 2004.

Africa924/shutterstock.com

An insight into another urban slum in Kenya was given by Norma Hayward following our visit there with Christians Aware. The slum we visited is on the edge of Kiambu, near Nairobi. Norma wrote:

> In spite of films and TV, nothing can prepare you for the reality of the Riruta slums. Accompanied by church leaders, whose courage we recognised in working in this area, we met the drug addicts injecting themselves, the alcoholics, the prostitutes, the AIDS sufferers, the women selling illegally brewed beer, her female customers with their small children, the man sharing a room about 12 feet square with 19 others, all sleeping on the bare concrete floor in order to share the rent owed to a private landlord. We saw the rubbish, the squalor, the needles, the open drains, the illegal brewery, the children not at school because they had no uniform, the shacks with no water or electricity; goats, hens, ducks move around in the middle of it all. It's surprising how you get used to the smell.

The local church is there in the middle of all the squalor, trying to make a difference by providing clean water, sold at 30 pence for 20 litres. There is also a small and very inspiring daughter church called the Congo Church. It was sad and at the same time hopeful to contrast this chapel, with its plain

Congo church.

A.C.K CONGO CHURCH
DIOCESE OF Mt.KENYA SOUTH
SERVICES:
SUNDAY SCHOOL 8·30 am – 9·45 am

SWAHILI SERVICE 10·00 am – 11·30 am

altar, with a clean white cloth and a simple cross, with the scene immediately outside the door, where noise and filth prevailed and where the people were understandably drunk. Congo Church has about 70 in the congregation. There is also a special service for the drug addicts, during which they are offered counselling towards rehabilitation and a good meal.

The hope for the slum communities I visited in Kenya and for slum communities everywhere is that they are communities. As we moved round, tip toing over the filth and trying to ignore the smells, we were aware of people who supported each other. We met people who used to live in slums and who are now, through education and work, affluent and living elsewhere, and who remembered their former lives with affection rather than with fear. I can honestly say that I have never been fearful in a slum community. I have been seen as an object of interest and sometimes as a possible source of a few coins.

Nowhere was community care and pride more apparent in the Riruta slum than in the excellent church school. This is a primary school with very low fees of £12.00 a term. The meals are free. There is also a computer room, though without connection to the internet. A cooperative bank has been set up inside the school and people are encouraged to save until they are eligible for a loan of up to three times the amount of their savings. We saw some of the small shops set up by the loans. Without the loans people earn a little in the slums by collecting up the rubbish and then selling it.

We saw children whose parents had raised the money needed to send them there by taking out loans in the cooperative bank and by developing businesses. There are only 34 children to a class and the teaching is good because the teachers know the children well and care very much about their welfare. There are nutritious school meals and healthy children. There is hope for the future of the children which is based on faith and love in action.

Hope seemed almost lost when I was in Kenya in September 2011 and an oil pipeline blew up in the Sinai slum area of Nairobi causing a hundred deaths. Many more people were severely injured. The oil pipeline comes from Mombasa and Eldoret to Nairobi. There was a leak and storm water drove the oil into the slum areas, where people tried to scoop it up. Cooking pots were everywhere and were the probable cause of the explosion. One journalist, Murithi Mutiga, wrote:

> **Life in the slums is a death sentence, so why worry about the dangers of oil spill.**

She continued: 'Slum dwellers in Kenya are an anonymous entity at the best of times – the millions of Nairobians that pour out of the city's underbelly to repair its cars, sweep its streets, construct its skyscrapers and guard its mansions.'[23]

There is a long way to go for the slum dwellers of Kenya and of the world.

---

23 *Daily Nation*, September 13th, 2011.

For as the rain cometh down, and the snow from heaven, and returneth not thither, but watereth the earth, and maketh it bring forth and bud, that it may give seed to the sower, and bread to the eater: so shall my word be that goeth forth out of my mouth: it shall not return unto me void, but it shall accomplish that which I please, and it shall prosper in the thing whereto I sent it. For ye shall go out with joy, and be led forth with peace: the mountains and the hills shall break forth before you into singing, and all the trees of the field shall clap their hands. Instead of the thorn shall come up the fir tree, and instead of the briar shall come up the myrtle tree: and it shall be to the Lord for a name, for an everlasting sign that shall not be cut off.[24]

For the Lord thy God bringeth thee into a good land, a land of brooks of water, of fountains and depths that spring out of valleys and hills; a land of wheat, and barley, and vines, and fig trees, and pomegranates, a land of olive oil, and honey; a land wherein thou shalt eat bread without scarceness, thou shalt not lack anything in it, a land whose stones are iron and out of whose hills thou mayest dig brass.[25]

24 Isaiah 55.10–13.
25 Deuteronomy 8.7–9.

A warning voice comes from Antonia Byatt in her book *Ragnarok*. She feels that religion may lull people into a false sense of security. Christianity is most likely to do this, because it teaches about the truth of the resurrection.

Ragnarok is a Norse myth with an end of black nothingness which Byatt sees as a warning of the end of our planet earth through misuse.

The Norse gods are like humans, both greedy and stupid. They know that the end, Ragnarok, is coming, but are unable to make themselves do anything about it. As the earth they themselves made is destroyed they are also destroyed. Everything is drowned in blackness.

Especially sad is the end of 'Yggdrasil', the tree. The legend teaches that: 'In the beginning was the tree.' The tree was at the centre of everything; it held the world together and many creatures lived in it. Its leaves opened to the sun and its branches provided pasture. It was the source of goodness and was constantly renewed, until the end.[26]

---

26 A.S. Byatt, *Ragnarok: The End of the Gods*, Canongate, 2011.

Tree nursery in Kenya.

Goal 8

Develop a Global Partnership for Development

'I certainly never feel discouraged. I can't myself raise the winds that might blow us, or this ship, into a better world. But I can at least put up the sail so that when the wind comes I can catch it.' *E. F. Schumacher*[1]

Working together between nations and at all other levels is never easy.

The dangers of the developed nations patronising the developing nations are always there. The need for the developed nations to listen and to work together with the developing nations is clear, so that they become committed to the global partnership working and moving forward. Honesty is also needed, including the recognition that both rich and poor nations may be givers and receivers.

For example, the huge issue of the dreadful material poverty existing in the richest countries of the world must, in honest sharing, be acknowledged and tackled. I included examples of poverty in the western world in Chapter 1.

The challenge to develop farming, manufacturing industries and trade in the developing world and at the same time to work for fairness and the development of farming in the western world must be faced.

Recently, strong calls are being made for the voices of the poor to be heard. Christian Aid has affirmed this need as it looks beyond the MDGs to future partnerships and work. The European Union is also looking ahead to the post MDG agenda. Consultations are underway in many areas, but **there is a long way to go.**

1 Barbara Wood, *Alias Papa: A Life of Fritz Schumacher*, Green Books, 2011.

Opposite: painting by Andrew Macara

The image maker

The following story of the image maker brings home the need for people across the world to listen to and learn from each other and then to work together. The legend is of a holy man who lived long ago in a remote village in India. He lived alone and grew food in a small garden. He expressed his vision of the divine by creating beautiful images and each one took several months to make. He began in meditation and then he lovingly carved his image in soft beeswax. He then mixed clay and pasted it all over the image and waited for it to dry. Next he warmed the beeswax and poured it out of the clay. He then chose silver, bronze or gold, melted it and poured it into the clay mould, allowing it to set. Finally he cracked the clay mould to reveal the bright and shining image, a vision of the divine. The holy man always kept each image until he was able to give it to the right person.

The reputation of the holy man spread for hundreds of miles and a king in a distant part of India heard of him and sent a servant to buy an image. The servant walked for months, until he found the village of the holy man. He explained that the king would like an image. The holy man began to ask questions about the king, but the servant unceremoniously brandished a large bag of money as payment for an image. The holy man explained that he never sold his images, he simply wanted them to go to people who were seekers of the divine and who saw the images as a way. The servant was baffled, but then he threw the money to the ground, grabbed the image and ran.

The holy man lost his vision and creativity and fell ill. He tried to make images but failed and finally he closed his home and set off to find the king. He walked until he came to the palace, where he was kept waiting until the king ordered the servants to let him in. He explained that he never took money for his images and that the servant had forced the money upon him. He said, '*A mistake was made.*' There was a deep silence, until the king said, '*Yes, a mistake was made.*' The bag of money was returned to the king and the holy man returned home. The first image he made was a present for the king.

This story is a reminder of how easy it is for us all to assume that other people have the same values as ourselves and of how hard, but also how necessary, it is to achieve true partnership across the world.

TARGET – deal comprehensively with developing countries' debt and address special needs of landlocked countries and small island developing states

The burden of servicing external debt has fallen over the last six years by 6% in most developing countries. The debts of 23 of the poorest countries have been eased. However, debts in developing areas are growing again in 2012, due to the global economic crisis.

When the **Millennium Development Goals** were agreed by the United Nations they committed the international community to working together to achieve a coordinated vision and action plan for the future. This vision was not new but perhaps began after World War Two with the formation of the United Nations itself in the 1940s. At the beginning of the 1960s John Kennedy launched the UN Decade of Development. He said, *'If a free society cannot help the many who are poor, it can never serve the few who are rich.'*

The decade set a target for every industrialised country that 1% of the GNP should be given for official development assistance, ODA. Many people and organisations had a sense of urgency and a vision of development and justice spreading across the world. At the end of the decade most developing countries had raised their GNP but a small new middle class had emerged and most of the people, the poor, were not touched. By the 1970s the 1% figure had been reduced to 0.7%, where it remains and is still not reached. The UK is hopefully on track to meet this target.

In 1973 the Organisation of Petroleum Exporting Countries group was formed, oil prices soared, wealthy states arose in the Middle East and the age of debt began in the developing world.

By the 1980s the globalisation of the world economy saw the growth of 'Pacific tiger' nations: Hong Kong, Singapore, South Korea and Taiwan together with some Asian and Latin American countries. Africa on the other hand was in decline. By 1990 the debts of the poorest countries, mostly in Africa, had doubled and aid had reduced. Many countries were forced into structural adjustment programmes in order to get help from the International Monetary Fund.

This was a time when non-governmental organisations were needed and became more visible. Their work has gone on into the 21st century and is still needed. Most of the heavily indebted poor countries, HIPCs, continue to struggle, even though there have been many cancellations of debts. The over a billion extremely poor people are even worse off than they were at the end of the twentieth Ccentury.

Aid to developing countries is at a record high but it remains 19 billion dollars short of the promises made at the Gleneagles conference in 2005.[2] Development assistance to Africa has risen but has not reached the Gleneagles projection. It is growing again but not quickly enough.

Development aid has in fact fallen over the last 5 years, largely due to a decline in debt relief grants. Help given by NGOs, the private sector and some special funds have become important, for example, the global fund to fight AIDS.

Total aid remains well below the UN target

International aid has always been controversial. There is a clear distinction between aid given by governments, which is nearly always, partly at least, for the benefit of the donor, and aid given by non-governmental organisations and by individuals, which is much more likely to be given in partnership with those receiving it.

In general the link between aid given and poverty reduction is not very clear. Most aid is given to governments and is tied up with bureaucracy, special contracts and investments. Some of it is used to relieve debt.

There is hope in the annual report published in June 2012 by the UK Department for International Development.[3] The key challenges for the department cover most of the MDGs. Andrew Mitchell pointed out that, over a two year period, 12 million children have been vaccinated, 12.2 million bed nets have been distributed, land and property rights have been improved for 1.1 million people, emergency food has reached 6 million people and fairer elections achieved in 5 countries.[4] The hope now is that when the UK takes over the G8 presidency in 2013 there may be a new commitment to reducing the number of child deaths from malnutrition. It is

2 CAFOD report – 'A thousand days: an end and a new beginning.' 2012.
3 www.dfid.gov.uk.
4 'Faith, Poverty and Justice' – Lambeth Palace Inter-Faith Event with DFID, 26th June, 2012.

estimated that more than 2 million children a year die in this way. Global partnership must hopefully also include the commitment to change of the countries with high levels of malnutrition.

A hopeful example of international partnership was the meeting called by David Cameron towards the end of the 2012 Olympic Games, when world leaders were asked to help malnourished children. Plans announced include funding for research into drought resistant and vitamin enriched crops. GlaxoSmithKline and Unilever will be partners in making nutritious food available to the poorest families. Save the Children is planning a programme for Kenya which will use mobile phone technology to track hunger hot spots and then to give resources. The plans will hopefully be the first of many.

The rise of the multi-national companies is a key factor in development or lack of it. They have gained control of many developing economies and there are good examples of what is being done, as above, but the companies have not generally made a good contribution to the raising of living standards in the developing world.

An example of the power of the multinational companies was exposed in *The Guardian* recently.[5] It was pointed out that in 2011 two thirds of the United States world food aid was given to three US based grain companies, who then provide and transport the grain to the developing world. It was further explained that only 40 cents of every taxpayer dollar goes on food, the rest going into the pockets of agribusiness and the cost of the transport. Patrick Woodall, a researcher at 'Food and Water Watch' has drawn attention to the fact that the companies benefitting from the way American food aid is given are the same companies that are encouraging poor countries to grow non-food crops for export. The way food aid works in America is under review. Many people would like to see the food aid bought close to where it is needed but others see the aid programmes having a double purpose of helping the world's poor and also helping American companies and workers. There is also the issue of aid being used to get rid of US farming and fishing surpluses. However, the 2012 drought in America has led to reduced output in every area of farming, with the corn harvest forecast to be the lowest since 1995 and 40% of what is produced going into bio-fuels. The impact on the world's poor is likely to be disastrous, as there will inevitably be less food aid. Oxfam America has called for urgent action.

It is encouraging that the European Community changed its policy in 1996 when it moved to giving aid in cash. Canada also freed its aid from national ties in 2010.

In the last quarter of the twentieth century the multinational companies have increased from 7,000 to 38,000 and now control two thirds of the world's trade.[6] The way some of the companies produce their goods for the

---

5 Ibid.
6 Oswaldo de Rivero, *The Myth of Development*, Zed Books, 2001.

world market is worrying, because people often have to work long hours in hard conditions. The only aim of many of the companies is profit. Any company, of course, has to be profitable to continue in existence, but the least the big companies can do is to make sure they give fair wages, provide good conditions of work and pay their taxes. Sadly this is not always done unless some scandal is revealed, and then improvements are made. Some people would argue that poorly paid work is better than no work of course. The least we in the west should do is to demand transparency, and then hopefully we may go on to work for justice for workers in every aspect of their work and lives; in farming, manufacture and sales.

Sometimes companies operate in free trade zones, where normal taxes and regulations do not apply. In Sri Lanka the garment industry is in a free trade zone, where undoubtedly the workers, mostly women, receive higher wages than they do outside the zone. Outside the zone they are likely to work as servants to tourists, on coconut, rubber and tea plantations and as sex workers. Some women also go to work in the Middle East. It is estimated that 70% of women workers in the country work in the free trade zone, most of them are young, under 25 years, their work is monotonous, their hours are long and they soon suffer from eye problems. The wages may be higher than those of other women workers, but they are low when the profits of the companies are taken into account. Trade unions are not encouraged in the free trade zone which makes it hard for the women to improve their conditions. There are advisory councils but as their name indicates, they can only advise. Most of the women who work in the free trade zones obviously go there to earn money and are unlikely to challenge the system. A few Sri Lankan women, one a colleague who has now died, do campaign for a better and more equal life for women. Bernadeen Silva was a true campaigner for justice for the people of Sri Lanka, especially the women. She wrote:

Bernadine Silva

'We must be alert, we must not allow capitalism to programme us into conformity, or give up the struggle on the assumption that it is a historical process and wait till history corrects and ushers in an egalitarian society... The free trade zone has brought a vast number of women together. However difficult it may be – because of the legal framework of the FTZ – to organize the women within it, to become aware of the need to understand their needs, is an opportunity not to be missed.'[7]

7 *Remembering Bernadeen*, edited by Selvy Tiruchandran, Deepika Udagama, Suriya Wickremasinghe, Women's Education and Research Centre, 2009.

One of the problems of the way companies operate is that many of the poor people who are not employed by them become dissatisfied with their traditional lives. When they see the alternatives close by, they feel even more helpless than they did before. I remember being in a camp in an African country where we were building a goat house when a big pineapple company invited the British visitors to look round the pineapple estate. Following the visit sacks of free pineapples were delivered to the camp. African friends were angry because they had seen the pineapples growing but had never tasted them before our visit.

> **Often developing countries themselves may be to blame for not having strong enough links to poor people, who are therefore outside the capitalist system altogether or exploited by it.**

Someone who had excellent links to the poor people of his country was **Julius Nyerere**, the first president of Tanzania. He always knew that the people of his country, mostly poor people, were the key to its future. He had links with people on every level and particularly with the poor majority. His vision, which was expressed best in the Arusha Declaration of 1967, was of a future of freedom, equality and dignity for all the people of his country. He worked hard to reduce the importance of the tribes in Tanzania, partly by moving people into collective 'ujama' villages. The villages did not work out well and people began to move back to their traditional homes, but the building of national consciousness and the reduction of tribal loyalties was largely successful in Tanzania and today people do not talk as much about the tribe they come from.

Education was the key to the future for Julius Nyerere. I have visited the Arusha Secondary School and read the statement he wrote which has been placed in the entrance hall. He addressed all those who would come to the school in the future and compared them with someone who had been given all the food in a village where people were starving so that he might summon the strength to travel, work and bring fresh supplies back to the village. The person who takes the food and does not then help and work with others who remain poor is a traitor. The statement went on to challenge the future pupils who will be educated in the school:

> **'If any of the young men and women who are given an education by the people of this republic adopt attitudes of superiority, or fail to use their knowledge to help the development of this country, then they are betraying our union.'**

It is important for the western world to have links with every strata of society in the developing world. This is a major key to the post 2015 agenda for sustainable development.

A major problem has been the failure of western governments and non-governmental organisations to understand the nature of societies in the developing world, where there is very little 'civil society' to take responsibility. Civil society is made up of those people, across society and through the public sphere, who strive, often voluntarily, to make a country work at every level. Most people in developing societies even today are not educated or organised. Many people are in so many ways pre-industrial and therefore living simply from day to day. Planning ahead is hard and sometimes impossible.

I will always remember landing in Nairobi and then being driven for hours into the semi-desert, arriving with a group of young people in the middle of the night. The Kenyan hosts had visited the place many times and had asked for mattresses and food to be ready, but there was nothing. We spent what remained of the night trying to sleep without the mattresses. The next day everything was sorted out and I later asked one of the local community members why nothing had been done. His answer was a surprise. He explained that the community had not believed that the group from Nairobi and England would come, because no-one had ever been to stay with them before.

In many African countries agriculturalists have been working for years to try to persuade people to accept dairy goats, to help to provide milk to fight malnutrition amongst the children, but this has proved an uphill struggle and very often the goats are still killed and eaten. Machinery given to African people is often abandoned once its newness has worn off and repairs are needed.

Christians Aware sends groups to many countries in the developing world. There are regular visits to Eastern Zambia where participants work with local people in building projects, sometimes in hospitals and health centres. A recent group came back to tell the sad story of the 2004 gift of an electrical incubator by the Swedish Government. The incubator was the latest and most efficient machine, designed to save the lives of new and premature babies. Sadly the incubator was fairly complicated to operate

An improvised incubator.

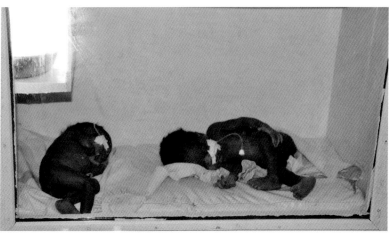

and therefore it stood in a corner and in 2011, when the visitors were there, it had never been used. A simple box with a glass front which is heated by a light bulb is still used for the many premature babies.

More effort needs to be made towards investment in models for development that will enable people to improve their traditional ways of living and surviving. This way forward gives confidence and new energy. One campaigner for a radical change in the 1960s and 1970s was Fritz Schumacher. His most famous publication was *Small is Beautiful. Economics as if People Mattered*, written in 1973. He, influenced by Mahatma Gandhi, believed in the value of all human beings and spoke out against a capitalist system which put profits before people. Following his travels in India, he suggested that change for a better life might begin where the people were, and that changes should be worked out by and with them. His approach was to start all economic reasoning from the needs of the people and thus to help the poor to help themselves. He pointed out that small steps should be taken, so that uneducated people could keep up and also be given confidence. He said:

'Find out what people are doing and help them to do it better.'

Appropriate technology was and is needed, so that people can work with it and not be mystified and fearful. This was the beginning of what became known as 'development from the bottom up'. Schumacher also challenged communities everywhere to work against the temptation of people to concentrate only in cities. He had spent the Second World War in internment in England and had worked on a farm. He loved this time and said it was his greatest learning experience. He wanted to revitalise farming and non-agricultural activities in rural areas and to link them to creative city life.

Many non-governmental organisations and some governments began to work with this model, including the base communities of Latin America and those who promoted African Socialism in Zambia and Tanzania.

Barbara Wood has written about intermediate technology:

'It gave hope to people at all levels, to the farmer who could improve his output by a better designed hand plough, to the builder who could make more mud bricks with a more efficient hand press, to the potter whose handmade pots grew at twice the rate on a wheel powered by foot pedal or even a small engine rather than a wheel spun by hand.' [8]

There are many recent examples of this approach including the improvement of the traditional pit latrines by the introduction of two chimneys to circulate the air. Oxfam[9] has developed a clay, water, mud and donkey dung cooking stove which is economical of fuel. It is being used in the Democratic

---

8 Ibid.
9 www.oxfam.org.uk.

Republic of the Congo. The stove is designed to use very little fuel and yet to reach a high temperature. This contribution is making a difference to women's lives because they no longer have to spend a long time every day looking for fuel.

There are improved ploughs and carts. I have been involved in building many small water catchment dams and tanks in Africa. Their value is not simply in the water they save but in the sharing of the people working together to build them. Water harvesting is now a very important part of life all over the developing world.

Following directly from the pioneering of Schumacher was the work of the Intermediate Technology Development Group, begun in 1966 and now called 'Practical Action'.[10] The charity works in Latin America, Southern Africa, East Africa and South Asia. The work aims to develop appropriate technologies in agro-processing, food production, energy, transport and disaster mitigation.

For example in rural Nepal, where the majority of the population still does not have access to basic energy services, Practical Action has established an 'Energy Village' demonstrating how renewable energies – micro hydro, solar and wind – can make an enormous benefit to income generation and local development without increasing carbon dioxide emissions.

Practical Action's Score Stove project.

10 www.practicalaction.org.

The New Economics Foundation began, in the footsteps of Schumacher, in 1986.[11] It is a 'think and do tank' putting people and the planet first. It was one of the pioneers in raising the issue of international debt. It aims to work with people in every section of society in the UK and internationally.

I have written about the work of Mohammed Yunus and the development of micro credit in Chapter Three. The Grameen Bank made self-reliance a reality for many in the developing world. What may be needed for the future is for more investment to be in very small sums of money for more people in more countries. Partnerships for development can only begin to happen when work for the poor of the world becomes work with the poor, who themselves become workers and leaders for change.

Charles Kingsley's *Water Babies* was published in 1863. The main purpose of the book was the utter condemnation of the way the children of the poor were treated in England in the 19th century, especially the child labourers. It was also an opportunity to write about a vision of something better. Water was not just the means of washing Tom the little chimney sweep and the other children, it was also symbolical of a movement into a new life, like the water of Christian Baptism. A 1978 film adaptation of the *Water Babies* showed the movement to a new life wonderfully when Tom was being chased by a landowner and jumped into a raging torrent and sank deep into the water, changing as he did so into a bright cartoon character who tackled the forces of evil before returning to the world as a new boy, who could also challenge the evil of exploitation in the real world. He was now himself the visionary leader who was passionate for change.

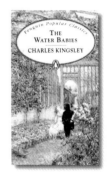

TARGET – develop further an open, rule-based, predictable, non-discriminatory trading and financial system

Trade has been a normal part of everyday life everywhere from the dawn of humanity. It is now practised on many different levels, and is local, national and global. In the 21st century we are more aware of where we trade and of the many issues arising.

---

11 www.neweconomics.org.

The **Trade Justice** movement is an international movement made up of non-governmental organisations who work for changes in world trade towards justice for the poor of the world.[12] Campaigns are organised to challenge governments and international bodies, including the World Trade Organisation, the International Monetary Fund and the World Bank. The challenge is for change in current trading practices away from growth and towards a just and sustainable system. The November 2011 camp outside St. Paul's Cathedral aimed to challenge the trading practices of the Stock Exchange and to encourage people to think about possibilities for global economic justice. Consumers are asked to find out about what they buy and to insist on 'fair trade'.

yampi/shutterstock.com

One large barrier to fairer trade is agricultural subsidies paid to farmers and agribusinesses in the developed world, which make it difficult if not impossible for developing world farmers to compete. The European Union's Common Agricultural Policy traditionally gave direct subsidies for agricultural produce but in 2003 the 'Single Farm Payment' was introduced.

---

12 www.tjm.org.uk.

Sugar is a good example of the negative effects of farm subsidies given to farmers in the developed world. America and the European Union now produce too much sugar, which is subsidised and sold cheaply or sent to poor countries. In 1975 Europe imported sugar and is now the second largest exporter. The world sugar price has gone down and small farmers in the developing world have gone out of business, sometimes leaving the sugar cane standing in the fields.

This is not a simple issue. It might be argued that sugar beet, grown in temperate climates, should be used for fuel, thus giving the advantage in food production to cane sugar production in the developing world. There is still the issue however of whether the cane sugar comes from small farms or big tropical plantations.

If the farm subsidies do end it is not clear what will happen. The farmers of the developing world may have more markets, though the big agribusinesses everywhere in the world will continue to dominate. The future of the small farmers of the developed world is not at all clear. There is an encouraging story from New Zealand, where there have been no agricultural subsidies since 1984 and where farming continues to flourish. New Zealand is a founding member of the Cairns Group which works to improve market access for agricultural exports.

Market access for most developing countries is not improving very much and there has been little progress in reducing the barriers to exports from developing countries to developed countries.

Trade justice campaigns focus particularly on the need for access by developing countries to the markets of the developed world. When the developing countries export to developed countries they very often still face tariff barriers which are much higher than those faced by other developed countries. The barriers sometimes cost the developing countries twice as much as they receive in aid.

The World Trade Organisation, WTO, replaced the General Agreement on Tariffs and Trade in 1995. It has 155 members, including the European Union and China, and 29 observer governments. Iran is the largest non-member. It provides a framework for trade negotiations and deals with the regulation of trade between participating countries. It also offers a process for the resolution of disputes.

The Doha Development Round was launched in 2001, with a special focus on the needs of developing countries. The 2005 WTO agreement on textiles and clothes freed up trade in these areas. In 2008 the meeting broke down over a dispute between the exporters of bulk agricultural commodities and countries with many subsistence farmers on the terms of a protection for farmers from surges in imports. Currently the future of the Doha Round is very uncertain, with 21 areas where the original deadline was missed. The main stumbling block is the agricultural subsidies in the developed world. Further, trade related assistance needs to be increased. Developing countries need technical assistance and the development of infrastructure. Technical cooperation has actually fallen in the last 5 years.

The General Council of the WTO has many committees, working groups and subsidiary bodies. Subsidiary bodies are:

○ The Trade Negotiations Committee, TNC, deals with trade talks rounds.

○ The Council for Trade in Goods has eleven committees and several groups relating to textiles.

○ The Council for Trade-Related Aspects of Intellectual Property Rights, TRIPS, was negotiated in 1994 and established minimum standards for intellectual property regulation for all nations, and it includes enforcement procedures.

○ The Council for Trade in Services is responsible for overseeing the working of the General Agreement on Trade in Services, GATS which was introduced in 1995. The plan, referring to the sale and delivery of intangible products, aims to bring the service sector into the multilateral trading system. Some examples of trade in services are banking, check-ups done by a doctor and Information Technology. Tourism is a service sector.

Two recent films, directed by Marc and Nick Francis, look at the impact of international trade when the global partnership is weak and one-sided. The first film, Black Gold, was made in 2006, about the international coffee trade. The coffee growers in the film are in southern and western Ethiopia, where the farmers are suffering low prices for their coffee. The manager of the coffee farmers' cooperative is Tadesse Meskela, who visits coffee growing areas in the region. He also goes to a coffee processing centre and auction house. He even travels to the UK and the USA and realises the huge gap between the setting of the coffee prices and the reality of the lives of the farmers.

The second film, When China Met Africa, was made in 2011 and illustrates China's trade movement into Africa and a new and deeper involvement in Zambia, supported by the government there. There are three stories: of a farm owner and his workers, of a manager of a Chinese company building a new road and of a Zambian trade minister. The difficulties of communication are obvious. The film shows Chinese people buying large plots of scrub, and hiring locals to clear and farm the land. The notion of partnership between Zambia and China is unreal. The possibility of a new colonialism is very real.

For global partnership, beneficial to all those taking part, to be real, fair trade is essential.

The International Fair Trade Association began in 1989 and is an umbrella group of organizations in more than 70 countries, defining fair trade as reflecting 'concern for the social, economic and environmental well-being of marginalized small producers' and 'not maximizing profit at their expense'.

Fair trade is growing and is one hopeful area in the global partnership. It undoubtedly improves the quality of life for at least 7 million people.

Buying fairly traded goods makes people aware of the unfairness of some world trade and of the need for change. Fair trade sales are constantly going up and have reached nearly half a billion pounds.

There are different forms of fair trade. The fair trade mark is reasonably well known. Producers and retailers have to be certified by the international fair trade labelling organisation. In Britain this is administered by the **Fair Trade Foundation**, which began in 1992.[13] The main aim of the foundation is education within the United Kingdom. Members know that if they manage to start people thinking about fair trade they are more likely to go on to support it and thus to support producers in the developing world.

Some companies have organised their own fair trade schemes. There is also 'ethical trade' which may take place when all the rules for fair trade labelling cannot be met.

The Rainforest Alliance[14] has a green tree frog as its logo and is supported by Greenpeace, working to ensure sustainability in forests, farms, and hotels. The alliance, based in New York, launched its first sustainable

13 www.fairtrade.org.uk.
14 www.rainforest-alliance.org.

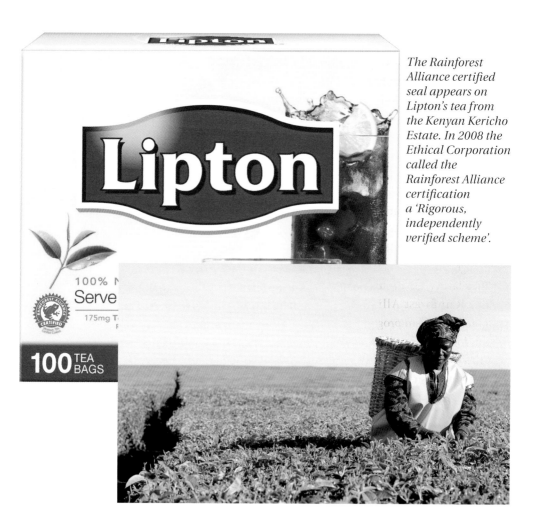

The Rainforest Alliance certified seal appears on Lipton's tea from the Kenyan Kericho Estate. In 2008 the Ethical Corporation called the Rainforest Alliance certification a 'Rigorous, independently verified scheme'.

forest programme in 1989. There is training and general education, school programmes, conservation projects and carbon offset projects. The 'Smart-Wood' programme gives certificates so that buyers can be sure that their wood protects biodiversity and that local workers have rights. This scheme is very special because it requires the prior consent of indigenous people for any scheme.

The alliance works to find buyers for the wood who in their turn become green builders and companies.

There is a sustainable agriculture programme which gives certificates to tropical farms which reduce their use of chemicals and look after the land and the workers. There must be no discrimination in the hiring of workers and no employment of children under 15 years. There also has to be eco-system conservation, the protection of wild animals and waterways. Crops included are coffee,[15] bananas, cocoa, oranges, cut flowers, ferns and tea.

The Rainforest Alliance differs from the Fair Trade Foundation in being linked to the international markets. It doesn't offer a fixed minimum price,

---

15 McDonald's coffee comes from ethically certified sources and carries the Rainforest Alliance logo.

so that if an international market collapses there is no lower price to protect the producers. The buyers on the other hand do not suffer, because if the price of a product drops then so does the price paid. No doubt the hope is that this system encourages more businesses to join the schemes and thus to ensure their success.

The Chiquita owned banana farms in Latin America are all Rainforest Alliance certified. Unilever plans to have all its Lipton Tea plantations certified by 2015. Efforts are made to encourage the buying of the products from the certified farms in 12 countries.

The Rainforest Alliance introduced its sustainable tourism programme in 2000, supporting local certification and developing partnerships with tour operators and hotels. There is a directory of sustainable tourism businesses in Latin America and the Caribbean.

Some Principles of Fair Trade

A fair price...

...is essential for trade to be fair, but whether this should be a guaranteed price is widely discussed and approaches vary greatly. The Fairtrade Foundation and the Rainforest Alliance have different views and approaches, as I have explained above. The Rainforest Alliance works with small and large producers and businesses. The Fairtrade Foundation works most often with associations of small farmers or cooperatives, but has recently included larger farms and plantations so that its labels are included in some of the larger supermarkets.

Divine chocolate[16] is a special pioneering project because the cocoa farmers in Ghana actually own shares in the company, a much more equal relationship than simply receiving a fair price for their produce.

In the early 1990s some Ghana cocoa farmers set up a farmers' cooperative called Kuapa Kokoo to work for the environment

---

16 www.divinechocolate.com.

and to sell their own cocoa to the government cocoa marketing company. Kuapa Kokoo now has about 40,000 members. It weighs, bags and transports the cocoa to market and deals with the paperwork. The cocoa is high quality and sells all over the world. In 1997 the cocoa farmers decided to develop their own chocolate bar which would be fairly traded.

In 1998 the Day Chocolate Company was set up with many investors. In the same year the Divine milk chocolate bar was launched in the UK, where the chocolate eaten per person is the highest in the world. The Kuapa Kokoo share in the Day Chocolate Company, now called the Divine Chocolate Company, was a first in the fair trade world. Kuapa Kokoo participates in decisions about how Divine is produced and sold. Two representatives from Kuapa Kokoo are directors on the company's board, and one board meeting a year is held in Ghana. As shareholders, the farmers also receive a share of the profits from the sale of the many varieties of Divine Chocolate.

In 2000 Comic Relief launched a new children's chocolate bar called 'Dubble' in support of African cocoa farmers. In 2007 Divine chocolate was launched in America.

A long-term relationship...

...between the producer and the buyer is helpful. Many relationships and products take years to develop. Munguishi coffee has been imported from Tanzania by Christians Aware for about 20 years and things have changed over that time. The first Munguishi coffee came from the farm of the Diocese of Mount Kilimanjaro, because there is a link with the Diocese of Leicester, where the Christians Aware office is based. The money raised through the sale of the coffee in the UK first went to pay a good price to

100% Arabica

the diocese so that the workers could be paid well. The profit made was then given to the diocesan centre for the training of lay people in farming, health and pastoral work. The profit from the coffee still goes the training centre, but the diocesan farm has ceased to grow coffee which is now bought from small farms in the Arusha and Moshe area. The workers on the small farms have good conditions and pay. They also grow their own food crops. The coffee is roasted and packed in the UK by Ethical Addictions.[17] One important area is the Manoshi village which is the centre for a number of very small coffee farms on the slopes of Mount Kilimanjaro. The coffee is excellent because the water from the mountain is pure and the volcanic soil is very rich. The farmers have tripled their income by working with Ethical Addictions. This is partly because a much higher price is paid for the coffee than was paid before, but also because the payment goes to the individual farmers and not to a cooperative. What we

17 Ethical Addictions is a 'passionate coffee company': www.eacoffee.co.uk

might call 'direct trade' cuts out a number of intermediary people so that the original producer receives a higher price. It is important that direct trade companies are transparent in their businesses, so that their work can be seen and judged as fair and just, or not.

Money is needed by farmers throughout the farming year...

Fair trade buyers will advance money to farmers against their future crop(s), which they are contracted to deliver. In this way there is no temptation for the money to be given up as interest to moneylenders.

Much of the Kenyan tea is organised so that the small tea farmer may benefit. The tea farms are owned by the farmers, who harvest the tea leaves and take them to the factory, which may be owned by the government, though recently there are more cooperatively owned factories. The tea leaves are prepared by the factory. They are dried, shredded and put into bags from where they go to tea exchanges around the world, including the London tea exchange. The benefit to the farmer is that he or she is paid for the tea when it first arrives in the factory and also receives a bonus when the tea is sold on the tea exchange.

The transfer of knowledge and skills is important...

The normal markets may gradually be encouraged to offer better prices. The buyers and also shoppers may learn about the crops and about resulting products. The producers may also learn improved methods and may share these with members of their communities.

Fair Trade products have now moved into most supermarkets. This move was largely pioneered by Café Direct and is both practical and educational, as the supermarkets are so popular. Many supermarket 'own labels' are now fairly traded. The Cooperative is perhaps the best example of this. The availability of cookery books which recommend fairly traded ingredients is an excellent way of teaching people about fair trade.[18]

The Bishopton Trading Company uses fairtrade organic cotton and is keen to share the reasons for this with its customers. The cotton, grown in Gujarat in Western India, is free from expensive and polluting pesticides. Suma peanut butter is promoted as organic and fairly traded. It is made from organic peanuts grown in China, where the peanuts are cleaned and shelled. The fairtrade premiums have enabled the farmers to plant trees to combat erosion and to build schools. Many cut flowers are now marketed as offering a better deal for producers in the developing world, and also better wages

---

18 *Food, Festivals and Faith*, Christians Aware, 2009. *The Fairtrade Everyday Cookbook*, edited by Sophie Grigson, Dorling Kindersley, 2008.

and conditions for workers. Buyers of flowers will be encouraged by this, but will also want to ask how much land and water are used to grow the flowers.

Efforts have been made recently for children and young people who play ball games to be aware of fair trade sports balls, where the fair trade certification relates to the labour of the workers rather than to the raw materials. Pakistan is the world's primary exporter of sports balls and around 40% of the Sialkot working population is dependent, directly or indirectly, on this industry for their livelihood. The region is particularly well-known for its production of hand-stitched balls and estimates suggest that as many as 60% of the world's footballs are made in Talon workshops around Sialkot, where people are traditionally landless and amongst the poorest in the country. Talon pays the national minimum wage. There is no child labour and separate small work places are offered for men and women, where there is good lighting and ventilation. The fair trade premium is used for education and health. It is interesting that there are more women workers than men, perhaps because the women are more likely to use the fair trade premium for their children and to join micro-credit schemes.

Farmers may receive a 'fair trade premium', which is used for community projects...

The projects may be in the area of farming, health and education. The community decides how to use the premium.

The Cadbury Cocoa Partnership is ten years old, during which time 45 million pounds has been donated to cocoa growing communities in Ghana, India and Indonesia, in partnership with the United Nations, for the development of community projects. Financial literacy and good sustainable farming practice have been valuable educational courses arranged for farmers. Farmers are encouraged to grow food crops between the cocoa trees.

A concern for children has led to the introduction of bicycle donations so that they can get to school easily, and solar lanterns, so that they can read after dark. The schools also have the solar lanterns. In 2009 Cadbury launched its dairy milk chocolate bar as a fair trade product and at the same time announced that it will not use cocoa produced by African child labour in its 'main chocolate range'.

Cadbury is now owned by Kraft Foods but the cocoa partnership will continue.

Labour conditions must be safe and workers must receive a living wage...

This is a difficult area because it is not always easy to find out what working conditions are like either at home or overseas. Sweat shops exist in most countries. They are places where workers work for 7 days a week, with no holidays, they do not receive decent wages and are not allowed to form unions. Some companies have signed the Ethical Trading Initiative, which is a good start in ethical trading, but there is a long way to go.

Burma particularly has a poor human rights record, including the allowing of very poor conditions for workers, many of whom are forced to work for little or for nothing at all. One example of forced labour is the use of the Rohingya people to build the road from Maungdaw to Buthidaung in 2008, to plant nut saplings and to cultivate paddy fields.[19]

An example of the difficulty of knowing about working conditions comes from Conor Woodman who has written about lobster fishing in Nicaragua,[20] where people risk their lives diving for lobsters which have been caught in traps, which are then sent to American companies. It is not possible for people who buy the lobsters to know that divers have risked their lives to reach the traps.

Harmful chemicals are not acceptable...

The World Health Organisation estimate is that 20,000 deaths occur in developing countries every year from poisoning by agricultural pesticides used on crops, and particularly on cotton. Organic cotton is now available.

Another example of the use of chemicals is in the flower industry. A lot of work has been done recently on whether harmful chemicals are used in the growing of flowers for export from the developing world. The chemicals are especially harmful for pregnant women. Colombia grows many flowers for export and many of the 9,000 flower workers have been exposed to harmful chemicals for many years. Research is now being done to improve matters in Colombia, and some progress is being made. Kenya is perhaps the best example of a country where efforts are being made by many flower growers to grow the flowers in a way which is not harmful to the workers. One farm which is a fair trade flower farm is Ravine Roses in Western Kenya. Here there is a water purifying system and organic pest control. However, there is always the question of whether flowers should be grown for export at all, because they take up a lot of land and use a lot of water.

---

19 Benedict Rogers, *Burma: A nation at the crossroads*, Rider, Random House, 2012.
20 Conor Woodman, *Unfair Trade*, Random House Business Books, 2011.

No forced child labour is acceptable...

I have already included a section on child labour in Chapter 4. There are many areas of production where child labour is used. One of the largest areas is in cocoa growing and harvesting. In the past the chocolate companies have normally bought cocoa from farms where child labour is used, particularly in West Africa. However, the companies are now much more aware of the harm the children may come to, including injury or death from the machetes used to cut the cocoa pods, and from pesticides. A further problem in cocoa harvesting is that the hours are long and the pods ripen throughout the year, so that there is no long space for education. Another problem is that children may have to carry very heavy loads of cocoa beans.

The Ivory Coast exports at least 35% of the world's cocoa and more than half the people there live in dire poverty. Not only are roughly 200,000 children involved in the work on the plantations, but it is estimated that at least 12,000 of the children are trafficked.[21] The government has said that low prices given for the cocoa may force small farmers to use the slave labour. In 2001 the UK and US threatened boycotts and chocolate companies promised to start refusing to do business with farms using forced child labour. In 2012 the European Union passed a resolution to fight child labour and to support existing voluntary agreements by chocolate companies to stop child labour. This was criticised as having 'no bite'.

It is vital to encourage the buying of fairly traded chocolate, totally free from child labour. It is essential also to check the full range of products of a company, as some may be fairly traded and others not.

Farmers are encouraged to introduce their own income generating projects...

...instead of always sending their primary produce to the developed world. This challenge is not easy.

Orange growing in Nepal is an income generating project for poor communities

One well established income generation project takes locally produced mandarin oranges, and processes then to make fresh orange juice. Farmers benefit from a direct ethical crop purchasing system, based on payment per kilogram by the processor, eliminating the previous system of middle men who would buy the whole crop, usually on disadvantageous terms to the grower. Processing is carried out at a factory local to the growers, giving employment to displaced persons. All seems to indicate a successful

---

21 International Labour Organisation, 2005.

income generation project, but although in many respects this is true, there is another side to the story.

Planting an orange orchard takes capital, and there is no significant return for seven years. Only the larger and wealthier farmers are able to raise the finance to do this, and then wait for seven years for the trees to mature. Studies have shown that replacing rice and maize crops with orange production reduces the labour required, but increases the financial return per unit of land. So the landless labourers suffer reduced employment, whilst the land owner benefits. Independent surveys show widening of the income gap between rich and poor in villages with orange orchards.

The latest data from Nepal shows that 39% of children suffer from moderate to severe malnutrition, and 49% have stunted growth, as a result of poor diet. Any project to replace staple food production with cash crops must be questioned, not just from the headline grabbing global industrial giants, but including what at first sight seem good local initiatives.

Traidcraft has given the example of three new items factory and farm workers may buy using their fair trade premium payments for selling fair trade charcoal.[22] The new items are bicycles, bread ovens and donkey carts. The charcoal comes from acacia trees which are cut down so that food can be grown and cattle grazed. The wood is baked in portable kilns and the charcoal is then processed in the factory. This work is approved by the Forest Stewardship Council.

Fair trade is increasing and sales have reached nearly half a billion pounds, but fair trade still accounts for only a very small percentage of world trade. There is a long way to go.

A useful book is *The Good Shopping Guide*, which includes sections on home and office, energy, travel, money, food and drink, health and beauty, fashion and networking.[23] The foreword to the book points out that we all leave an ethical footprint every time we shop. There is a challenge from the authors:

'We believe that the key to a progressive 21st century lies in the persuasive power of intelligent consumer action.'

22 www.traidcraft.co.uk.
23 *The Good Shopping Guide*, the Ethical Marketing Group, 2011.

Target – to provide access to affordable essential drugs in developing countries

Health is a human right which the world's poor are so often denied. It is easy to see, by reference to the three MDGs which are about the need to improve health, Goals 4, 5 and 6, that there is a very long way to go. For instance, conditions such as diarrhoea can be prevented or treated and are hardly noteworthy in rich countries. In the developing world they are killers of large numbers of people.

It is frustrating that drugs are easily available for many illnesses now, but that this availability is normally for those who can afford them or for those who live in a country where there is a health service, like the UK. Poor availability and high prices continue to be barriers to access to essential drugs in the developing world.

Many countries have made progress in increasing access to medicines and treatments for HIV/AIDS, malaria and tuberculosis. The Global Fund to Fight Aids, tuberculosis and malaria, with other funds, has helped, but **there is a long way to go.**

Support is needed to tackle cancer, diabetes, respiratory disease and heart disease. Sixty percent of all deaths are in these areas, most in low and middle income countries. There is a wide variation in national spending on medicines per head of populations. Free provision of drugs is also patchy, mainly because of inefficiencies in government planning, purchase and distribution.

What does **global partnership** mean when there are such HUGE GAPS in health provision in the world TODAY?

It is important to remember that access to essential drugs is defined as having the medicines continually available and affordable at both public and private health facilities and within one hour's walk from the homes of the people.

Most developing countries have published an essential medicines list and 71% of countries have a national medicines policy. Two thirds of people find that drugs do not reach them because they are far too expensive. People are also victims of false drugs being sold to them. When medicines are not available in public clinics the people have the choice of going to a private clinic, where medicine provision is normally good, or of going without the medicines. Most people have to go without.

Progress requires national governments to eliminate taxes and duties on essential medicines, to adopt generic drugs as an alternative to higher priced original and brand named medicines, to reduce trade and distribution mark ups on the prices of essential medicines and to make sure that they are widely available. Monitoring is also essential.

Progress requires global pressure to be put on pharmaceutical companies to reduce their prices for developing countries and also to produce and promote generic medicines. The Doha Declaration states that 'Trade Related Aspects of Intellectual Property Rights', TRIPS, should be interpreted as consistent with the goal to promote access to medicines for all.

Research funding must be improved to develop medicines relevant to developing countries.

There is always the issue of education in the use of the medicines, because they are worthless or even dangerous unless they are used properly. I remember looking at what seemed to be a perfectly clear and sensible poster for the prevention of malaria in an African village. The poster showed pictures of three people standing in a row. The first picture was of a person who was ill from malaria, the second of the same person taking an anti-malarial tablet and the third of the same person, now well and smiling. When the poster was discussed with a local African village group the participants began in the middle of the poster, with the person taking the pill, after which they saw him either getting better or worse. They concluded that it was not worth taking the pills at all.

TARGET – in cooperation with the private sector, to make available the benefits of new technologies, especially information and communications

Solar powered battery chargers enable communications equipment to be widely available, even in villages with no access to mains electricity or to electric generators. Cheap wind-up basic computers have recently been distributed to many African schools.

Mobile phones are expanding and improving communications in developing countries. The number of mobile phones soared from less than 500 million to 2.7 billion by 2006 and there are now 4.2 billion mobile phones in the developing world.[24] More than 22% of Africa's population has a mobile phone. They are not all professional people but a wide cross section, including the Maasai who use them when they go on journeys.

Communication through the use of mobile phones is particularly important in remote rural areas, and especially in Africa. I have written about mobile phone use for the emergency delivery of babies. I have recently been in remote areas of Kenya where the only means of finding the way was the use of the mobile phone. The problem my group experienced was that the batteries of the phones do have to be charged from time to time, and sometimes this requires a long journey, usually on foot, into the nearest

24 World Bank.

town. Now there are sometimes the solar powered battery chargers. A new development also is the wind-up battery charger which, once it is introduced widely, will be very good news.

The mobile phone brings many new opportunities for the development of farming and other businesses and for education on many levels. It is estimated that the use of the mobile phone has led to an average growth of 0.8% in the economies of developing countries.

Ghana is an example of a country which has worked with the World Bank and other partners to promote the use of mobile phones, run by Ghana Telecom. It is estimated that there are more than 3 million mobile phone users. There are roughly 30,000 people who earn a living by selling phone calls on their mobile phones. Ghana is also becoming known as a place, like India, which the Western world can turn to for outsourcing work. An outsourcing centre is now being supported by the World Bank. International businesses are also settling in Accra. The economy is growing enough now for many professional Ghanaians to go back home to work from all over the world and the local middle class is growing. The gap between the professional groups and the poor is also growing. Hunger and disease have not gone away and 60% of young Ghanaians are out of work.

The use of mobile phones mostly preceded the use of the internet in the developing world. Broadband access and internet use has made communication between the developed and the developing world much easier. News and current affairs are exchanged much more than they used to be for instance.

Internet usage is growing in the developing world, but is not nearly as widespread as the use of mobile phones. It is estimated that only 7% of Africans have access to broadband, but this percentage will hopefully grow quickly. Also the bandwidth is normally low and distribution is very uneven. Frequent electricity blackouts in many countries also make the internet unreliable, but this need not be a permanent situation.

Access to information is central to economic development, so the more available and reliable it is the more the economies of the developing world may grow. On a simple level farmers and others can find out what is right or wrong with their crops and can sometimes learn how to take their harvests to a later stage of production. They can also find out what their produce is worth on national and international markets.

Some countries, including Nigeria, have encouraged the development of entertainment on line, providing new work for those engaged in it. Nigeria has the popular 'Real Nolly' movies, now launched as a 'YouTube' channel. Real Nolly has digital distribution rights to Nigeria's Nollywood films, which are available to viewers free of charge. The channel earns money through advertising.

The good news is that successful internet connections are making the MDGs for health, education and employment more possible. They thus also have a contribution to make to poverty reduction and thus to the reduction of the gap between the rich and the poor, and between the developed and the developing world.

Partnership for development is possible

When Fritz Schumacher wrote *A Guide for the Perplexed*, he called for a turning around, a 'metanoia' in how we see the world. He wrote:

> The art of living is always to make a good thing out of a bad thing. Only if we know we have actually descended into infernal regions... can we summon the courage and imagination needed for a 'turning around', a metanoia. This then leads to seeing the world in a new light, namely a place where the things modern man talks about and always fails to accomplish can actually be done.[25]

Portable solar power platforms.

---

25 E.F. Schumacher, *A Guide for the Perplexed*, Jonathon Cape, 1977.

A challenge for global partnership from Traidcraft

Global Partnership is about working for a world freed from the scandal of poverty, where trade is just, and people and communities can flourish.

Why we're here [26]

To sit on the chill stone floor
in an ancient church
and listen to voices from the two thirds world;
to listen to questions
to share anger
to express hope –
that's why we're here.
It makes up for all those righteous pews,
comfy chairs
and politeness.
It's why we're who we are,
in our cheerful diversity.

To stand shoulder to shoulder,
moved, moving,
on the edge of dancing
to African drumming
which echoes from the vaulted roof
and rocks the walls of the abbey –
that makes sense
of churchgoing.
It reminds us of who we are:
the people of God on the move.

To be encouraged, excited,
incited to take to the streets;
to go out of that grand doorway,
like royalty, the common people,
together and one by one;
to leave in a great wave
like the start of a marathon –
with a message
for the people in power –
this makes sense;
It's why we're here,
doing our best to be
the human race.

26 Jan Sutch Pickard, *Between High and Low Water: Sojourner Songs*, Wild Goose Publications, 2008.

A Resource for global partnership

World Shaped Mission is an Anglican resource for study and action towards global partnership. There are sections on many aspects of mission, and running through them all are themes of listening to partners, receiving and giving and working together for our world.[27]

27 Janice Price and the World Mission and Anglican Communion Panel, *World Shaped Mission: Exploring new frameworks for the Church of England in world mission*, Church House Publishing, 2012.

Afterword

But there is a long way to go...

In 1948 the United Nations published its 'Universal Declaration of Human Rights.' Article 25 is:

> Everyone has the right to a standard of living adequate for the health and well-being of himself and his family, including food, clothing, housing and medical care and necessary social services, and the right to security in the event of unemployment, sickness, disability, widowhood, old age or other lack of livelihood in circumstances beyond his control.

> Motherhood and childhood are entitled to special care and assistance. All children, whether born in or out of wedlock, shall enjoy the same social protection.

More than 20 years later the Zambian poet Jonathon Chileshi asked:

> How is the victory over poverty to be won?
> How is the gap between the rich
> and the poor nations of the world to be closed?
> How can the nations of Africa
> begin to trade in manufactured goods
> as well as agricultural produce?
> Christians must come to grips
> with this complex subject of international economics.
> Sympathy is not enough,
> for in this area of life,
> Love without justice is an impossibility.

The fact that the declaration and also the poem were written so long ago, and that the situation is much the same or, in some areas of life, worse in the twentyfirst century is scandalous. There have been improvements but insufficient overall impact by those who signed the UN declaration. The existence of the World Bank and the International Monetary Fund over the same period of time has also made an inadequate impact. Chapter 8 demonstrated that world trade arrangements have hardly improved and big business continues to dominate. The commitment by people of the world faiths to poverty alleviation was seen in the 1992 declaration, 'Towards a Global Ethic'. There are good projects, and this book includes many. The Golden Rule, to treat others as you would wish to be treated yourself, has shone through in action for the poor by religious people and others. The sadness is that the big picture does not change very much.

A sign of hope for the future was 'Faith, Poverty and Justice', the June 2012 interfaith event held at Lambeth Palace. A new paper from the government Department for International Development was launched, setting out principles to guide DFID's relationship with faith groups towards building understanding and cooperation to overcome poverty. The Archbishop of Canterbury spoke of '...the honour due to human beings', and of shared commitment to sustainable development. Shared work will include the identification of three countries for learning and action. Andrew Mitchell, then Secretary of State, wrote at the beginning of the paper, '*Faith groups are doing excellent work in providing not only humanitarian relief, but delivering health, education and other services in some of the most troubled parts of the world. I look forward to the closer partnership with people of faith who play a unique role in fighting poverty.*'

One important achievement by people of faith has been the demonstrations at summit meetings of the rich countries. The work of Jubilee 2000 led to the cancellation of many debts, but this process is now, as I pointed out in Chapter 8, being reversed, due to the world economic crisis. This book has looked at many reasons why, although a great deal of progress has been made, life is not improving for many of those who live in the developing world or for those who are poor anywhere in the world.

Citizens of Spain protest in Barcelona for a change of the alliance between politicians and the financial elites, October 15, 2011.

matthi/shutterstock.com

The eight Millennium Development Goals examined in this book have been adopted through the United Nations, and therefore by the international community as a whole; every government and person is responsible for striving to reach the targets set for 2015.

The MDGs have been excellent in arousing the world to an awareness of what needs to be done, and, as this book makes clear, good progress has been made in many areas and much more may be achieved before 2015.

A sign of hope has been that most of the governments of the developing world have introduced programmes towards the reaching of the goals. There have been really good developments in Africa and this must be affirmed ,even though, partly due to the worldwide economic crisis, most of the goals will not be reached by 2015. It is interesting that many government programmes are pointing towards 2030 as the time when their work will hopefully be complete.

But there is a long way to go...
...some major areas of concern are:
- 1 in 5 workers and their families live in extreme poverty;[1]
- 96 million children in the world are not in school;
- One quarter of children in the developing world are undernourished. This figure is growing rather than being reduced, largely due to the increase in world food prices. 8.1 million children still die before their fifth birthday;
- Women continue to represent 70% of the world's poor;
- 6 out of 10 women globally experience physical or sexual violence in their lifetime;
- Over 500,000 women in developing countries continue to die annually in pregnancy or childbirth. Goal 5 states that most of these deaths are preventable;
- Over 33 million people are living with HIV;
- Carbon dioxide emissions are still increasing. Forests continue to disappear. Overfishing of the oceans is rising;
- Over a third of the growing urban populations in developing countries live in slums;
- Aid to developing countries is falling. The debt burden of developing countries, having fallen, is rising again;
- International trade negotiations are many years behind schedule;
- Sub-Saharan Africa is still the poorest area of the world.

The economic crisis in the Eurozone has affected and will continue to affect progress in the developing world. There are plunging demands for imports to Europe. The crisis is also affecting the 'BRIC' nations of Brasil,

---

1 CAFOD report – '1,000 days: An end and a new beginning'.

People protesting against government spending cuts and tax rises in Aliados Square, September 15, 2012 in Porto, Portugal. dinozzaver/shutterstock.com

Russia, India and China. India has already reduced its exports instead of growing them, and many small textile businesses have closed down. It is also harder for BRIC nations to import from Europe, because the prices are now inevitably higher. Investors are already moving away and this may be most serious for China. There are fears that the rapid expansion of exports and building projects and other developments in China have depended too heavily on investment from outside the country. China is aware of this and is reducing its exports and imports, including those with Brasil, which will in turn affect this the biggest growing economy in Latin America.

The Christian Aid report 'Poverty: we're all in this together' has issued a challenge to immediate action by the whole world to reach the MDGs. The report also calls for sustainable work beyond the MDGs, including an understanding of the many types of poverty and a commitment to their eradication. Further discussion and decision making in the developing world should be both national and local, with a true voice for the poor.

The focus on poor people at the local level brings back famous voices of the 1970s. Both Paulo Freire and Fritz Schumacher called for the release of people's awareness and creativity for change.[2] In Africa, Kenneth Kaunda and Julius Nyerere spoke, wrote and acted for the self-reliance, work and dignity of African Socialism.

During 2008 Lambeth Conference of Anglican bishops from all over the world there was a London walk of witness which drew the attention of the world to the need for commitment and work towards achieving a new humanity. Every person has the right to know what it means to be a human

Wall of witness, Lambeth Conference 2008.

---

2 Paulo Freire, *Pedagogy of the Oppressed*, Penguin Books, 1973. E.F. Schumacher, *Small is Beautiful*, Blond & Briggs, 1973.

being, to be whole and to flourish. Few people in any part of the world have this awareness. There were three main messages. The first was 'Keep the Promise', a reminder to world leaders that the MDGs were commitments they had made. The second message was 'Halve Poverty by 2015'. The third message was 'Do Justice, Love Mercy'. Many people on the march carried the poverty and justice bible, which highlights two thousand verses from the scriptures relating to poverty and justice.

The 'Micah Movement'[3] raises the idea of human flourishing and also of human responsibility. All people are challenged to '...*do justly, and to love mercy, and to walk humbly with thy God...*' (Micah 6.8). The movement challenges Christians to:

Share the good news – the whole Gospel of Jesus as revealed in the Bible;

Show mercy – turn compassion into action on behalf of the poor;

Fight for justice – speak up for those who have no voice;

Show humility – walk the talk in our own conduct.

All human beings can be givers as well as receivers

Rabindranath Tagore was a Bengali poet who recognised the value of every person as creative and also as capable of giving. One of the stories he told in his 'Gitanjali' is about a beggar woman on the streets of Calcutta. The woman was extremely poor and was standing by the side of the street with a begging bowl. An Indian prince rode down the road on a big horse and he stopped in front of her. She thought her fortune had changed until the prince said, 'What have you to give to me?' The woman was horrified and pointed out that she had nothing, but the prince repeated his question,, until the woman wished he would just go away. Finally, as he refused to leave, the woman went into her cardboard shelter and took out a wooden bowl of rice, her only food. She picked out a few grains of the rice, and gave them to the prince. he thanked her and rode off down the street. The woman was almost in despair. She turned and went into her shelter and took out the bowl of rice to cook supper when she noticed some small shining bits in the bowl. She took them out and realised that they were exactly the same size and number as the grains

Tagore in 1925.

3 www.micahchallenge.org.

of rice she had given to the prince. Furthermore the grains were pure gold. She was devastated, asking, 'Why didn't I give him more, why didn't I give him everything?'

Poor and rich individuals, groups and countries must be challenged to work for change. The rich countries must be challenged to realise their responsibilities and to work with poor countries as equals. A 2012 Christian Aid report[4] points out that inequality in access to and use of natural resources is driving both global poverty and environmental destruction all over the world. Consumption patterns in the developed world and amongst the middle classes everywhere are leading to the degradation of natural resources.

Working with all people and countries as equals involves giving respect to each other's values, listening and learning. It also involves doing the many practical things necessary to bridge the huge material gap between the rich and the poor worlds. A recent book seeks to show how almost everything is affected by how equal a society is.[5]

The issue of equality must also include the achievement of equality between women and men and it must go far beyond the original MDG 3, which stuck to very simple and measureable areas. I went far beyond MDG 3 in this book, and would expect future work also to move on to the more hidden and hard to measure areas of the abuse of women, often within their own homes.

womenseducationproject.org

---

4 *The Rich, the poor and the future of the Earth: Equity in a constrained World*, Christian Aid, 2012.

5 Richard Wilkinson and Kate Pickett, *The Spirit Level: Why Equality is Better for Everyone*, Penguin Books, 2010.

The issue of women's economic inequality and the worsened impact on women of the global economic crisis is tackled in a series of papers published by Oxfam and Practical Action.[6] The papers, from many countries and situations, make it clear that there is a very long way to go before economic equality for women is reached. The hope is that governments will read, learn and act for change.

The United Nations has started to consult and plan for the post-2015 world. In September 2013 there will be a review of the MDGs and proposals for work beyond them.

There is now a 'Beyond 2015' campaign, which is being co-chaired by CAFOD and which is working closely with the United Nations and the UK Government.

The 2012 Christian aid report suggests that all work towards a more equal and sustainable future must ensure more equal access to global resources. In fact equality must be the yardstick by which each area of human development is tackled. New goals should be **sustainable development goals** which hold all countries to account for their responsibility for delivering poverty reduction and a sustainable future. There must be more effort to involve the private sector and to create and execute global plans for climate change, biodiversity and resilient development.

The suggestion is that the new approach will need to ensure that the poorest and most marginalised people are focused on. The poorest should have access to natural resources where they live. Those who have not been helped by the MDGs must be the centre of attention, including many women, disabled people, many tribal people and some religious and ethnic minorities.

Also, the MDGs, with the exception of Goal 8, were mostly focused on the developing world. It is vital that post 2015 work challenges the developed world in its responsibilities to share and to work for true equality, for true justice. The work of Christians Aware aims to raise awareness of the true equality which exists between all people, rich and poor, old and young, women and men.

The key phrase in Progressio's plan for 2012 to 15 is 'People Powered Development'. It is inspiring in its commitment to work with people at the local level, to be the catalyst which energises them to new ideas and work.

There is little hope of achieving equality through sustainable development goals at the moment. A lot of work has to be done to change attitudes and to create commitment. The first earth summit was held in Rio de Janeiro in 1992, when there were high hopes that campaigns for sustainable living would get underway and would be successful. The second earth summit

---

6 *Gender and the Economic Crisis,* edited by Ruth Pearson and Caroline Sweetman, Practical Action & Oxfam, 2011.

closed in Rio de Janeiro on 23rd June 2012 amidst great disappointment. At the end of the summit many statements of goodwill were made, but nothing really practical was agreed. The conference was described by many people as a non-event: it was hard to find positive reports in any of the newspapers.

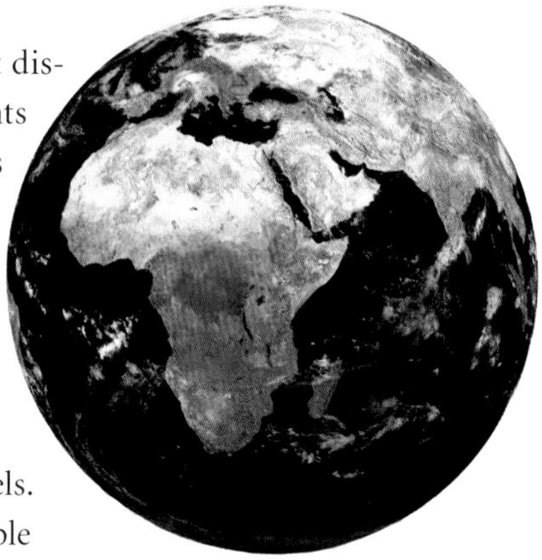

- There were no efforts to make targets for sustainable development.
- There was no effort to stop the burning of fossil fuels.
- There was no effort to support research for renewable energy and no attempt to make it cheaper.
- China and India were both determined that any reduction in carbon emissions should not be made by them but by the western world.
- American oil, car and airline companies lobbied to stop extra taxes on oil or gas.

The banks campaigned to stop any imposition of a tax for financial transactions, sometimes called the 'Tobin Tax', after James Tobin who first introduced the idea in 1972. Tobin suggested a tax on currency market transactions whilst today it is suggested that a wider range of transactions are included. The proceeds of such a tax could, if it was ever adopted, be used to help the poorest countries, especially in the area of climate change.

Commitment to work to alleviate climate change has become unpopular. I attended a conference a few years ago when the speaker said that climate change was simply caused by natural forces, and not by human behaviour. His view has become popular, and can be an excuse for inaction in the area of carbon emissions. The Republican Party in America has adopted this view because they see work to reduce carbon emissions as leading to a reduction in human freedom and enterprise. The suggestion is that countries of the world must work to adapt to increasing temperatures, although the present pattern of 'global weirding', pointing to extreme temperatures in the USA and in Europe, is making many people very thoughtful..

Increased carbon dioxide in the atmosphere, caused by human cultures and lifestyles, does undoubtedly lead to an increase in temperatures, and something can be done about it if there is the will. Those who support work to tackle the results of climate change suggest carbon taxes and targets for efficient use of resources. Regulations to encourage environmentally friendly behaviour can also be encouraged.

The way forward clearly involves a new commitment to education for change. One way to educate is through film. An excellent film set in a devastated world of 2055, where a lone man (the late Pete Postlethwaite) asks himself why nothing was done earlier to combat climate change.[7]

7 The Age of Stupid, Franny Armstrong, Spanner Films/Passion Pictures, 2009.

Another film, WALL-E is a children's film which depicts the planet covered in rubbish because of human greed and consumption.[8] Mike Berners-Lee, the founding director of 'Small World Consulting' has written a very useful book.[9] In *How Bad Are Bananas?* Mike has worked on the assumption that readers will wish to help the planet and has offered a good guide to carbon footprints from under 10 grams to one million tonnes and beyond. It is possible to read, learn and change. There are many surprises and bananas turn out to be good.

Education for sustainable development groups is growing, especially in the world's schools. One practical project, 'Care for Creation', looks at how people bring their spiritual and religious beliefs into their work for the environment and works to offer programmes for action. One programme has been to encourage children and adults to work for biodiversity in churchyards.

The Quaker action pack on sustainable development [10] offers a learning and planning resource for local meetings and groups to work towards becoming low carbon and sustainable. The pack includes sustainability stories, reflections, exercises and questionnaires, ideas for action and resources.

The 'Transition' Movement began in Totnes and is spreading around the world.[11] It offers resources to communities wishing to reduce their carbon emissions, including 'Transition guides'. Eco-Congregation is a programme offering churches help to change towards an environmentally friendly future.[12]

A Quest for Juniper

This inspiring project, in the Esk Valley in Yorkshire, is an example of work for the environment and of good education of learning by doing, where children became absorbed in the project. The way forward for every country must be for education to be exciting and compelling.

The project began very simply, with an attempt to restore a quarry. Peter Woods was commissioned to prepare a plan to restore the whinstone quarry Force Garth in 1993. The original working quarry had been planned to be out of sight, but then became an eye sore when the Pennine Way opened on the opposite bank of the River Tees, offering walkers a full view into the ugly and redundant quarry. The hope of the restoration was to create a quarry landscape to match the surrounding countryside, with mixed woodland and scattered boulders. Birch and rowan trees were found, and

8 WALL-E Disney/Pixar, 2008.

9 Mike Berners-Lee, *How Bad are Bananas? The Carbon Footprint of Everything,* Profile Books, 2010.

10 *Sustainability Toolkit. Becoming a low carbon, sustainable community,* Living Witness. Quakers for Sustainability, 2011 www.quaker.org.uk.

11 R. Hopkins, *The Transition Handbook, From Oil Dependency to Local Resilience,* Green Books, 2008.

12 www.ecocongregation.org.

also plenty of boulders, but the landscape also included juniper, which had been one of the earliest trees in the area but had declined so that new sources were hard to find. Peter managed to discover a forester who was growing small juniper plants and to enlist him to propagate the berries for the quarry scheme. A juniper project was set up which spread to include a wider area of Upper Teesdale and then the even wider area of the North Yorkshire Moors. It took six years for the small trees to grow enough to be planted out in what became the 'Save the Juniper campaign'. In 2001 local primary schools and one secondary school joined the campaign and each school became responsible for a triangle of 6 trees, to be planted within pollinating distance of old trees. The children prepared the ground, planted the saplings and added stakes and protection. The children also took on-going responsibility for the trees, making sure the land immediately surrounding the trees was kept clear and that the trees had enough water. The scheme is now supported by the North Yorkshire Moors National Parks, the clumps of juniper have been fenced and a bio-diversity action plan has been set up. The children have continued to be involved in the care of the trees and further in the collection and sorting of ripe berries for propagation. Each year more juniper are ready for planting and more children are involved.

Education for change involves changing attitudes, towards a realisation of the truth that all people are equal and that in every human encounter there is something to learn as well as something to give. There are no 'we' and 'they' situations, but only 'us', working together for a good future for us all.

- The Quaker 'Sustainability Toolkit'[14] offers many ideas for practical action including energy and the use of buildings and gardens, consumption and the use of waste, and dealing with money.
- David Bellamy has produced many resources towards sustainability.[15]

Awareness Raising...

- Plan events, write articles, give talks.

Networking...

- Work begun in small groups may spread to national and international groupings. The use of the internet, e-mail, skype etc is vital.

Travel...

- Go to the developing world, to listen and learn, contact those who are travelling for business and suggest they meet local people to listen and learn. Check out which airlines are working to become 'green' and use them.[16] Everyone may give talks on return.[17]

Give...

- Choose a percentage of your income to give regularly to poverty reduction programmes. Buy presents through a development charity.

Pray...

- Choose an issue or country to pray for every week. Introduce this idea in your church.

There is a long way to go...

'Because of the circumstances in which I travelled, first as a student and later as a doctor, I came into close contact with poverty, hunger and disease; with the inability to treat a child because of lack of money; with the stupefaction provoked by continual hunger and punishment... And I began to realise that there were things that were almost as important to me as... making a significant contribution to medical science: I wanted to help those people.'
Ernesto 'Che' Guevara, 1960

14 See footnote 4.
15 David Bellamy, *A Hundred Ways to Save the Earth*.
16 Christians Aware has a green airlines list – www.christiansaware.co.uk.
17 Ailsa Moore and Barbara Butler, *Go to the People*, Christians Aware, 2000, is an excellent resource.

Reality Check

Afghanistan and the MDGs
– a progress report

By David Page, Chair of Trustees of Afghanaid*

Afghanistan did not sign up to the original Millennium Development Goals in September 2000. It was being governed by the Taliban regime at the time, which was only recognised by three other countries. It signed up in 2003, after the international community had dislodged the Taliban following the attack on the twin towers and a new internationally recognised interim government had been installed. Even then Afghanistan was not given the same timetable to meet its MDGs as other nations.

The international intervention of 2001 brought hopes of an end to two decades of war in Afghanistan, which had taken an enormous toll in what was already an extremely poor country. The Soviet invasion of 1979, the resistance by western-backed Mujahideen, the subsequent civil war and the eventual emergence of the Taliban, who subdued the rest of the country by force of arms: this long history of conflict resulted in the destruction of much of the country's infrastructure, the flight of millions of its inhabitants, including most of its middle class, and the plummeting of its human development indicators. In 2001, Afghanistan was more or less at the bottom of the UN Development Index, with only one or two Sub-Saharan countries for company.

For these very persuasive reasons, the UN accepted that Afghanistan could not be expected to meet its MDG targets by 2015, like the rest of the world, which was working to a baseline of 1990. It was agreed that it would be given until 2020 – a further 5 years – and it was hoped that with the help of substantial international help it would be able to catch up.[1]

There were eight MDGs in the original UN agreement and Afghanistan added a ninth of its own – Enhancing Security – which reflected the fact that Afghans define lack of security as their greatest problem. This MDG involved the destruction of anti-personnel mines, both emplaced and stockpiled, the reduction of the misuse of weapons, and – crucially for the

* Afghanaid is a British charity which has been operating in Afghanistan since 1983. It works in some of the poorest parts of the country to help disadvantaged communities improve their livelihoods and with communities vulnerable to the repeated cycles of natural disasters to overcome their suffering. Its vision is of a peaceful and secure Afghanistan, where Afghans exercise their rights to political freedom and economic opportunity and where institutions are accountable to the people.

Photo opposite courtesy Afghanaid

future – the creation of a professional Afghan national army by 2010. This last MDG remains at the heart of the exit strategies of the US, Britain and other western countries, who have announced that they will cease active military operations by 2015. This new Afghan army has already begun to take over security responsibilities in more peaceful areas but critics say it is still quite a long way from achieving sufficient strength or operational capacity for a national role. Discipline and morale are also problematic among local militia and police, as has been shown by a spate of attacks on international training forces. There are also concerns about its lack of ethnic balance which is going to affect its acceptability among the Pashtuns in the south and east of the country. But this MDG is one of three which are officially regarded as 'on track'.[2]

Among the other key development areas, primary education has been transformed since the difficult days of the Taliban when only one million children were in school and none of them were girls. The energetic Education Minister, Farooq Wardak, told a meeting of European school children in London in November 2011 that there are now 8.4 million Afghan children in primary school, of whom 39% are girls. Even more impressively, women make up 31% of nearly 200,000 primary school teachers. But by the minister's own account, 4.2 million children of school age have no access to a school, 50% of existing schools do not have adequate buildings and only 36% of teachers have any qualifications. There is still some way to go to achieve universal primary school education by 2020. According to the minister, 16,000 schools will need to be constructed and another 250,000 teachers recruited. It is a tall order and it depends on continuing international support and political and security developments in Afghanistan after 2014. But it is a measure of growing confidence that it is seen as an 'achievable' goal.[3]

The development of secondary and tertiary education has made far less progress, and the proportion of girls in these sectors is much lower than in primary education. This is not necessarily because of cultural resistance to educating girls, though that plays its part. It is also because there is an even greater shortage of women teachers at secondary level and there is cultural resistance to young women being taught by men. Lack of access to suitable secondary schools is another issue which needs to be addressed. The empowerment of women – in so far as it is measured for the MDGs in terms of their share of jobs which require education – will only make progress once these hurdles are overcome. But at other levels of society – as office bearers in community development councils or as small-scale entrepreneurs – women have been making significant progress and are growing in confidence in these new occupations.

Health is a key area for the MDGs and one which has seen measurable progress. In Afghanistan, the death rate of women in childbirth and the morality rate among children under five have been among the highest in the world; and progress in changing this appalling situation has been pain-fully slow. Over the past ten years, there has been considerable investment in health infrastructure and the percentage of the population within strik-ing distance of a health clinic has greatly increased. According to a recent government survey, health facilities have increased from 450 to 1800 and the number of midwives from 400 to 2000, though these numbers remain small to serve a country with 40,000 villages and a population of 26 million.[4] A survey of public opinion in Afghanistan carried out in 2011 for ACBAR, a leading umbrella group of NGOs, produced some heart-rending stories of pregnant mothers struggling to reach clinics, only to find that they were closed or that no trained medical staff were present. Shortage of medicines is also a critical weakness.[5] In both health and education, there is a national shortage of trained personnel, which is compounded for people living in remote and inaccessible places by the fact that qualified people do not wish to serve there. This is not a problem peculiar to Afghanistan but it makes progress more difficult to achieve, particularly in a situation of deteriorat-ing security. The UNDP development report of 2010 showed only limited progress in health indicators.[6] A more recent survey by the Afghan Ministry of Public Health suggested much more significant improvements: that life expectancy, which has been as low as 45 for some time, had risen to between 62 and 64 years for both men and women, and that the percentage of chil-dren dying before the age of 5 had been halved.[7] However, these statistics have been widely questioned and the UNDP Human Development Index for 2011 indicated a much more modest improvement for life expectancy to 48.7 years.[8] According to other reports, immunisation against tuberculosis and preventative treatment for malaria have also been effective in reducing disease – another MDG goal which is on track to be achieved.[9]

Progress has been much slower in the eradication of extreme poverty and hunger, which is the first MDG goal and one which is critical to the achievement of some of the others. (If families do not have enough to eat, they find it much more difficult to send their children to school). In this field, unfortunately the indicators have been moving in the wrong direction. At Afghanistan's five year assessment in 2008, the percentage of those below the 'minimum level of dietary energy consumption (2100 calories a day)' had risen from 30% to 39%. A study of vulnerability in the same year indicated that 68% of the population was affected by some form of food insecurity;[10] and this may have increased recently s because of the severe drought which affected the northern provinces of the country. In a country where 75% of the population is reportedly dependent on agriculture, and a majority on rain-fed agriculture, progress is severely constrained by climatic conditions and development has to be focussed as much on improving the capacity of rural communities to deal with disasters as on helping them to max-imise food production. Unfortunately, for many years neither the Afghan government nor the donor community gave agriculture the importance it deserves. An Oxfam report published in 2008 calculated that only about $300–400 million had been spent on agriculture over the previous six years, a figure dwarfed by one month's US military expenditure.[11] This serious omission is now being corrected with the emergence of several National Priority Programmes with a focus on agriculture on a par with those already making a difference in governance, education and health.

The campaign to meet the MDG targets is being run by the Afghan government and its various ministries, with technical and financial support from the international community. Since 2001, there have been regular international conferences in different world capitals to underwrite donor support for the Afghan government's national development strategy. The most recent were in Chicago and Tokyo in May and July 2012, at which the international community pledged $4.1 billion dollars annually over three years for the Afghan armed services after 2014 and $16 billion to underwrite development until 2017. A key objective throughout has been to re-build the capacity of the Afghan government after a long period of institutional attrition and middle class migration. Initially, far too much was expected of the fledgling national government and progress was painfully slow. Ten years later, ministries are working more efficiently, though much more needs to be done to build the capacity of government at provincial and district level, where development plans are implemented. The donor community is now committed to channelling 50% of all development aid through the Afghan government. But service delivery in health, education and other fields of development continues to depend on the facilitation of national and international NGOs, like Afghanaid, who have a history of engagement with local communities, a track record of working in remote areas and the trained personnel to deliver development programmes.

Much of Afghanaid's work is directly related to the achievement of the MDGs – particularly the eradication of poverty and the empowerment of women. Helping communities to deal with food insecurity is a priority, whether through improved agricultural productivity, better storage and conservation or diversification into new areas of employment. Afghanaid provides farmers and their families with access to improved varieties of crops – whether wheat or vegetables or fruit – and helps them to improve their market links. Our engineers work with local communities to repair roads and bridges, restore old irrigation channels, re-build schools and provide electricity in remote areas through micro-hydro schemes. Much of our work is focussed on improving governance and mobilising local communities to decide their own development priorities. As a facilitating partner for the Afghan government's National Solidarity Programme (NSP), over the past nine years we have helped to establish elected community development councils in over two thousand villages in four provinces

FOR REFLECTION

'And I heard a great voice out of heaven saying, Behold the tabernacle of God is with men, and he will dwell with them, and they shall be his people, and God himself shall be with them, and be their God. And God shall wipe all tears from their eyes, and there shall be no more death, neither sorrow nor crying, neither shall there be any more pain; for the former things are passed away. And he that sat upon the throne said, Behold I make all things new.' Revelation 21.3–5

Potential Group and Individual Action for Change

Study...

- Read, listen to news, form a study circle, join a class.[13]
- Discuss the human condition which makes the world as it is. How may this change?
- **Encourage research to find out how global warming is affecting weather patterns.**

Advocacy...

- Organise meetings, get to know your Member of Parliament, lobby and campaign.
- One worthwhile campaign is for the reform of the world trade system towards the rich countries and companies assuming more responsibility for economic development in the poorer nations and communities.
- Other much needed campaigns: climate change, corporate responsibility, migrants.
- Those campaigning from within the developing world might work for more transparency in economic policies and in elections and in some cases for an end to the violence which so often causes poverty. The death of Maria Colvin brought out some of her work on the poverty and suffering caused by war.
- The use of natural resources for the benefit of the people could be highlighted more often. I pointed to the work being done for the environment through tree planting in Kenya. Another example is the on-going work of some churches in the Philippines to save the environment by stopping excess mining for minerals by certain mining companies.

Practical Action...

- Buy fairly traded products. Promote fair trade by designing exhibitions and evenings focusing on particular products and issues. Perhaps a 'cocoa campaign' may be enjoyable and educational. Promote campaigns, organise prayer services.
- A good time to write and organise services and special prayers is harvest festival.

13 *Working Together, Ten Bible Studies Inspired by the Millennium Development Goals*, Christian Aid.

– Badakhshan, Nuristan, Samangan and Ghor – and have helped them to implement their development plans with funds provided by the central government. This programme has given villagers a say in their own development for the first time and is also helping to empower village women, who are now emerging as office bearers in many councils. Much of our work focuses on providing opportunities for women, whether through women's resource centres, savings groups or small business development. We have trained over 2500 women as local leaders and hundreds of our women trainees are now running their own small businesses.[12] It is going to take time for women to benefit from secondary education but at the village level there are positive signs of change.

One of the worries for the future is that this progress may not be sustained. As the USA and Britain plan an end to active military engagement by 2015, there is much uncertainty in Afghanistan about what the future may bring. The pledges made at the Tokyo conference in July 2012 have helped to dispel some fears that, despite talk of a 'decade of transformation',[13] Afghanistan will cease to be a priority and aid budgets will be cut. But there are continuing concerns that peace talks with the Taliban, which western countries are encouraging as a means of achieving a political settlement, may involve surrendering progress in such fields as media freedom or women's education and rights.

The uncertainty is compounded by growing insecurity in parts of the country which were previously relatively peaceful. ISAF may have regained the initiative in Helmand but in Ghor province to the north, where Afghanaid works, instability is spreading and development is becoming more difficult. Even in Badakhshan in the north east, armed opposition groups have emerged in some districts and are trying to dictate the terms of development to government and to NGOs. Many of these groups are not strictly linked to the Taliban, though the Taliban now have shadow governments in almost all provinces.

In the West, the press and the public have focussed increasingly on the death toll among their soldiers and have grown weary of a war which was not expected and has gone on too long. The growth of corruption has also played its part in the disillusionment of the public, both in Afghanistan and elsewhere. There has been much less publicity for the real achievements – in governance and development – which have begun to make a difference to the lives of ordinary people. Whatever the weaknesses of day to day government, the country now has a constitution which enshrines people's rights and provides the means for peaceful political change. There is a relatively free media and an increasingly vociferous civil society. Power is not always wielded democratically but most Afghans would not wish to put the clock back to 2001. In terms of development, Afghanistan has made measurable if limited progress since 2001 in meeting its MDG targets and

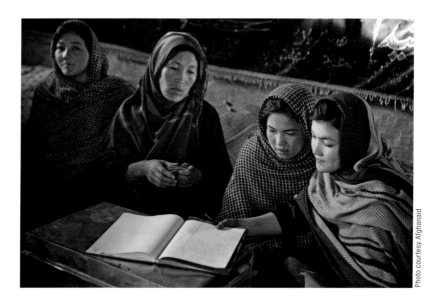

Photo courtesy Afghanaid

in other important areas. But it is still one of the world's poorest countries and it will need international support for the next twenty years at least to change that. As the west prepares to disengage militarily, it is a saddening reflection that so many billions of dollars have been spent on fighting the Taliban and comparatively few on meeting the real development needs of the people. Afghanistan is an old country with a very young population which longs for a better future. What it desperately needs is an orderly end to the fighting and a sustained peace dividend.

Endnotes

1 http://www.unama.unmissions.org/Portals/UNAMA/Documents/MDG-2005-vision2020.pdf.

2 http://www.undp.org.af/Publications/KeyDocuments/2008_MDGAnnualProgressR.pdf.

3 Speech by Farooq Wardak, House of Commons, London, 24 November 2011.

4 Afghan Health Ministry survey 2010, quoted in the Guardian, 1 December 2011, p 36.

5 ACBAR report on *Health and Education, 10 years after: Quantity not Quality*, by Althea-Maria Rivas, September 2011.

6 http://hdr.undp.org/en/reports/global/hdr2010.

7 Afghan Health Ministry Survey, 2010, quoted in the Guardian, 1 December 2011.

8 http://hdrstats.undp.org/en/countries/profiles/AFG..

9 http://www.undp.org.af/Publications/KeyDocuments/2008_MDGAnnualProgressR.pdf.

10 Afghanistan National Risk and Vulnerability Assessment, 2008. http://ec.europa.eu/europeaid/where/asia/documents/afgh_nrva_2007-08_full_report_en.pdf.

11 *Afghanistan: Development and Humanitarian Priorities*, Oxfam Report 2008, p 10 http://www.oxfam.org.uk/resources/policy/conflict_disasters/downloads/afghanistan_priorities.pdf.

12 For more details of Afghanaid's work, see http://www.afghanaid.org.uk/pages/projects.

13 The International Afghanistan Conference in Bonn, 5 December 2011, conference conclusions.

Beyond the MDGs

A few extra ways forward

Many useful organisations and resources are listed throughout the book. Here are just a few other suggestions.

A global campaign – www.beyond2015.org. This is a network of 380 civil society organisations and 80 countries. Its main hope is to create a post 2015 development framework to succeed the MDGs.

Bond – www.bond.org.uk. A national network of UK non-governmental development organisations. There are 358 ngos working for development advocacy. Bond includes the European policy Group.

Act Alliance – www.actalliance.org. A network of non-governmental organisations working together for humanitarian assistance, advocacy and long term development in 140 countries. The secretariat is in Geneva.

APRODEV – a European network of development agencies related to the World Council of Churches. This network aims to influence European Development policies.

The Methodist Church is working for all countries to achieve sustainable development goals. This work arose from the Durban conference.

Trace the Tax Campaign is for it to become a legal requirement for companies to report profit and tax across the world. At the moment it is estimated that multinational companies report just a fraction of the profits they make in poor countries and hide the true amounts in offshore accounts, thus not paying the tax. It is estimated that this costs developing countries $160 billion, which would be enough to enable the reaching of the MDGs several times over. It is also twice the amount poor countries receive in international aid.

> All ways forward beyond 2015 must be with the 'world's poor people' as equal partners.
>
> There is a long way to go...

Acknowledgements

The Millennium Development Goals have provided a sturdy framework around which this book has grown. The achievement of the goals remains vital for the future of the whole world.

First of all I would like to thank all my friends in the developing world, who have inspired me to attempt to write this book. My hope is that the book will give readers an insight into the lives of other people which will lead them to new understanding, appreciation and shared work for the future of our one world.

My work in Christians Aware has made it possible for me to visit the developing world and to organise and attend conferences where people from around the world have been present. I am grateful for all the opportunities I have had for listening and learning and for sharing in a new way.

I am grateful to everyone who has contributed to the book by providing an article, a story or an illustration. The contributions come from direct experience and offer an invaluable resource.

I have acknowledged the photographs in the book which are not my own and I would like to thank everyone who has provided them. I have found it very creative to include them in this book. Many of them speak much more powerfully than words. We have sought appropriate permission for all the images – we apologise if any accreditation is incorrect and would be glad to make any amendment required in future printings.

My book includes works of art and I wish to recognise the generosity of all the artists who have shared their work. Anne Gregson, a Quaker, has provided the front cover and many of the paintings included throughout the book. I am indebted to Anne for her readiness to share. Jyoti Sahi is a long-standing colleague who has often spoken and led workshops at Christians Aware events. He is a Roman Catholic who works to integrate his Christian faith with the rich cultures and faiths of India. I have been inspired by visits to his ashram near Bangalore and am always moved by his paintings, woodcuts and other artworks. I am continually grateful for his friendship and support.

Solomon Raj is a Lutheran artist and writer who lives in Eastern India and specializes in batik work and wood block prints. Solomon has spoken to me of his work and ideas over a number of years, especially his grief from living in a country where the gap between the rich and the poor is so wide. Petra Röhr-Rouendaal is a German artist who visits Africa regularly and who paints the people and places she loves. She is a good friend and support. Beate Dehnen is also German and a Quaker who lives in England. She works with Christians Aware and with refugee children. She is an artist and an inspiring teacher of art and theology.

In my preparations and writing of this book I have been very encouraged by Bob Fyffe of Churches Together in Britain and Ireland who has been enthusiastic in his support and, as General Secretary of CTBI, has published the book. My thanks are due to Bob and to CTBI.

David McLeod is someone with a wide publishing background and I have been very fortunate that he has been the person working with me and responsible for the layout of the book. David has also shared in a lot of discussion with me, particularly about the illustrations for the book and he has provided many of them. He has been an invaluable colleague in this venture and I am very grateful for his support.

Amanda Fitton has worked tirelessly in the Christians Aware office to seek the necessary permissions for the publication of the book. She has been a great support and I am very thankful to her.

Finally, I would like to thank the members of my family, especially my husband Tom, for their patience and encouragement in this venture.

Barbara Butler

About Christians Aware

Christians Aware is an international and interdenominational educational charity working to develop multicultural and interfaith understanding and friendship locally, nationally and internationally. Its aim is to work for justice, peace and development. The focus is on listening to encourage awareness and action.

It does this with a programme of focus groups, conferences, international exchanges, work-camps and publications. 'Travel with Awareness' is a book of guidance for the international visits which are often to places where there are or have been situations of conflict, such as Palestine, Israel and Rwanda. Groups also visit places where there are acute development needs, including primary health care, education and water harvesting.

The words of Ronald Wynne are important:

'Do not try to teach anyone anything until you have learnt something from them.'

Christians Aware
2 Saxby Street
Leicester LE2 0ND
0116 254 0770
Email: barbarabutler@christiansaware.co.uk
Website: www.christiansaware.co.uk